2673

11.21

D0469185

The
YOUNGER
Evangelicals

The
YOUNGER
Evangelicals

Facing the
CHALLENGES
of the New
WORLD

Robert E. Webber

Baker Books

A Division of Baker Book House Co
Grand Rapids, Michigan 49516

Published by Baker Books
a division of Baker Book House Company
P.O. Box 6287, Grand Rapids, MI 49516-6287

Fourth printing, October 2004

Printed in the United States of America

Library of Congress Cataloging-in-Publication Data
Webber, Robert.
    The younger evangelicals : facing the challenges of the new world / Robert E. Webber.
        p.   cm.
    Includes bibliographical references (p.) and indexes.
    ISBN 0-8010-9152-7
    1. Evangelicalism—United States. I. Title.
BR1642.U5W43 2002
270.8′3—dc21   2002008644

For current information about all releases from Baker Book House, visit our web site:
http://www.bakerbooks.com

To my students at
Wheaton College
1968–2000

Every teacher of the law who has been instructed about the kingdom of heaven is like the owner of a house who brings out of his storeroom new treasures as well as old.

JESUS

Contents

Tables

The tables in this volume attempt to present the differences between *traditional, pragmatic,* and *younger* evangelicals. I intend them to show general directions and cannot, because of their brevity, capture various nuances. Please use these tables as guides for thought and discussion, not as statements of absolute accuracy.

Illustrations

Acknowledgments

A book like *The Younger Evangelicals* could not have been written without the input of a lot of people.

I first need to thank Northern Seminary for appointing me to the Myers Chair of Ministry with its greatly reduced teaching load. This much needed release from teaching has given me the time to do the research and writing of this book.

Second, my thanks to the people at Baker Books. They trusted my hunch there was a story here and gave me a contract with confidence that what I thought about the twenty-somethings was indeed true. It turns out the story is more extensive than either of us dreamed. Thanks, too, for the able editing of Chad Allen, who is also a twenty-something. He looked, not only at the writing, but also at the ideas through the eyes of "someone who thinks this way."

Then there were the many people who helped me reflect on the changes being made by the twenty-somethings. Thanks to my twenty-six-year-old Northern Seminary assistant, Ashley Olsen, who is alive to our postmodern world, especially in worship, spirituality, and all the arts. There is that special group of very bright young men, Wheaton students who served as my focus group. Thanks for the many luncheons in the college cafeteria where we pored over the ideas and worked through so many issues. These students, Joseph Clair, Tim Leininger, and Joel Handy, also made lengthy contributions to the manuscript, as did Ashley Olsen. Tullian Tchividjian, minister to young adults at Cedar Springs Presbyterian Church in Knoxville, Tennessee, sent a perceptive article, unsolicited, at just the right time.

Thanks, too, to Rob Bell, pastor of Mars Hill Bible Church in Grand Rapids, Michigan; to Joe McDonald and Kurt Vickman from Christ Presbyterian Church in Minneapolis for their description of youth worship; to Ron Martoi, pastor of Westwinds Community Church in Jackson, Michigan; to Steve Skaff, a former Wheaton student; to Julie Vigors, a Bethel Seminary student; and to many others who contributed.

Many people contributed by answering an email questionnaire. Most of them provided me with extensive answers to my questions. Their insights are quoted throughout the manuscript. A special word of appreciation goes to the following people: Chris Alford, minister of music at Smithwood Baptist Church, Knoxville, Tennessee; Jason Archer, youth pastor, Spring Arbor, Michigan, Free Methodist Church; Tory Baucum, teacher in the Beeson program at Asbury Seminary in Wilmore, Kentucky; Paul Christenson, minister of music and worship, West Court Street Church of God, Indiana; David Clark, professor of theology, Bethel Theological Seminary, Minnesota; Don Curran, graduate student in ministry, Berkeley University, California; Nathan Coleson, coleader of Breaking Bread, a street ministry to homeless people in Chicago; Dale Dirksen, director of worship arts, Briercrest College Seminary, Saskatchewan, Canada; David Di Sabatino, editor of *Worship Leader Magazine*, California; Tim Erdell, librarian and assistant professor of religion and philosophy, Bethel College, Indiana; John Green, executive director, Emmaus Ministries, Chicago; Dawn Haglund, pastoral ministry, D.C. Vineyard; Paul Jones, student, Regent College, Vancouver; Russell Jung, racial reconciliation, New Hope Covenant Church, Oakland, California; Jonathan Nelms, minister of music and worship, First Baptist Church, Cooksville, Tennessee; Bruce McEvoy, student, Northern Seminary, Lombard, Illinois; Frank Nihart, music minister, First Baptist Church, Troy, Alabama; Kyle Roberts, graduate student, Trinity Evangelical Divinity School, Deerfield, Illinois; James Stump, assistant professor of philosophy, Bethel College, Minneapolis; David Taylor, pastor of arts and teaching ministries, Hope Chapel, Austin, Texas; and Bernie Van De Walle, assistant professor of theology, Canadian Bible College, Regina, Canada. In the event I have missed one or two contributors, I apologize.

I also need to acknowledge that I drew from the website material of several twenty-somethings. Acknowledgment of these writers and of the websites that contained their material is made in the footnotes. Here I wish simply to admit how much I learned from these younger thinkers and to express thanks for their contributions to my thoughts.

Finally, I owe a debt of gratitude to those who work with me day by day. A special word of thanks goes to Carmen Martinez who has so faithfully worked as my assistant at the Institute for Worship Studies, the Illinois office. Her tireless work at the computer and her cheerful servanthood attitude are a constant encouragement to me. And then, there is my wife, Joanne. How could I ever thank her enough? Her sharp and critical mind keeps me accountable. Her willingness to give me the time to write is a freedom without which this book could not have been written.

Thanks to all these very special people who have enriched my life and continue to do so.

Introduction

This is a book about an emerging generation of leaders, the younger evangelicals. It is also a book about all evangelicals because it tells the story of evangelical roots in the twentieth century and how and why evangelicalism in the next century will be different.

Evangelical Christianity is in a state of change. The change taking place is not abrupt, nor simple. This book interprets the changing face of evangelicalism since about 1950 and projects where evangelicalism is going in the next decades. History is best told after the fact, yet there are discernible shifts and seeds of thought that will probably flower in the near future. Consequently, I interpret what I have seen and project what I foresee. But I do so recognizing the complexity of change and with the underlying conviction that evangelicalism has an unchanging message for a changing culture.

Not everyone will read this book in the same way. If you were born before 1975, you may read from the perspective of the twentieth century. If you were born after 1975, you will probably read from the perspective of the twenty-first century. But this is a generalization. You may break the mold.

I write from both perspectives. I was born in 1933 and have spent my whole life in the evangelical world. Like others my age, I was shaped by the issues of the twentieth century with its emphasis on reason and science. But I have been shaped by the shift into the twenty-first century as well. I straddle the two paradigms, as do many of us who are seeking to make sense of the enormous changes currently taking place.

For those of us born before 1975, it is a stretch to understand the "new world" and to affirm the younger evangelicals' response to it. For those born after 1975, it is a stretch of equal proportion to understand and appreciate the modern worldview and the response of the twentieth-century evangelical to it.

Right now these two paradigms—the older evangelicalism built around twentieth-century culture and the evangelicalism being formed around the twenty-first century—are in conflict. This clash is birthing a new set of leaders—the younger evangelicals. Despite the clash, both twentieth- and twenty-first-century evangelicals have much in common.

Regardless of when you were born or whether you accept the evangelicalism of yesterday or find yourself in search of a new evangelicalism, I invite you to enter the story of the transition from an older evangelicalism to the younger evangelicalism with an open mind and heart and a willingness to change as together we enter a new period of evangelical history.

Who Are the Evangelicals?

First, all evangelicals stand in continuity with each other throughout the history of the church. Our commonality is expressed in the four uses of the word evangelical: biblical, theological, historical, and cultural. The *biblical* use of evangelical simply refers to the *euangelion*, the good news that salvation has arrived in Jesus Christ. This common linguistic use belongs to the whole church and to all who affirm faith in Jesus Christ and the gospel.

The second use of evangelical is *theological*. It refers to those who affirm Scripture as the authoritative Word of God and accept the creeds of the early church as accurate reflections of the gospel: the Apostles' Creed summarizes the faith; the Nicene Creed confesses the trinity as essential to the Christian faith; the Chalcedon Creed affirms that Jesus is fully God and fully man. Evangelicals affirm these creedal convictions.

The *historical* usage of evangelical refers to all those movements in history that have attempted to restore a vital historic Christianity to the church at those moments when the church has become dead in spirit or has departed from the faith of the fathers. For example, evangelical renewal is found among the monastics, the outburst of spirituality in the medieval era, the Protestant Reformation, pietism, the Oxford movement, and the rise of the evangelical awakenings facilitated by John Wesley, Jonathan Edwards, Billy Sunday, and Billy Graham, to name a few.

Fourth, the most complex use of evangelical is the modern Protestant *cultural* usage of the word. A cultural evangelical is defined by the biblical, theological, and historical uses of the term but goes one step further to be rooted in a particular paradigm of thought. For example, modern evangelicalism has identified with the Cartesian emphasis on reason and the empirical method. These culturally defined evangelicals have used the modern paradigm of thought to develop a particular kind of evangelicalism encased in a culture that elevates reason and the attainment of propositional truth. They have created a culturally bound evangelicalism embedded in the modern paradigm of thought. The current dilemma of twentieth-century modern evangelicalism is that the twentieth-century cultural paradigm in which the evangelical faith was explained, proclaimed, and defended has come to an end. Because culture is in a new paradigm, the old wineskins are collapsing. It is not the faith that needs to be changed but the paradigm or the wineskin in which Christianity is communicated. The current transition from the old to the new paradigm has created a great deal of dissonance and confusion.

What is happening now in North America and around the world is a new evangelical awakening (in the sense of the biblical, theological, and historical usages of the word). This awakening is happening concurrently with the beginning of the twenty-first century. Some are resisting this change and insisting on the preservation of the old paradigm. Others are rushing to make alliances with the new cultural conditions without carefully considering how an evangelical faith that is grounded in Scripture and informed by the history of the church should be translated into a new cultural context. This book is about the changes being introduced by the next generation of leaders, a generation I have called the younger evangelicals.

I have situated the younger evangelical within the larger period of history from 1950 to the present. During this period of time there are many kinds of evangelical leadership. The first evangelical leadership came from the more traditional twentieth-century evangelicals; it emerged after World War II and functioned as the dominant evangelical image until about 1975. The second paradigm of evangelical leadership is found among those who introduced new ideas such as those reflected by the church growth movement, the megachurch movement, contemporary worship, and seeker churches. This movement has dominated evangelical Christianity since the late seventies.

But now a different movement, a new evangelical paradigm, is emerging. This group, the younger evangelicals, is introducing vast changes into the evangelical way of thinking and doing the faith. They are the new leaders who will form a new kind of evangelicalism to dominate the next twenty-five years of evangelical thought and ministry. Table 1 puts these three groups into perspective and identifies a prominent leader of each paradigm.

Who Are the Younger Evangelicals?

I use the word *younger* in a variety of ways—to refer to those who are young in age, those who are young in spirit, and to refer to the movement they represent as a new or young movement.

Table 1
Overview of Traditional, Pragmatic, and Younger Evangelicals

	Traditional Evangelicals	Pragmatic Evangelicals	Younger Evangelicals
Approximate Year of Origin	1950	1975	2000
In History	After World War II	After the 1960s	After modernism and Sept. 11, 2001
Leader	Billy Graham	Bill Hybels	Brian McLaren

First, *younger evangelicals* refers to those who are *young in age*. My interest is in capturing the thinking of the college and seminary student in particular, the "twenty-something." Such students are thinking about what it means to be an evangelical in the twenty-first century. Their leadership in the academy and in the church is already being felt. A major concern of this book is where these movers and shakers are likely to lead the evangelical community in the early decades of the twenty-first century.

Second, there are older leaders from the previous generation who are already addressing the matter of the evangelical faith and practice in the twenty-first century. They are *young in spirit*. They have been teaching, pastoring, leading parachurch organizations, writing articles and books. These persons have encouraged the young in age to start to think differently and to provide new leadership in the church and academy. These older leaders are vital to the new awakening in every area of thought and ministry. I will profile them, their ideas, and influence, and show how they impact the thought patterns of the young in age. Together, these young in age and young in spirit represent a new or younger movement.

Here, then, is how I am using the phrase *younger evangelical*. The younger evangelical is anyone, older or younger, who deals thoughtfully with the shift from twentieth- to twenty-first-century culture. He or she is committed to construct a biblically rooted, historically informed, and culturally aware new evangelical witness in the twenty-first century.

These younger evangelicals constitute *a new kind of leader for the twenty-first century*. These new leaders seek to maintain historic Christianity in a new setting. They are evangelical in their faith and practice but very different than *traditional* or *pragmatic* evangelicals of the twentieth century.

Younger evangelicals affirm the twentieth-century evangelicals for contextualizing the faith in the culture of the twentieth century and believe they did what had to be done to communicate in the old culture. Twentieth-century evangelicals held fast to a biblically informed and historically tested faith, but they saw it, explained it, and presented it in a cultural situation that no longer exists.

The younger evangelicals stand in the same tradition. They want a faith that is biblically informed and historically tested as well. But, because they are products of a new culture, the younger evangelicals explain and present the faith differently. The clash between twentieth- and twenty-first-century evangelicals is not over truth but over the cultural garb in which truth is clothed. The commitment to construct an evangelical faith for a new cultural setting refocuses the way truth is presented, explained, and lived out.

The younger evangelical wants to release the historic substance of faith from its twentieth-century enculturation in the Enlightenment and recontextualize it with the new cultural condition of the twenty-first century. This contextual methodology is no different than the method the Reformers used to deconstruct the church's reliance on the medievally culturalized form of Christianity in order to release the faith to be contextualized into the cultural situation of the emerging English and European culture. Evangelicals have carried out this process of deconstruction and reconstruction repeatedly throughout history. Those who resist this process in the current debate deny the evangelical commitment to a changeless faith indigenized into various cultures.

A study of the cultural shift from the twentieth to the twenty-first century lies beyond the scope of this writing. Because the focus of this book is on the younger evangelical response to the new cultural situation, I am assuming a general acquaintance with the cultural shifts. The bibliography will point the reader to a wide variety of literature on the subject, and table 2 summarizes the major shifts that account for the rise of the new cultural situation.

Table 2
Comparison of Traditional, Pragmatic, and Younger Evangelicals

	Traditional Evangelicals 1950–1975	Pragmatic Evangelicals 1975–2000	Younger Evangelicals 2000–
Cultural Situation	Modern worldview Industrial society Post–WW II	Transitional paradigm Technological society Vietnam War	Postmodern worldview Internet society War on terrorism
Communication Styles	Print Verbal	Broadcast Presentational	Internet Interactive
Generation	Booster Traditional	Boomer Innovative	"Twenty-Something" Deconstruction/ Reconstruction
Attitude toward History	Maintain distinctives of twentieth-century fundamentals	Get a fresh start Ahistorical	Draw from the wisdom of the past The road to the future runs through the past

(continued)

Table 2
Comparison of Traditional, Pragmatic, and Younger Evangelicals

	Traditional Evangelicals 1950–1975	Pragmatic Evangelicals 1975–2000	Younger Evangelicals 2000–
Theological Commitment	Christianity as a rational worldview	Christianity as therapy Answers needs	Christianity as a community of faith Ancient/Reformation
Apologetics Style	Evidential Foundational	Christianity as meaning-giver Experiential Personal faith	Embrace the metanarrative Embodied apologetic Communal faith
Ecclesial Paradigm	Constantinian church Civil Religion	Culturally sensitive church Market driven	Missional church Countercultural
Church Style	Neighborhood churches Rural	Megachurch Suburban Market targeted	Small church Back to cities Intercultural
Leadership Style	Pastor centered	Managerial model CEO	Team ministry Priesthood of all
Youth Ministry	Church-centered programs	Outreach programs Weekend fun retreats	Prayer, Bible study, worship, social service
Education	Sunday school Information centered	Target generational groups and needs	Intergenerational formation in community
Spirituality	Keep the rules	Prosperity and success	Authentic embodiment
Worship	Traditional	Contemporary	Convergence
Art	Restrained	Art as illustration	Incarnational embodiment
Evangelism	Mass evangelism	Seeker service	Process evangelism
Activists	Beginnings of evangelical social action	Need-driven social action (i.e., divorce groups, drug rehab, etc.)	Rebuild cities and neighborhoods

Where Are the Younger Evangelicals Found?

Twentieth-century evangelicals maintained distinctions between groups such as fundamentalists, neoevangelicals, ethnic evangelicals, mainliners, Reformed evangelicals, Holiness, Pentecostal, and charismatic types, as well as historic churches such as Orthodox and Catholic. But the new movement of the younger evangelicals doesn't have tight boundaries. They come from every branch of the church, every denomination, every parachurch movement, and every ethnic background. While my research has been primarily with the North American phenomena, I am aware of similar kinds of thinking in England, Scotland, New Zealand, Australia, the European countries, Africa, Asia, and Latin America. This movement, the emergence of the younger evangelicals, is worldwide. It cannot be contained or circumscribed, because it is taking root in every branch of Christianity, in every geographical location, and in every culture.

I admittedly interpret the phenomena of this movement from my own perspective. I was born, reared, educated, and have conducted my vocational life from within the distinctives of the American evangelical movement since the fifties. Many who read this book will have shared a journey similar to mine in the twentieth century. Others, especially the young, will have experienced only the evangelicalism of the last two decades of the twentieth century. While I write out of the experience of the latter half of the twentieth century, the primary focus of this book is on the younger evangelicals and the leadership they bring to a new cultural situation. The leadership of the younger evangelicals comes from *within* twentieth-century traditional and pragmatic evangelicalism yet breaks from it to find a new voice in the twenty-first century.

How to Read This Book

In part 1 I introduce the younger evangelicals. Chapter 1, "A Century of Evangelicals," presents an overview of twentieth-century evangelicalism. I briefly interpret the cycles of evangelical history from fundamentalism to the growth of a highly diverse evangelicalism at the end of the century. I suggest that there are three dominant movements at the end of the century poised for leadership in the twenty-first century: the traditionalists, the pragmatists, and the newly emerging younger evangelicals (see table 2). In chapter 2, "A New Kind of Evangelical," I introduce the primary characteristics of the younger evangelicals that will shape the kind of leadership they offer to the church in the twenty-first century.

In part 2, "The Younger Evangelical Thinkers," first I show how younger evangelicals have been influenced by new forms of communications (chapter 3). Then I demonstrate how their new approach to communications has impacted their approach to history, theology, apologetics, and ecclesiology. No longer shaped by the primacy of print communication, the younger evangelicals are moving evangelical thought in new directions. These new movements include a shift from the ahistorical attitude of the twentieth century to a new appreciation of tradition (chapter 4); a shift in theology from propositionalism toward a story-oriented theology (chapter 5); a shift in apologetics from rational arguments to an appreciation for truth verified through communal embodiment (chapter 6); and a shift in ecclesiology from a preoccupation with the invisible church to a new interest in the church visible (chapter 7). In all these shifts the younger evangelicals are reflecting their commitment to move toward an *ancient-future faith*. By ancient-future faith, I mean an evangelicalism connected to the past, especially to the church fathers, the sixteenth-century Reformers, and the Wesleyan movement.[1]

Part 3, "The Younger Evangelical Practitioners," describes how the younger evangelicals differ from twentieth-century evangelicals in how they do church. The first, and perhaps the underlying, shift is from the market-driven church to the missional church (chapter 8). Everything else falls in line with this shift. Pastors are moving from power to servanthood (chapter 9); youth ministers from parties to prayer (chapter 10); educators from information to formation (chapter 11); spiritual directors from legalism to freedom (chapter 12); worship leaders from programs to narrative (chapter 13); artists from constraint to expression (chapter 14); evangelists from rallies to relationship (chapter 15); and activists from theory to action (chapter 16). These fundamental shifts reflect the influence of the pre-Constantinian church. The younger evangelicals look to the early church and how it thrived in the secular and pagan world of the first three centuries to find principles for the church in our current culture.

The final chapter, "A New Kind of Leadership for the Twenty-First Century," focuses on the kind of leadership emerging from the younger evangelical. It is a leadership characterized by missiological, theological, formative, and cultural reflection.

We live in a complex time of history. It is certainly a time of disarray, confusion, and open-endedness. But it is a new day for the church. A new spirit of renewal and reform is sweeping over North America and around the world. The younger evangelicals are on the forefront of this movement, and they will lead evangelical Christianity into a new chapter of its history in the early decades of the twenty-first century.

Introduction to the
Younger Evangelicals

We begin our study of the younger evangelicals by understanding their roots in the twentieth century. Most younger evangelicals were born since 1975 and know little of twentieth-century evangelical history. In order for them to understand themselves and in order for older evangelicals to understand them, they need to be situated in the history of the rise of the movement from which they derived. I address this matter in chapter 1, "A Century of Evangelicals."

The burden of the book is to show how different the younger evangelical is from traditional and pragmatic evangelicals, the two dominant evangelical groups at the end of the twentieth century. Therefore, I map out the primary characteristics of the younger evangelical. My goal is to provide a general insight into their characteristics at the very outset of the book. I address this matter in chapter 2, "A New Kind of Evangelical."

1

A Century
of Evangelicals

Although the younger evangelicals began to appear at the end of the twentieth century, they are inextricably linked with the history and developments of the entire century, particularly the movements of the last half of the century. Therefore, I will begin the study of the younger evangelicals by placing them in the context of a century of evangelicals.

In the broadest sense, American evangelical history goes back to the very beginning of the church. "The Chicago Call," a prophetic document issued to evangelicals by a representative body of evangelicals in 1977, recognizes that "throughout the church's history there has existed an evangelical impulse to proclaim the saving, unmerited grace of Christ, and to reform the church according to the Scriptures."[1] The evangelical story of the twentieth century stands in the tradition of the "impulse to reform the church." But it also has its own unique story determined by the cultural context of the twentieth century.

The rise of twentieth-century evangelicalism came at a crucial time in American history. The new leaders of the American economic and political machinery were moving America toward material wealth and power around the globe while building great cities at home. On the religious scene the spirit of rational inquiry and confidence in scientific knowledge resulted in the questioning of traditional Christianity. Doubts were raised about a supernatural worldview and the literal interpretation of Scripture. The result was the widespread doctrines of liberalism. Jesus was no longer viewed as a supernatural being but a prophet who preached love.[2]

When conservatives reacted against the liberal message, they set into motion the issues that dominated the evangelical history of the twentieth century. The fundamentalist-liberal conflict gave twentieth-century evangelicalism a unique stamp, defining it as a type of evangelical reform different from any of its predecessors—different than the Reformation of the sixteenth century, the rise of seventeenth-century pietism, Puritanism, the nineteenth-century evangelical awakenings of Wesley, the revivalism of Jonathan Edwards or of Charles Finney or of any evangelical who ministered prior to the twentieth century.

This unique context of twentieth-century evangelicalism has shaped the mindset of the twentieth-century evangelical. In particular three movements of twentieth-century evangelical thought have dominated the last seventy-five years. They are *fundamentalism, neoevangelicalism,* and *diversity evangelicalism.* Each of these three umbrella movements has gone through a cycle including charismatic origins, the development of organizations and institutions, and a fixed institutional form. Each of these movements has hearkened back to the original issues that fueled the fundamentalist-modernist controversy but with less and less intensity over time. By the end of the twentieth century, the issues that originally created the rift between fundamentalism and modernism had grown increasingly dim, as the movement of culture reformed and rearranged the issues in each camp. In each cycle a minority sought to resurrect the old questions again and again, but by the end of the century evangelicalism was by and large a movement that had gone far beyond the issues that defined it in the beginning of the century.

Looking back over the twentieth century one can see that each of these three movements has created a proliferation of churches, mission agencies, publishing houses, social organizations, colleges, Bible schools, seminaries, theological systems, and ethical rules. Each group engages in "sibling rivalries" with the other groups and competes for the most lasting ideological inheritance. Two characteristics each have in common is that they belong to the twentieth century, and they have all passed through the stages of development into institutional form. Each group has its elite, its adherents to the core beliefs, and its mavericks who push the envelope.

This chapter is a brief overview of these three movements. It is important to understand these three modes of evangelical thought because they set the stage for understanding the younger evangelicals who are *not of the twentieth century and its mindset.* To know these younger evangelicals, it is necessary to set them in the paradigm shift from the twentieth- to the twenty-first century and grasp how they differ from their predecessors. Then and only then will we understand why postmodern evangelical leadership of the twenty-first century looks and will continue to look very different than evangelical leadership of the twentieth century.

But first, before we look at the twenty-first-century younger evangelical, let's survey the three cycles of evangelical history of the twentieth century (see table 3).

Table 3
Three Cycles of Evangelicals in the Twentieth Century

	Origins	Fundamentalism	Neoevangelicalism	Evangelical Diversity
Time Period	1910–1925	1925–1945	1945–1966	1966–2000
Description	Origins of the Fundamentalist Movement	Anti-intellectual Antiecumenical Anti–social action	Prointellectual Proecumenical Pro–social action	The period between 1966 and 2000 represents an ever-widening diversity in intellectual expressions, in ecumenical relationship, and in the diversity of social concerns

Because twentieth-century evangelicalism constitutes a vast amount of material, I will organize my comments about each of the three cycles of evangelicalism by looking at the attitude of each toward (1) intellectual thought; (2) ecumenical engagement; and (3) social action. My concern is to highlight shifts and developments to see the increasing distance made from the original fundamentalism rather than to provide a comprehensive history. My goal is to describe the setting for the emergence of the fourth cycle, the younger evangelicals who are now a full century away from the debates that formed twentieth-century evangelicalism. I see this new group as a fresh start, a new beginning for an evangelicalism of a different kind.

The Fundamentalist-Modernist Controversy

The story of the origins of fundamentalism in America has been thoroughly detailed by George Marsden.[3] Marsden points out that turn-of-the-twentieth-century evangelicalism was "the dominant religious force in American life."[4] It was characterized by a rigorous foundationalism—an intellectual frame of reference that adhered to the scientific method of empiricism and to the ability of the mind to arrive at factual propositional truth. While conflicts with the growth of liberalism were already brewing at the turn of the twentieth century, the notion of breaking from the established church and beginning a "separate" movement had not been birthed.

Evangelicals and their denominational associations were comfortably rooted in Calvinism, Puritanism, Wesleyan revivalism, and the rise of dispensational thought. Even though there were tensions between these various traditions, evangelicals were united in their commitment to the historic faith, to the Bible as authoritative, and to the Great Commission. Evangelicals were also deeply involved in social action and "The ideal of building a Christian civilization."[5] They were the heirs of the social action derived from the Calvinist and Puritan commitment to the transformation of culture and to the aggressive and effective social reform that stemmed from the Wesleyan revivals. In brief, early twentieth-century evangelicalism was characterized by a rigorous intellectualism, was a movement "within" the major denominations, and was highly sensitive to social concerns.

But the cultural setting at the beginning of the twentieth century was unsettling. The decline of Christendom and the emergence of secularism were becoming increasingly apparent. Walter Lippmann in *Preface to Morals* complained that the "irreligion of the modern world" was "magical to a degree for which there is, I think, no counterpart."[6] The profound spiritual crisis which was to affect the entire twentieth century was already making a subtle appearance.

The foe was modernism and its commitment to evolution. Evolution had emerged as a worldview. It was a new answer to the basic questions: Where did we come from? Why are we here? Where are we going? If evolution was right, there was no need for creation. If man originated from chance and was in charge of his own meaning and history, there was no need for Christian redemption or eschatology. William Jennings Bryan, three-time candidate for president of the United States and vociferous foe of evolution, declared this new hypothesis "is the only thing that has seriously menaced religion since the birth of Christ; and it menaces . . . civilization as well as religion."[7]

The story of how evangelicals won the debate but lost the war over evolution constituted a turning point. Marsden speaks of the enormous impact of the debate: "It would be difficult to overestimate the impact of the 'Monkey Trial' at Dayton, Tennessee, in transforming fundamentalism."[8] The "Monkey Trial" Marsden mentions, also known as the Scopes trial, refers to the 1925 Tennessee legal case in which the state succeeded in having John T. Scopes convicted for illegally teaching evolution in public schools. This trial marked the end of the initial controversy and the beginning of a new kind of fundamentalist saga in the years between 1925 and 1945.

Cycle One: Fundamentalism from 1925 to 1945

The first phase of twentieth-century fundamentalism was known as much for what it was against as for what it was for: First, it was against an intellectual engagement with new thought. Second, it was a time during which the fundamentalists separated from the "liberal" denominations and began their own independent coalitions. Third, it retreated from social engagement with the world.

Anti-intellectual

The first characteristic of fundamentalism was its anti-intellectualism. Historian George Dollar asserts that the movement was "shaped by a desire to strike back at everything modern—the higher criticism, evolutionism, the social gospel, rational criticism of any kind."[9]

While fundamentalism was "anti-intellectual" toward the new movements of thought, it remained rooted in the intellectual thought of "Scottish Common Sense Realism" and to the Baconian system of thought. Common Sense philosophy insisted that "facts" could be known directly. This conviction derived from Descartes' emphasis on knowledge gained through the empirical method. One could study the facts and obtain through observation and reason knowledge that was propositional. While this method was originally known as the "scientific method," it was soon applied to religious knowledge as well. Francis Bacon had taught a method of analysis that consisted of gathering data, classifying it, and interpreting it. Common sense and Baconian analysis were applied to Scripture to determine truth. The inerrant Bible was the source for data fed into the evidential process of knowing truth.

The view of inerrancy, that "every single word of the text had been divinely inspired," figured prominently in the fundamentalist rejection of evolution, historical and literary criticism, and any attempt to interpret Scripture in any way other than a literal reading of each word. Inerrancy extended to all scientific statements, to historical references, and to all numbers found in the prophecies of future events. There was little room for symbol, poetry, or any kind of imaginative speech.

Fundamentalists became "the people of one book." Having no need for philosophy, sociology, history, science, and the arts and disciplines that dominated the intellectual world, the fundamentalist rejected the "philosophy of the world" in favor of "Biblicism."

This was true of my fundamentalist college education, which was marked by a distinct negative attitude toward things intellectual. For example, the fundamentalist school where I was educated did not have a philosophy department because "all you need is the Bible." They offered one course in philosophy to meet state requirements for students in the educational department, but this was a course designed to show why all philosophical speculation was foolish and should be avoided. The opening lecture of the course always dealt with Paul's statement in Colossians 2:8: "See to it that no one takes you captive through hollow and deceptive philosophy, which depends on human tradition and the basic principles of this world rather than on Christ." No attempt was made to put this verse in the context of Hellenistic philosophical thought or in relationship to the growing threat of first-century Gnosticism. It was treated as a blanket statement against the study of all philosophy, a stance that would be taken in that course to teach how the study of philosophy was a waste of time. This attitude still dominates fundamentalist Biblicism, a view that is based on the modern philosophy of rationalism and the scientific method of hermeneutics. This method results in propositions of faith that deliver guaranteed truth, a hermeneutic not widely accepted by the younger evangelical.

Antiecumenical

A second characteristic of fundamentalism was its antiecumenical outlook. The antiecumenical attitude of fundamentalism is understandable given the growing institutionalization of liberal thought in the early part of the century. The antiecumenical attitude was justified when one considers the power exercised by denominational leaders over fundamentalist pastors and churches.

Liberals were not nearly as liberal as they thought. A true liberal spirit is inclusive, magnanimous, and open to others' points of view. But the liberalism of the early to middle part of the twentieth century was anything but liberal when it came to the fundamentalists. Most liberals were scornful of fundamentalist views, demeaning of the people who held these views, extremely controlling, and very proud and arrogant. They considered their reduction of Christianity to the love of God and neighbor as right. Marsden refers to the "increasingly aggressive and ambitious character of interdenominational Protestant liberalism in the immediate postwar years"[10] and writes of a liberal agenda that "repeatedly asserted . . . the eradication of the defective forms of Christianity associated with conservatism."[11] This mean-spirited attitude of the liberals and the control they gained over the mainline denominations caused many fundamentalists to feel their own personal survival and the continuation of their ministry was more important than fighting a losing battle. As my own father did, many pastors and congregations "gave up" and formed new denominations as well as numerous independent churches where they were free from the liberals and their psychological persecution.

A case in point may be taken from the life of young Charles Fuller in the early twenties. Fuller taught Sunday school at the Presbyterian church in Placentia, California. The class, with a fundamentalist point of view, grew so large by 1925 that it created a rift with the pastor, whose sympathies did not lie with the fundamentalist cause. Instead of fighting with the pastor, Fuller took his class out of the church and reorganized his people as the Calvary Church of Placentia.[12] This scenario was repeated in numerous churches and denominational bodies, producing a whole new class of independent churches and new conservative denominations throughout America.

The emergence of their antiecumenical stance is understandable, but it came at the expense of the biblical mandate regarding the unity of the church. However, fundamentalists insisted that unity must be based on truth. Consequently, fundamentalists viewed the liberal denominations as apostate. Fundamentalists saw their exodus from the mainline church as a divine call to "come out from them and be ye separate" (See 2 Cor. 6:17). They viewed themselves as the continuation of the pure church unified through doctrinal consensus. However, their inability to agree on "true truth" led to more splits and to deep divisions among even the fundamentalist groups. To this day a central argument of many fundamentalists is that unity and even fellowship with other Christians must be based on unity in all matters of faith and doctrines.

Anti–Social Action

A third characteristic of fundamentalism was the stand it took against social action. After 1925 fundamentalists withdrew from social action. This shift has been called "The Great Reversal." There are many reasons why this reversal took place. Society had become highly individualistic, and fundamentalist evangelism reflected this shift especially. Marsden reports that "[Dwight L.] Moody dropped direct social involvement for the same reason that he avoided controversial theology—both threatened to distract from his primary concern for evangelism."[13]

The rise and spread of a premillennial eschatology also played a part in the demise of social action. The new prophets turned their backs against nineteenth-century postmillennialism in which the moral and social progress of that century was seen as the upward movement toward the achievement of the kingdom by the church. Now the world, with the growth of secularism and the demise of Christendom, was getting "worse and worse," and, as the premillennium doctrine asserted, would become increasingly worse until Jesus returned.[14]

The attitude toward social action became "Why bother? . . . We can let it get worse and perhaps hasten the return of Jesus." While these movements did effect an antisocial stance among fundamentalists, none were as crucial to the fundamentalist loss of interest in social action as the liberal commitment to social action. Who wanted to look like the liberals anyway?

Liberals, having rejected doctrine as the touchstone of Christianity, moved toward a more pragmatic position which interpreted Christianity in terms of action. Truth was not what you thought but what you did. Jesus' agenda was interpreted as a social movement spoiled by the metaphysical interpretation given to it by Paul. Paul, it was argued, had ruined true Christianity, and now liberal nineteenth-century scholarship had restored the true teaching of Jesus. It separated Jesus from Paul, arguing that Paul had Hellenized the gospel. The bible of this new liberal Christianity was Walter Rauschenbusch's *A Theology for the Social Gospel*.[15] Rauschenbusch argued for a new version of postmillennialism in which the church would eventually convert the world to Christianity and establish God's kingdom of love over the entire earth. Fundamentalists viewed the liberal involvement in social issues as a substitution for truth. In this way, they paved the way for a doctrinaire fundamentalism that neglected social concern.

Fundamentalists had good reason, given their historical origins, to be anti-intellectual, antiecumenical, and anti–social action. There is, of course, much more to fundamentalism than the three "anti's" I have described. But these three attitudes unveil the spirit of fundamentalism and give us an insight into its heart. What began as a defense of the faith, a movement of intellectual strength and courage, became by the middle of the forties a movement of legalism. Its approach to theology became doctrinaire and legalistic; it rejected any social action on the part of the church; and it viewed all other denominations and Christian groups as apostate. Frozen in their ways, the fundamentalists were to receive a jolt when their own children broke from the circle to start the neoevangelical movement.

Cycle Two: The "New" Evangelical

A new generation of evangelical leaders emerged in America after World War II. In the immediate aftermath of the war, America became "upbeat": World War II veterans returned with an agenda to begin their lives again, to marry and have children, to return to school, to start new businesses, to integrate into society. This new cultural impulse generated a new breed of evangelicals who were anxious to disassociate themselves from the fundamentalism of the past and from its negative persona. According to historian Tim Weber, they "launched a well coordinated strategy to achieve their goals."[16] This strategy included a new name, "new evangelicalism"; the organization of the National Association of Evangelicals (NAE) in 1943; the founding of Fuller Seminary in 1947; the establishment of *Christianity Today* in 1949; the development of specialized ministries such as Young Life, Youth for Christ, and Campus Crusade for Christ; and the emergence of Billy Graham as the movement's central figure.[17] The story can be told in terms of the movement's challenge to fundamentalist anti-intellectualism, antiecumenism, and anti–social action.

Challenge to Anti-intellectualism

The first broadside directed against fundamentalist anti-intellectualism came through Carl F. H. Henry's *Remaking the Modern Mind*, published in 1946. Henry argued that fundamentalism "developed a disastrous isolation from the questions on which the future direction of civilization hung" and that fundamentalists were prepared to "fall all over each other in the rush to make it clear that they have no message which is relevant to modern political, sociological, economic and educational tension." Henry traced the philosophical roots of liberalism with its notions of the evolutionary progress of history and the inherent goodness of man to show the fallacy of Western thought, the demise of Christian influence in culture, and to call on the new evangelicals to "seize the opportunity to build a new mind for the forthcoming era."[18]

The "new mind" that the leaders of the new evangelical movement had in mind was the "Reformed paradigm," the one that had been taught at "the old Princeton Seminary, where theology was rationalistic (in the Scottish common-sense style), ready to do battle for the faith, and firmly tied to the doctrine of biblical inerrancy."[19] The theology of the "new" evangelicalism was actually a form of old fundamentalism that excluded Wesleyan evangelicalism's emphasis on free will and marched under the intellectual banner of a reformative fundamentalism.

Challenge to Anti–Social Action

It was also Carl Henry who took the fundamentalists to task for their anti–social action attitude. His book, *The Uneasy Conscience of Modern Fundamentalism*, published in 1947, called on fundamentalists to quit their internal squabbles and turn their attention to the practical application of their doctrines. "For the first protracted period in its history, Evangelical Christianity stands divorced from the great social movements" wrote Henry.[20]

Harold Ockenga, the young and brilliant pastor of Park Street Church in Boston, wrote the introduction to Henry's book and stated: "If the Bible-believing Christian is on the wrong side of social problems such as war, race, class, labor, liquor, imperialism, etc.," then "it's time to get over the fence on the right side."[21] Marsden notes that "the call for more social involvement among fundamentalists was little more than that—a call. In reality, this theme received relatively little attention."[22] The focus was primarily on the task of reformulating an intellectually sound evangelicalism and establishing missions and evangelism around the world. These were the twin goals of Fuller Seminary, the focal point for the story of the new evangelicalism.

Challenge to Antiecumenism

The challenge to the antiecumenical stance of fundamentalism also emerged within Fuller Seminary. Harold Ockenga had become friends with Hungarian theologian Bela Vassaday, who had not been part of the fundamentalist controversy. He was a founder of the World Council of Churches and a disciple of Karl Barth whose credentials as an evangelical were suspect. Vassaday's appointment to the Fuller faculty turned out to be "too much" for fundamentalist Fuller supporters to handle. Francis Schaeffer, who by now was quite well known and influential in the new evangelical circles, declared that Karl Barth was not an evangelical because, Schaeffer wrote, he will say "the Bible is infallible but he *will not say* that the Bible is inerrant."[23] Vassaday, who had survived under communism, saw the fundamentalism that still lurked within evangelicalism as a "spiritual totalitarianism" and privately wrote to a friend that "he had never experienced a seminary so Evangelical in doctrine and so un-Evangelical in practice."[24] Vassaday eventually left Fuller Seminary in 1950.

However, it was the emergence of Billy Graham and his evangelistic crusades that pushed the ecumenical issue. When I entered Bob Jones University in the early 1950s Billy Graham was still in the good graces of Bob Jones Sr., who spoke well of him and introduced him to the student body with warm accolades. All that changed because of Billy Graham's New York crusade in 1957. Graham insisted he would not go to New York unless he had the support of all the churches. Graham's choice in 1955 to reject the exclusive support of the fundamentalists and accept the invitation extended by the Protestant council of the city of New York to hold his New York crusade under their auspices became a point of irreparable breach between fundamentalism and the new evangelicalism. Bob Jones Sr. launched an aggressive campaign against Billy Graham and all those associated with the Graham outlook. Students' mailboxes were filled with anti-Graham literature, and Jones declared in chapel "Billy Graham is the tool of the devil in the twentieth century" and soon thereafter Bob Jones students were forbidden to attend his crusades and even to pray for him. Infraction of these rules resulted in immediate dismissal from the school. Bob Jones III, the current president and grandson of the founder, continues to echo the same sentiments as did his grandfather and father.

Tensions between fundamentalism and new evangelicalism continue to this day over the issues of intellectual engagement with the world of thought, commitment to social issues, and relations with the mainline church. The division between the two groups runs so deep that it is rare for fundamentalists to cooperate in any way with the new evangelicals who have dominated the second half of the twentieth century.

It is clear that evangelicals are "sons of the fundamentalists," but in many cases fundamentalist fathers and mothers see evangelicals as prodigal sons, sons who have wandered away from the family, sons who are now effectively disowned and removed from the will. But the separation that had occurred between the fundamentalists and the evangelicals was to repeat itself, at least to some degree, by the rise of evangelical diversity—a response to the changes taking place in society, namely the cultural revolution of the sixties and the spread of evangelicalism throughout the world and in many different cultures.

Cycle Three: The Rise of Evangelical Diversity

Sociologist Francis Fukuyama views the period between 1960 and 1990 as an aberration in American history. He comments on how this period of intense turmoil and change was "marked by seriously deteriorating social conditions"[25] such as the rise of crime, the inhabitability of the inner cities, the disruption of social institutions, the decline of marriages, the rise of divorce, out-of-wedlock births, the breakdown of values, the suspicion of institutions, the intensification of individualism, the demise of authority, and in general the collapse of modern society as we knew it. It was during this period of history that evangelicalism became subject to the rise of diversity and branched out in many different ways to address the growing cultural pluralism. During this period of history, new evangelicalism faced external challenges, internal challenges, and the development of new models of ministry. Fundamentalism stayed more intact because it was arrested in its development and frozen in its anti-intellectual, antiecumenical, and anti–social action stance. But evangelicals, having become free of fundamentalist control, interacted creatively with the cultural changes of this thirty-year period.

Just as it was a time of great change in culture, it was a time of great upheaval in the evangelical community, bringing enormous changes in its intellectual, ecumenical, and social life.

Intellectual Diversity

The seeds for *theological pluralism* within evangelicalism were already sown in the establishment of the National Association of Evangelicals (NAE) in 1943. This organization included members from the Wesleyan, Holiness, and Pentecostal traditions. While their viewpoints were held "in check" by the consensus of the Reformed leadership, this control was not to endure into the seventies. Donald Dayton, for example, challenged the tightly construed Reformed evangelicalism by tracing "another set of Evangelical roots" that went back to Wesleyan luminaries like Jonathan Blanchard (first president of Wheaton College), the well-known revivalist Charles Finney, and other Wesleyans who introduced social reform. Dayton concluded, "A great heritage of Evangelical social witness was buried and largely forgotten."[26] Through his writings and that of other Wesleyans who emerged to make their claim as "heirs of nineteenth-century evangelicalism," the Reformed leaders of new evangelicalism lost their theological control and had to allow the Wesleyan witness, which was a substantially different theological tradition, into the evangelical tent. Theological consensus was gone. Theological diversity was birthed.[27]

This theological pluralism became evident in the differences among evangelicals concerning *biblical inerrancy*. Mark Noll distinguishes between two attitudes toward biblical criticism that emerged within this new coalition between

Reformed and Wesleyan evangelicalism. The evangelicals with Reformed commitments tended toward the party of "critical anti-critics."[28] For them the purpose of scholarship was to "protect the Bible against its detractors." According
to Reformed scholars, modern research had overthrown the authority of the
Bible. Consequently, they "worked hard to support traditional notions of authorship, dating, literary transmission, and the Bible's historical and scientific
accuracy."[29]

My own seminary education in the late fifties and sixties was preoccupied
with these issues. Studies dealing with various books of the Bible almost never
dealt with their message but almost always with matters of authorship and internal consistencies. In most schools of Reformed evangelicalism, the Bible is still
taught from the critical perspective even though students who are removed from
the debate by two generations long for a study of the Bible that focuses on content and message.

On the other hand, evangelicals with Wesleyan commitments tended toward
what Noll calls the position of "believing critics."[30] According to Tim Weber,
they were more "willing to let go of traditional interpretations where the find-
ings of modern research were convincing, but they denied that they were rejecting the Bible's inspiration and authority when they did so."[31]

These two attitudes toward biblical criticism spilled over into the issue of inerrancy. Reformed evangelicals were committed to inerrancy, but the Wesleyan
element thought the word "inerrant" to be too precise and unnecessary. By the
middle of the sixties the debate broadened with some from the Reformed side
of evangelicalism wondering if the word "inerrant" was useful any longer. The
turning point came at a meeting in June of 1966 at Gordon College where a
group of fifty scholars met to solve the problem but discovered "irreconcilable
differences in their approach to the Bible."[32] The failure to come to consensus
on inerrancy provoked Harold Lindsell to write *Battle for the Bible* in 1977. Lindsell argued that no question "is more important than the one that has to do with
the basis of our religious knowledge."[33] He claimed that "for two thousand years
the Christian church has agreed that the Bible is completely trustworthy; it is
infallible or inerrant."[34] Lindsell contended that "embracing a doctrine of errant
scripture . . . will finally lead to apostasy."[35] In effect, Lindsell laid down the
gauntlet that subscription to biblical inerrancy was the mark of a true evangelical. His book resulted in a torrent of literature in agreement and disagreement
with his thesis and eventually led to the International Council of Biblical Inerrancy. This council met in Chicago in 1978 and produced the "Chicago Statement on Biblical Inerrancy."[36] While a statement was issued, no real consensus
on inerrancy was forged in the evangelical tent.

For institutions committed to a Reformed evangelicalism like Gordon-Conwell Seminary; Trinity Evangelical Divinity School in Deerfield, Illinois; and
Wheaton College, strict adherence to biblical inerrancy as articulated by Harold

Lindsell has become "a political weapon for institutional control."[37] Other evangelical schools like Fuller and Asbury Seminaries as well as colleges like Westmont and Messiah do not require subscription to the word "inerrant." Lindsell, not happy with this situation, wrote, "The term *Evangelical* has been so debased that it has lost its usefulness" and suggested that those who believe in the strict use of the word "inerrant" should call themselves fundamentalists.[38] But pluralism about this matter has prevailed. In most organizations and institutions of evangelicalism, people work side by side believing differently about how "inerrant" should be used.

One impact of the inerrancy issue is that it spread the parameters of evangelicalism beyond the Calvinist/Wesleyan constituency to include two large denominations, the Southern Baptists and the Lutheran church, Missouri Synod. Evangelicalism, by 1980, had grown far beyond its small beginnings in the fundamentalist/modernist controversy of the Presbyterian church.

A third broadening of evangelical theology was rooted in *the recovery of the ancient tradition*. A group of forty leaders met to write "The Chicago Call" in 1977.[39] The writers of this call urged evangelicals to move toward a more historic faith. The call states, "In the past ten years or so, a number of evangelicals have been growing beyond the borders of what has, until now, been regarded as the limits of evangelicalism. In the same way that our current Evangelical fathers, Billy Graham, Harold Ockenga, Harold Lindsell, Carl F. H. Henry, and others grew beyond the borders of fundamentalism, so a new group of evangelicals following their example, have continued to look beyond the present limitations of the 'new' evangelicals toward a more inclusive and ultimately historic Christianity."[40] The call asked for evangelicals to return to their (1) historic roots and continuity, (2) biblical fidelity (without using the word inerrant), (3) creedal identity, (4) holistic salvation (justice as part of the salvific process), (5) integrity, (6) spirituality (devotional resources of the whole church), (7) church authority (return to the visible concept of the church), and (8) church unity.

"The Chicago Call" was largely ignored by the evangelical establishment even though its writers included well-known leaders like Donald Bloesch, Donald Dayton, Peter Gillquist, Thomas Howard, Richard Lovelace, and Eugene Osterhaven. Because there was no room in the evangelical subculture for this kind of witness to historic Christianity, some leaders who wanted to restore the ancient faith ultimately chose to move into historic churches such as the Anglican and Orthodox churches as well as the Catholic church. Interestingly, these leaders did not repudiate their evangelical roots. Instead, they insisted they were still evangelical but now more fulfilled evangelicals having moved into the historic church. The insistence on being an evangelical Anglican or evangelical Orthodox or evangelical Catholic added more movements to evangelicalism and served to highlight the already growing diversity.[41]

The fourth intellectual movement is what Tim Weber calls *pragmatic evangelicalism.*[42] This movement challenged the "old" way of doing evangelism and modeled a new tradition for church growth. This pragmatic nature of the seeker tradition shifted toward an *ahistorical* and *antitheological* stance. A method of evangelism that paid attention to marketing issues, sought to meet people's needs, and relied on a seeker service transferred easily into any theological tradition. It brought into its orbit scores of churches and ministers from struggling churches to learn about the new evangelism. It also created a flurry of theological writings that chided the movement for "dumbing down the faith."[43] By the end of the twentieth century, this movement, fueled by church-growth principles, the rise of the megachurch, and the popularity of contemporary worship, became the most influential of all late twentieth-century evangelical movements.

Fifth, the *openness of God* movement, ushered in by evangelical theologian Clark Pinnock, emerged.[44] Pinnock, a former Southern Baptist friend and protégé of Francis Schaeffer and committed Reformed theologian, did an about-face and became an Arminian. Influenced by the new science, Pinnock opened questions about the immutability of God and suggested God's relationship to the world is interactive. This movement, which began in the eighties, picked up some steam in the nineties with new spokespersons such as Gregory Boyd[45] and John Sanders.[46] While this movement is opposed particularly by Reformed evangelicals, the fact that it remains within evangelicalism speaks to the extent of intellectual diversity within evangelicalism by the end of the century.

By 1990 the intellectual diversity within the new widespread and unmanageable evangelicalism produced a theological wringing of hands. Movements to restore the evangelical center began to emerge. But where was that center? David Wells, in *No Place for Truth*,[47] saw the center in the Reformed faith; Stanley J. Grenz called for a revisioning of evangelical theology,[48] seeing the center in experience.

Christianity Today sponsored a conference that met in Florida in the summer of 2000 to draft "The Gospel of Jesus Christ: An Evangelical Celebration," a document in search of a unifying center.[49] The document's emphasis is "unity in the gospel," or agreement on the essentials of the Christian faith. No mention is made of a particular theological tradition, nor of inerrancy (although the Scripture is declared infallible), and an attempt is made to show that the gospel as presented in this document is affirmed by "the Patristic Rule of Faith, the historic creeds, the Reformation confessions, and the doctrinal bases of later Evangelical bodies," all of whom "witness to the substance of this biblical message."[50] Near the end of the document are these words: "Centuries ago it was truly said that in all things necessary there must be unity, in things less than necessary there must be liberty, and in all things there must be charity. We see all these gospel truths as necessary."[51] This declaration is an interesting note on which to end a century of intellectual turmoil and debate.

But has the debate ended? Has evangelicalism come to unity and peace? Probably not. And for this reason evangelicalism at the end of the century was no longer an American phenomena but a *global movement.* Already by the end of the century, new evangelical voices from Africa, Asia, and Latin America were raising new theological questions as William Dyrness has shown in *Learning about Theology from the Third World, Invitation to Cross-Cultural Theology,* and *Emerging Voices in Global Christian Theology.*[52] The intellectual structures of fundamentalism and of the new evangelicalism no longer define evangelical theology. By the end of the century, evangelicalism was a movement of great theological diversity.

The Ecumenical Spread

The period between 1965 and 2000 was also a time for the expansion of evangelical relations with the entire church. Six distinct movements have given rise to the ecumenical flavor of evangelicalism.

First, the intellectual pluralism discussed in the preceding section had the effect of breaking evangelicalism from its attachment to the Scottish Common Sense realism and the Baconian method of hermeneutics. It allowed traditions not rooted in this particular Western Enlightenment view to be included under the banner of evangelical. This shift cannot be underestimated. It wrenched the tight control of evangelicalism from Carl F. H. Henry, Harold Lindsell, and others who wanted evangelicalism to be contained by its original connection with the Presbyterian roots of fundamentalism. By the end of the century, *evangelical* was a word that could be used of people in every conservative tradition of Protestantism as well as groups within the Catholic and Orthodox traditions.[53] What was once a restricted evangelical isolationism became an *evangelical ecumenism.*

Second, the globalization of evangelical Christianity into Asia, Africa, and Latin America has expanded American evangelicalism beyond its former borders to reach across nearly every culture of the world and into new denominations that have flourished around the world. What once was confined to a small group of fundamentalists in the eastern United States is now a *global phenomena.*

Third, one major effect of globalization is the new multicultural face of evangelical Christianity. For most of the twentieth century, evangelicalism was almost exclusively white. Since 1960, African-Americans have emerged within the evangelical tent in America. But the worldwide impact of Asian, African, and Latin American presence in international conferences has created an international face for evangelical Christianity. What was once a white movement is now *multicultural.*

The fourth sign of ecumenical expansion within evangelicalism is the rise of distinctly evangelical movements within mainline denominations.

The fifth symbol of ecumenical expansion is the dialogue now occurring between evangelicals and Catholics. The most visible expression of this dialogue is found in the document, "Evangelicals and Catholics Together," which was released on March 29, 1994.[54] Even though the document speaks to "common convictions about faith and mission" and does not "speak officially for our communities,"[55] it has created a storm of protest by the Reformed evangelicals who consider Catholicism to be apostate and have thus advocated a stance of separation from the Catholics.

A sixth example of ecumenical dialogue is derived from the current discussions between evangelical and Orthodox communities. The leader of this movement is Brad Nassif. Nassif was converted under the ministry of Billy Graham and then went on to complete his graduate education in theology. "In 1990, Nassif founded and now leads the society for the study of eastern Orthodoxy and evangelicalism, a scholarly association that explores both religious communities."[56] A group that once listened only to the Reformed faith wants now to hear what the Eastern fathers have to say.

The Widening Social Concern

The third area in which evangelicalism burst beyond the borders of the new evangelicalism of the fifties and sixties was that of social concern. The evangelical leaders of the seventies felt the new evangelical initiatives in *social action* did not go far enough. Evangelicals generally supported the war in Vietnam, were behind Richard Nixon, and were arguing that capitalism was the form of economics ordained by God. The evangelicals who provided the vision and energy to become more socially active were Jim Wallis and Ron Sider. Wallis, as a student at Trinity Evangelical Divinity School in Deerfield, Illinois, began a highly controversial news journal called *The Post-American*, which eventually became *Sojourners* magazine. Wallis and Sider organized a conference on evangelical social action that met in Chicago over the Thanksgiving holiday in 1973. This conference of about one hundred evangelical leaders included a widespread body of adherents from the Reformed evangelical group such as Carl F. H. Henry to the Mennonite evangelical John Howard Yoder. But *The Chicago Declaration* produced by them reflected themes that were more expressive of the "left" side of evangelicalism.[57]

The Chicago Declaration document constituted a turning point in the evangelical social conscience. It reflects its situation in history, of course, which included the cold war, the indifference of most evangelicals to the problems of injustice around the world and of racism at home, and the rise of women's issues. The people invited also exemplify the growing ecumenical face of the evangelical church—Calvinists like Lewis Smedes, Wesleyans like Donald Dayton, Mennonites like Dale Brown—united in their concern for a new evangelical social conscience. This document succeeded in triggering a social awakening among evangelicals.[58] In succeeding years Ron Sider wrote *Rich Christians in an Age of Hunger*, which held its place on the bestseller list for years.[59]

In the years between 1974 and 1999, evangelical social action reached around the world through world relief and numerous other movements. A mature evangelical social conscience had been awakened to action that went far beyond the imagination of the new evangelical who had originally called for a return to social action. Evangelical social action at the end of the twentieth century was as vital and energetic as it was after the evangelical awakenings in England at the end of the nineteenth century. What began on an anti–social action platform was now the most socially active Christian community in the world.

A second expansion of social concern occurred in the rise of the women's movement. Leaders of this movement—Nancy Hardesty, Sharon Gallagher, Eunice Schatz, and Donna Simons—were present and involved in *The Chicago Declaration*. But they began their own movement with the publication of Letha Scanzoni and Nancy Hardesty's *All We're Meant to Be*.[60] They argued for a much more egalitarian view of the sexes, for "Women's Liberation" and for women's ordination. They founded the Evangelical Women's Caucus International to promote their feminist perspective. This group was controversial and made some headway within evangelical circles but became suspect in 1986 when, in a meeting in Fresno, California, a group called "Lesbians and Their Friends" emerged within the Women's Caucus. Lesbians and Their Friends called on the Caucus to recognize "the presence of a lesbian minority" and to take "a firm stand in favor of civil rights protection for homosexual persons." The resolution passed with eighty in favor, sixteen opposed, and twenty-three abstaining.[61] This vote resulted in a break in the ranks and the formation of a new group called "Christians for Biblical Equality." This new group has had a much larger impact on evangelical churches and women because it maintains a traditional stance on homosexuality.

To follow is a list of characteristics for each of the three shifts involved in the emergence of the younger evangelicals.

Social Diversity

The Moral Majority and the Christian Coalition
The Women's Movement
Worldwide social action
Evangelicals and Catholics in dialogue

Ecumenical Diversity

Mainline evangelicalism
Multicultural evangelicalism
Global evangelicalism
Ecumenical evangelicalism

Intellectual Diversity

Openness of God movement
Pragmatic evangelicalism
Recovery of the ancient tradition
Inerrancy questioned
Theological pluralism

In the meantime a men's caucus in support of homosexuality emerged.[62] Evangelicalism began as a "male" movement in early fundamentalism but since has been challenged to include women and homosexuals. While women have found a new place of leadership, gay and lesbian behavior is still rejected. But the issue lies at the doorstep of evangelicalism.

The third movement of social concern to affect evangelicals in the eighties was the rise of the Moral Majority, a political action group founded by evangelist Rev. Jerry Falwell.[63] Although this movement arose from within fundamentalism and was hotly contested by fundamentalists who argued against social action in favor of an exclusive emphasis on the "evangelism of souls," it struck a nerve among many evangelicals and drew them into a culture war against the loss of Christian values. The concern to stem the tide of the breakdown of the family, the high rate of abortion, the availability of pornography, the rise of permissive sex, the violence on television, and other expressions of moral collapse were addressed by hundreds of thousands of fundamentalists and evangelicals in movements that were an outgrowth of the Moral Majority. These included Focus on the Family,[64] Concerned Women of America,[65] and eventually the successor to the Moral Majority, the Christian Coalition.[66]

While these three matters—social action, women in positions of leadership, and Christian political action—are the major areas of social responsibility, evangelicals in general are involved proactively in every social issue confronted in America and around the world. Social responsibility is no longer an item of "extra" interest but a matter fundamental to the evangelical presentation of the Good News.

An Evangelicalism at the End of the Century

This brief overview of twentieth-century evangelicalism through the eyes of its intellectual agenda, ecumenical commitment, and social concern demonstrates that a great deal of change has occurred between the fundamentalism of 1925 and the evangelical diversity of 1999.

A movement that began as a highly confined dispute within the Presbyterian denomination and against modernism appeared doomed to obscurity in 1925. Its emergence in a new form after World War II was still contained to a small group of people centering around Fuller Seminary, *Christianity Today*, and Billy Graham. But this small group, reflecting its cultural situation, became enmeshed with the rise of pluralism, and the evangelical cause spread beyond its tiny borders to become an international movement as diverse as the world in which it was situated.

By the end of the century, evangelical leaders became highly concerned about the future of the evangelical movement. Evangelicals began to look for clarity and a unity of focus in the midst of what appeared to be an unwieldy diversity. Questions such as, "What is evangelicalism?" "Where is its center?" and "Where are we going?" began to emerge. The old issues that were organized around intellectualism, ecumenicalism, and social action were no longer rallying points.

Within the dizzying array of options, two strong movements were apparent at the end of the century. The first was a call to return to traditional evangelical Christianity defined as a return to a kind of prediverse evangelical faith. This movement faces the current cultural changes by calling people to build an evangelical Christianity rooted in theological propositionalism, evidential apologetics, a cautious pragmatic regard toward evangelical diversity, and a negative view to postmodernity.

The other movement contending for leadership at the end of the twentieth century was pragmatic evangelicalism. Its central church is Willow Creek Community Church and its most visible leader is Bill Hybels. This movement is a product of the church growth movement, the megachurch movement, and the contemporary worship movement. Through its association of Willow Creek churches and its huge conferences here in America and around the world, this movement has attracted many thousands of churches, impacted numerous pastors and lay leaders, and emerged as one of the most controversial movements of the twentieth century.

But beneath the surface, there is another movement that is now emerging. They are the younger evangelicals who are neither traditional nor pragmatic evangelicals. They share common elements of the faith such as the authority of Scripture, the affirmation of the trinity, the deity of Jesus, the efficacy of Jesus' death and resurrection, and the affirmation of the church as the body of Christ. But they differ with both the traditionalists and the pragmatists on how Christianity is presented and practiced in a twenty-first-century culture.

This book focuses on the younger evangelicals as the next generation of leaders, the first new evangelical movement of the twenty-first century. Because they are different than either the traditionalists or the pragmatists, I contrast them to both throughout the book.

I do not suggest that all evangelicals lie within one of these three movements. The spread of evangelical Christianity is far too complex to reduce it to three movements. My point is that the two most visible movements at the end of the twentieth century were the traditionalists and the pragmatists. There are certain schools, organizations, and publications that tend to be one or another. For example, seminaries like Gordon-Conwell in Boston, Trinity Evangelical Divinity School in Chicago, Covenant Seminary in St. Louis, and the magazine *World* represent the more traditional kind of leadership. On the other hand, the pragmatic evangelicals cluster around the megachurch movement represented by Saddleback Community Church in Orange County, California, and Willow Creek Community Church in the suburbs of Chicago. These are the internationally known *images* of these two movements. The younger evangelicals have not yet created highly visible and well-known images. Perhaps the best-known is www.emergentvillage.com. Another is www.theooze.com. Magazines such as *Faithworks* and *Regeneration Quarterly* are emerging as rallying points for younger evangelical thought. Churches like Mars Hill Fellowship in Seattle, Mars Hill Bible Church in Grand Rapids, and numerous smaller churches that will never gain national visibility are emerging.

There are also schools and publications that straddle the fence where you not only find traditionalists but also pragmatists and the emerging younger evangelicals. *Christianity Today* is the best example of a publication that seeks to represent the full diversity within evangelicalism. Fuller Theological Seminary contains a mixture of these three movements with a strong emphasis on the pragmatic and the emerging younger evangelicals.

The purpose of this book is to introduce the younger evangelicals, not to offer a study of the diversity of evangelicalism. My primary concern is to introduce the new kind of leadership found among the twenty-somethings. Therefore, the comparison I make with the traditionalists and the pragmatists are methodological. The focus of the book is the younger evangelicals, not the traditionalists, nor the pragmatists. In order to describe how the younger evangelicals practice being the church, however, I contrast them with other evangelicals, particularly the pragmatists.

2

A
New Kind
of Evangelical

In the previous chapter the younger evangelical was placed in the context of the history of twentieth-century evangelicalism. These younger evangelicals also need to be situated in the cultural revolution from the twentieth to the twenty-first century. It must be remembered that they were reared and educated in a different context than that of the traditionalist and the pragmatist.

For example, traditionalists were shaped by the Enlightenment emphasis on reason and science and by the postdepression and post–World War II emphasis on rebuilding society. Their approach to the church and to faith reflected a stable society. As changes came after the sixties, they generally resisted the change and opted for the security they had built into their traditional ways.

On the other hand, the pragmatists grew up in that era Francis Fukuyama called "The Great Disruption."[1] They were influenced by a hippie generation, by the civil rights revolution, by the war in Vietnam, by the first moon landing, by the *green* revolution, by Woodstock, and by a revolution against the past—its institutions and traditions. The byword was *new*. If it was new, it was good. If it was old, it was bad.

The late sixties and seventies were characterized by a deep reaction against all forms of tradition, including religious traditions. Chuck Fromm observes that "western civilization was suddenly and completely thrown into a state of violent flux and from the turmoil emerged a strange new figure—the counter culture anti-hero enemy of authority, committed free thinker, impassioned free lover, obsessive searcher."[2] These people became a generation of searchers.

The evangelical pragmatists emerged as the new religious gurus to create new ministries to appeal to the seekers. They adapted successful business models and created the market-driven megachurch based on the principles taught by the church growth movement.

Table 4
The Cycles of Traditional, Pragmatic, and Younger Evangelical Histories

	Traditional Evangelicals	Pragmatic Evangelicals	Younger Evangelicals
Era of Origin	Modern Post–World War II Era (1950–1970)	Revolution of the Sixties (1970–1980)	Postmodern, Post–9/11 Era (2000–?)
Organized	1970–1980	1980–1990	
Institutionalized	1970–1990	1990–2000	

Evangelical groups follow a cycle of birth led by charismatic leaders. Each new movement follows the pattern of becoming organized and eventually institutionalized. Later, a new group breaks from the parent group and the cycle begins again. The younger evangelicals represent the first new cycle of the twenty-first century. Older cycles continue to exist and minister, generally with decreasing effectiveness. Many subgroups exist within evangelicalism, but the traditional, pragmatic, and younger evangelicals represent the main voices of evangelicalism at the beginning of the twenty-first century.

While the traditional and pragmatic churches flourished and influenced the evangelical church across the globe, another new set of social conditions appeared to influence younger people in a new direction.

First, a strong sense of spirituality replaced the former mood of secular humanism. According to Wade Clark Roof, author of *Spiritual Marketplace*, "observing the religious scene today, one is struck by a distinct change of mood." The shift is from the search for "group identity and social location" to the quest "for an authentic inner life and personhood." "Religion," he writes, "has to do with two major foci of concerns—personal meaning and social belonging." The quest in the beginning of the twenty-first century is "around the first of these" and is so widespread that it "is now a province not just of theologians and journalists, but of ordinary people in cafes, coffee bars and bookstores across the country."

All this is happening, Roof notes, at a time when the West is undergoing a massive cultural change in which "discoveries in quantum physics and astronomy lead scientists to back away from Newtonian notions of a deterministic uni-

verse and to speak of awe, holism and even of an observer created universe."
These trends are also occurring at a "time when tradition as memory and its
hold on peoples' lives, or lack thereof, is widely discussed in intellectual circles,
most notably in the debates over modernity and postmodernity." He further
notes that the current "spiritual yearnings are leading many Americans beyond
the self-centered, therapeutic culture in which they grew up."[3]

"Journey" and "recovery" language keep the focus upon growth and self-de-
velopment, thereby reinforcing a personal, psychological account of the meaning of salvation. This personalized account of salvation reflects the "emphasis
away from the 'truth-oriented' posturing of the older religious conservatism."
He identifies this "older" faith with the "rationalistic and tough in demanding
assent to doctrinal formulations."[4] This has resulted in an "epistemological shift"
from the reason-based theology of the fundamentalists to a more experience-
based faith, "grounded in the whole person, in both body and mind." Spirituality, mocked by the secular humanists of the sixties, is now a common quest and a
respectable topic of conversation. Roof noted the rise in spiritual hunger prior
to the events of September 11, 2001. Since then, the quest for spiritual reality
has increased exponentially.

Conrad Cherry, director of The Center for Study of Religion and American
Culture at Indiana University/Purdue University, reports, "Prayer circles and
faith-based groups like True Love Waits or Fellowship of Christian Athletes
have proliferated in high schools and college campuses like so many WWJD
bracelets: Christian rock festivals and CDs rival their secular tent."[5] This search
for faith "may be the generation's most important signature" and is "more important than fashions, tastes or even behavior," says William Damon, director of
The Center on Adolescence at Stanford.[6]

Another characteristic of millennial youth (youth who witnessed the beginning of the twenty-first century) is their commitment to service. *U.S. News and
World Report* said "about a quarter of all high school students today regularly
perform community service, while an additional 40 percent do so occasionally."[7]
Newsweek estimates an even higher rate of service among teens, suggesting "as
many as 60 percent do some kind of community service, primarily through
faith-based organizations." James Youniss of the Catholic University of America
suggests that many youths do service "for a connection with the history of a system of meaning. Religion is one. Politics is one. Ethnicity is one."[8] We may now
add military service in the war on terrorism as another.

The matter of ethnicity is another characteristic of the young. *Newsweek* felt
this was such an important shift, an entire article, "Color My World," was devoted to the subject. The article reports that teens generally view race to be an
"outdated institution." Statistics seem to bear this out. "Thirty years ago, only
one in every 100 children born in the United States was of mixed race. Today
the number is 1 in 19."[9] Twenty-one-year-old Matt Kelly, founder of *Marvin*

Magazine, a publication with a circulation of thirty-two thousand that explores interracial relationships, claims, "Young people today want to mix it up and continually blur the boundaries."[10] Liz Short, the daughter of a white service-man and Korean mother, sums up the new attitude: "Just look around. It's great! Nobody is plain white or plain black, or plain anything. Eventually, I'm hoping every place will be like this."[11]

While religion, service to others, and interculturalism are among the strongest trends among young people, these are not all the trends. Another trend is a more conservative attitude toward sex. *Newsweek* reports that "teen pregnancy is down slightly . . . abstinence initiatives are now commonplace around the country."[12]

What does all of this add up to? Youth are open to the supernatural, ready to commit their lives to a cause they can believe in, ready for a leadership that sees the church as made up of many tribes and nations—a church that is intergenerational and intercultural. What will reach these youth and draw them into faith? The pragmatist's bywords were "big," "flashy," "slick," "entertaining," and "What's in it for me?" The younger evangelical's bywords are "real," "genuine," "relational," "honest," "mix it up," and "What can I do for others?"

The twenty-somethings appear to be the first generation of people coming out on the other side of a cultural paradigm shift. Wendy Murray Zoba writes, "Generation X grew up *enmeshed* in their parents' revolution, while the millennials are growing up *reacting* to the revolution."[13] According to William Strauss, "The millennial generation is coming of cognition age at a time when the adult community has determined the conditions of childhood to be unacceptable." He reports that boomers have become what "*The New York Times* has dubbed a 'do as I say, not as I did' generation of parents." These parents agree that millennial children are to be "shielded better than we were from media, sex, violence, and profanity." In school the new three R's are "rules, respect and responsibility."[14] These new trends reflect what is happening all over the world. Millennials are considerably more conservative than their predecessors. The twenty-somethings desire a stable society, a return to tradition.

The defining moment for these younger leaders, and indeed for American society, was the events of September 11, 2001, and the subsequent determination of America and most of the world to declare war on terrorism.

Younger evangelical David Taylor reflects the fears of those who have not known war:

> We have a hidden enemy who strikes not at our chest or across the jaw—in obvious, conventional places—but behind our kneecap, boxing our ears, crushing our pinky. They strike us down in places we don't expect: the Greyhound bus station, the Del office desk, the HEB grocery store on Saturday morning. And so we become angry at the air, at the unknown. We become restless. We become irritable,

like the kids in *Red Dawn*. We feel especially vulnerable. We don't know how to defend ourselves.[15]

On the other hand, we ask how engagement with terrorism may impact younger evangelicals' character and ministry. It may intensify what already distinguishes them: a radical, almost extreme commitment to the faith; a deep desire to create community; a longing for a worship that emphasizes the otherness of God's transcendence, yet the healing power of God's presence; a ministry not based on programs but on transformed lives; a commitment to rebuild the cities of the world and establish a presence of the kingdom that changes neighborhoods.

Characteristics of the Younger Evangelicals

I have briefly situated the younger evangelicals within evangelical history and Western culture in the final decade of the twentieth century. Much more could be said about the religious and cultural factors that have shaped their faith, but it is sufficient at this point to see that the context in which they grew up is very different than the context of both the traditionalist and the pragmatist. Therefore, their approach to faith and ministry is different. Because the younger evangelicals will present different thought patterns and approaches to ministry, it will be helpful to begin by noting several specific characteristics of the younger evangelicals.

First, the younger evangelicals are conscious that *they grew up in a postmodern world*. One young evangelical writes of ways postmodern thinking differs from modern thought. Postmoderns "no longer feel a need to bow the knee to the modern God of rationality." Postmoderns, he argues, "have a much broader conception of what 'counts' as reason" because they acknowledge that "*all* rationality (religious, scientific, or whatever) is laden with faith." Postmodern young people recognize that "thinking is highly indebted to others." Therefore, the younger evangelical rejects the modern notion of individualism and embraces community. And to be postmodern in a Christian way is "to embrace the kingdom of God and renounce the values of the world."[16] These commitments are commonly shared by younger evangelical leaders, as they face the realities of the postmodern world.

The younger evangelicals are marked in a very special way by the events of September 11, 2001. They know that the world will never be the same, that the ideals of prosperity and the hopes of a pre–September 11 world of peace will never happen. The rise of terror by militant fundamentalists is marking their world and creating an ideological battle of religions. Life will be marked by issues of peace and war, a new form of American patriotism, a wave of conservative political philosophy, a new form of civil religion, a new economic tightening of resources, and a more disciplined life. This cultural setting is radically different than the cultural setting of the post–World War II generation, which was resolved to rebuild their world, and of the post-sixties generation, which was bent on breaking from the past and asserting their freedom to reinvent ethics, religion, and the church.

The postmodern September 11, 2001, world has led to the *recovery of the biblical understanding of human nature.* The language of sin, evil, evildoers, and a reaffirmation of the deceit and wickedness of the human heart has once again emerged in our common vocabulary. The liberal notion of the inherent goodness of humankind and the more recent evangelical neglect of the language of sin and depravity have failed to plumb the depths of the wickedness that lurks in the human heart. The younger evangelical approaches humanity with a more realistic and biblical assessment of our estrangement from God.

This juxtaposition of a postmodern relativistic worldview with a post–September 11 world of terror and evil has created a *new context for ministry.* The climate of an apocalyptic age has resulted in a new openness to hear the gospel and to get connected with the church as a community of supporting people. The younger evangelicals now minister in a climate open to an evangelical awakening, an openness and vulnerability not known to their traditional and pragmatic evangelical predecessors.

Younger evangelicals freely acknowledge that *they differ with the pragmatist's approach to ministry.* Paul Keith is not attracted to "showy worship and things that please my felt needs."[17] Bernie Van De Walle finds "most, if not all, of the church-growth strategies based on method, almost revolting."[18] Dale Dirksen, a young college professor, sums up the younger evangelical difference with the pragmatists in these words: "This is not a mere generation gap, it's a total paradigm shift—the immense change of one civilization to another."[19]

This leads to another insight of the younger evangelicals. They know that *they must minister in a new paradigm* of thought. They must be different than the traditionalists. For example, younger evangelical David Clark writes, "There's no reason to think we need the sort of lab-like certainty that the modernists wanted. It's not found in science . . . we are fallible human beings who will never know it all."[20] Jonathan Nelms laments that "it is difficult to meet the emerging needs of a postmodern age within the bounds of a modern institution"[21] (i.e., the local church he serves). Kyle Roberts complains that "the problem with a mere 'propositionalism' (a modern idea) is that you lose the power and force of the imagination . . . you lose the story and in so doing you lose the vibrant stuff."[22] These younger evangelicals agree with Dawn Haglund, a recent graduate of Trinity Evangelical Divinity School, who feels "increased tensions and pulls from the modern paradigm." The "old paradigm," she writes, is "behave, believe, belong." But the new paradigm is "belong, believe, behave."[23]

The younger evangelicals know *they must stand for the absolutes of the Christian faith in a new way.* I can remember Francis Schaeffer shouting the law of contradiction saying, "A cannot be B and B cannot be A." For moderns, like Schaeffer, knowledge had to be clear and noncontradictory, but for postmoderns, things are complex and multidimensional. Tom Beaudoin says, "Gen X pop culture's theme [is] ambiguity."[24] But this doesn't mean postmoderns want to be handed a plate of relativism. Today, young people come to church because "it stands for something." But the gospel it stands for is presented as "story," not a noncontradictory, rationally defended, logically consistent fact apprehended by cognitive acquiescence.

In order for younger evangelicals to affirm the Christian story, they realize they must embrace the past. They *recognize that the road to the future runs through the past.* Dale Dirksen, a young college professor, observes that "there is a significant trend toward a greater valuing of history among our eighteen- to twenty-four-year-olds. They are very intrigued with old stuff, possibly because they have lived in a world with only new stuff their whole lives."[25] David Taylor, a pastor, concurs and writes, "We are in desperate need of a more robust consciousness of our tradition."[26]

This interest in story and tradition in no way suggests a lack of interest in current issues. On the contrary, *the younger evangelicals are primarily committed to the plight of the poor, especially in our urban centers.* They realize the old story must be lived out. Andrew Black contends that "new research suggests this generation [is] . . . looking for new ways to serve others. There is indeed apathy toward big programs, big ministries, big ideologies, and big solutions. But there is growing eagerness to work together to address problems on a more manageable level."[27] Research shows that 68 percent of younger evangelicals surveyed affirmed that the best way to change the situation of our broken world is by "practicing your ideals in everyday life." Todd Hunter concludes, "I see God raising up missional communities that can influence from the margins."[28] These younger evangelicals are inspired by nineteenth-century evangelicalism and its strong emphasis on a gospel that results in social action like that of John Wesley, the founder of the Methodist movement, and William and Catherine Booth, founders of the Salvation Army.

Another feature of the younger evangelicals is their *willingness to live by the rules.* They are the children of one of the most permissive eras of America. They have watched the results of throwing away traditions and mores that have shaped values for centuries. They have seen the results of permissiveness in a culture of broken homes and destroyed families. They have lived in a culture of violence demonstrated especially by the holocaust of abortion and the uncertainty of terrorism. They have lived in a time when drugs and condoms are readily available. But research shows there is a general turning away from the so-called freedom initiated by the sixties toward a much more stable and rule-keeping life. Author Mike Males points out that "it's grown-ups who have deteriorated, and this has occurred across race and income lines. Drug abuse, family chaos, family violence, and felony arrests have all skyrocketed among the thirty to fifty range." "Teenage crime," Males demonstrates, "is rarer today than it was twenty years ago, teen drug abuse is falling and teen pregnancy is not the national disaster so much as are poverty and abusive families."[29] The incidence of younger people from evangelical families who gravitate toward drugs, sex, and violence follows the same trend as society. Teens want rules and models of adults who live by the rules and embody in life what they say with their lips.

Another trait of younger evangelicals is their *facility with technology*. Throughout the twentieth century, evangelicals have always been quick to use and even dominate new advances in technology, especially new forms of communication. For example, Matt Redman, Andy Park, and Kevin Prosch of the website *Next-Wave* ask how we fulfill the Great Commission in a postmodern generation. They point to young "explorers" and "pioneers" who "share the conviction that we will have to substantially change the way we do church to be relevant to the postmodern era." They and other younger evangelicals have chosen to use the internet as a forum for thinking through church in the next generation.[30]

Technology underlies an additional feature of the younger evangelicals: *they are highly visual*. Sarah Diffenderfer, a student at Truett Theologial Seminary, thinks *Star Wars* is the movie that most clearly defines this generation of visual learners. It is, she writes, "a force that shapes our lives." Why has this visual extravaganza communicated so effectively? It is the story of human relationship visualized. According to Diffenderfer, "The movies tell of romance, of leaving home to find one's destiny, of the heartbreak of family betrayal, and ultimately of finding one's place in the universe."[31] *Star Wars* is a cultural experience that has shaped the younger evangelical way of knowing.

This emphasis on the visual points to another characteristic of the younger evangelicals: *they communicate through stories*. Story communication is a central feature of the twenty-first century. David Taylor says, "This frees the church to tell good stories." Stories make words visual and memorable. The propositionalism of modernity reduced everything to factual words, but now we are recovering the power of stories to shape and form our lives. There is no better or more meaningful story than that of God's involvement in history and in the stories of Israel and Jesus. This is the *good* story postmoderns are waiting to hear.[32]

Postmoderns *grasp the power of imagination*. David Taylor points to the modern "propensity, deeply engrained, towards literalism and rationalism." He decries the "resistance within churches to the use of the imagination" and refers to the "terrible fear" that many evangelicals have of the imaginative.[33] But younger evangelicals are calling for the recovery of the imagination. Thomas Hohstadt points out the relationship between imagination and actualization. Imagination, he claims, is the seat of creativity. "Since imagination locates itself in time," he explains, "it must also locate somewhere in space. Somewhere, in other words, it takes on a physical reality."[34] If you can dream it, you can create it.

My daughter Alexandra, who is an artist, was recently explaining to me the new evaluation of people as "generators" and "manifestors." Some people "generate" ideas in their imagination. Others come along and "manifest" these ideas by bringing them into reality. The younger evangelicals are dreamers who "generate" ideas in their imagination and workers who "manifest" these ideas in actual concrete realities. The freedom from rationalism, propositionalism, and logical analysis has revived the imagination, and we are beginning to see the fruits of empowered imagination in the new ministries formed by the younger evangelicals.

The recovery of imagination has led to a new emphasis among the younger evangelicals, *the resurgence of the arts*. The pragmatists reintroduced drama skits and the entertainment arts, but the younger evangelicals are returning to much greater appreciation and use of the classical arts. This new, more compelling use of the arts in the church corresponds to the return to classical Christian thought. David Taylor writes, "If our theology is not good, our art making will be bad; it will be sentimental, narrow minded, functionalist, and trite." Artists need to understand "why God has created us with imaginations and the ability to make art."[35] Art has to be understood not as mere illustration but in the greater context of the church, as it witnesses to the kingdom of God and to the ultimate redemption of all things as set forth by Isaiah's vision of the new creation. Younger evangelicals appreciate art not as mere presentations of the gospel message but as visions of a transformed and redeemed world. In other words, art is eschatological. It may point to the problems of this world, but Christian art points beyond to the redemption of this world.

Consistent with the resurgence of the arts is the younger evangelicals' *new appreciation of performative symbol*. Pragmatists taught us to strip our churches of all symbols and rituals that made Christianity visible. But the younger evangelicals are, more than any other Protestant generation, shaped by images, computer icons, and symbolic forms of communication that extend into every area of life. For them, the reduction of Christianity to a plainness that rejects symbol is strange and alienating. For example, there is a current recovery of the cross. Bruce McEvoy, a youth worker, describes a recent service that featured a cross behind a white sheet. "A light shone from the back to show the cross and a Jesus figure on it dying. The lights went out and the sheet was torn from top to bottom and the cross was left without a person on it." The younger people then gathered around the cross to sing "Turn Your Eyes upon Jesus."[36] According to McEvoy, this symbolic event resulted in a powerful experience of community.

The younger evangelicals yearn to *belong to a community*. They do not embrace the individualism birthed out of the Enlightenment and dominant in the twentieth century, nor are they attracted to the me-ism of the eighties. They have rejected the culture of narcissism and seek community. Jim Belcher writes, "They crave genuine relationships and authentic friendships. Some are hoping for the home they never had."[37] For example, Bernie Van De Walle writes of his experience in graduate school in another country. He says, "We found a church of 35 people made up of 13 distinct ethnic groups. Boy! I wish I was still in that church. It stood against all the wisdom of modern church growth and was the best community of which I have been a part."[38]

Van De Walle's experience points to another characteristic of younger evangelicals: they are *highly committed to multicultural communities of faith*. Postmoderns have grown up in a society that is more integrated than it has been in previous generations. Today there are three million mixed marriages. William Forey reminds us that "historically Christians responded to America's growing diversity by starting churches aimed at distinct ethnic groups. But as intermarriage and assimilation blur those ethnic lines . . . a new kind of multicultural church [is emerging]."[39] "It's a cultural trend that everyone is going to have to deal with,"[40] says Bill White, an Anglo pastor of a multiethnic church in south Florida that has forty nationalities represented in its membership.

This trend toward intercultural communities is complemented by the *commitment of the younger evangelical to intergenerational ministries*. Valerie and Dieter Zander, church planters in San Francisco, write, "Most generation X'ers know they need to be mentored. They've largely gotten over their youthful alienation and truly want guidance and leadership. The last thing they want, in their heart of hearts, is to be sent off on their own."[41] The younger evangelicals desire to be around their parents and grandparents, and their dislike of being separated into their own group runs counter to the advice given by church-growth movements that the way to grow a church is to target generations. Today's younger people seek out intergenerational communities where they mix and form relationships with all ages.

In spite of the fact that younger evangelicals have grown up in a relativistic world, they are not turned off by claims to absolute truth. If anything, *younger evangelicals are attracted to absolutes*. But they don't want to arrive at absolutes through evidence or logic. They are, as Todd Flanders has pointed out, attracted to the kind of absolute that Pascal referred to in his *Pensées*. They want truth that is a matter of "heart as well as mind." Pascal remarked that "truth is so obscured nowadays and lies so well established that unless we love the truth we shall never recognize it."[42] It is this approach to truth that is the path of postmoderns. The importance of truth is not so much that it is understood but that it is loved and lived.

It follows that an additional characteristic of younger evangelicals is their *readiness to commit*. Unlike the boomers, who didn't want to commit to anything, the twenty-somethings and the millennials are in search of something to which they can commit. One seventeen-year-old wrote to me, "We just want to commit and we will commit to anything."[43] The negative side is that young people might commit to a Hitler-like leader who promises stability through blind obedience. The positive side is that when this age group commits to the Christian faith, they do so with passion and a sense of turning their whole life over to God.

This willingness to commit is related to the younger evangelical method of learning, which is *shared wisdom*. For them, stating truths to which they are asked to commit is too modern. It's related to propositions and conclusions that have been developed by others outside their intimate community. Younger evangelicals enjoy the process of shared experiences from which they derive a sense of wisdom and direction.

What the younger evangelical is after is *authenticity*. This is another way in which they differ from the pragmatists. The pragmatists were attracted to transparency that demanded "highly personal information." In a *Regeneration Quarterly* article, Cherie Harder points out that these honesty sessions are when people divulge "past hurts, injustices, abuses, sins, failures, inadequacies, insecurities, complexes, and anxieties." The problem, Harder says, is that these honesty sessions have become "an essential part of godly worship" for many churches. The urge to be transparent fits the "therapeutic culture" and has become a kind of Christian exhibitionism. The shift among younger evangelicals is toward being real and authentic.[44] Jason Archer puts it this way: "I long to see the church led by people who care little about being successful as the world sees it and care so much about being in touch with God and in community with the people of God that the reality of God's power is powerfully unleashed."[45] Younger evangelicals are tired of people wallowing around in the mud of their past or beating their breasts about all their successes. They just want people to be real.

These characteristics of the younger evangelical are equally shared by the thinkers and the practitioners. The thinkers are struggling with the theological side of being evangelical in a postmodern terrorist world, while the practitioners are dealing with matters of doing: How do you present Christianity in an authentic way in the twenty-first century?

I have made this division between the thinkers and the practitioners to serve as handles to understand the younger evangelical leadership. I do not mean to imply that the thinkers are not concerned about practice and that the practitioners are not concerned about thinking. They are.

These two groups are moving toward each other and learning from one another. The more time they spend together, the more they tend to get on the same page, recognizing that thought and action are not disparate movements but complementary realities. This *realization of the unity between thought and action* is a postmodern insight and another characteristic of the younger evangelical.

In the modern world hard distinctions were made between the academic and so-called practical disciplines. Theology was seen as an academic discipline, while ecclesiology, worship, and the church in the world were seen as the more practical disciplines. In the postmodern world of the interrelationship of all things, no such distinction is made. Younger evangelicals see "practical theology as a theological understanding" and "theological engagement as practical understanding."

In sum the younger evangelical is different than the traditional and the pragmatic evangelical. The traditionalist is the last generation of the modern worldview with its emphasis on reason and science; the pragmatist is the generation shaped by the great disruption of 1960–1990. The pragmatists represent a transitional group of leaders who were influenced by the tumultuous cultural revolution that ushered civilization into the twenty-first century. The younger evangelical is the first cycle of new evangelicals in the twenty-first century. Like their predecessors, they are committed evangelicals, but the religious and cultural context that has shaped their particular approach to faith and practice is on the other side of the twentieth-century culture. Society has moved into the new culture of the twenty-first century. And the younger evangelicals are the first generation to lead us into what it means to be evangelical in the new cultural condition of the new century. In the remaining chapters of this book, we will explore how the younger evangelicals think and practice the faith, and we'll look at the new kind of leadership they will offer to the evangelical community in the new world.

Characteristics of the Younger Evangelical

1. Grew up in a postmodern world
2. Marked by a post–9/11 era
3. Have recovered the biblical understanding of human nature
4. Are aware of a new context for ministry
5. Differ with the pragmatist approach to ministry
6. Minister in a new paradigm of thought
7. Stand for the absolutes of the Christian faith in a new way
8. Recognize the road to the future runs through the past
9. Committed to the plight of the poor, especially in urban centers
10. Willing to live by the rules
11. Facility with technology
12. Highly visual
13. Communicate through stories
14. Grasp the power of imagination
15. Advocate the resurgence of the arts
16. Appreciate the power of performative symbol
17. Long for community
18. Committed to multicultural communities of faith
19. Committed to intergenerational ministry
20. Attracted to absolutes
21. Ready to commit
22. Search for shared wisdom
23. Demand authenticity
24. Realize the unity between thought and action

The Younger
Evangelical Thinkers

By the latter part of the twentieth century the pragmatic evangelicals with their megachurches were the most obvious respondents to postmodern culture. However, by the turn of the twenty-first century a new group of thinkers were looking at postmodern thought and culture from a different perspective. In the summer of 2000 a group of younger evangelicals gathered under the auspices of the Regeneration Forum to discuss postmodernism and to search for an appropriate response. This gathering was featured in *Christianity Today.*

The *Christianity Today* article reported that "postmodern Christians are trying to redefine the relation of faith and knowledge, that instead of coming to the faith rationally, true knowledge requires the Holy Spirit to work an ontological change in the human heart."[1] Because this view sounds like classic Augustinianism, the interviewer wanted to know, "What's new about postmodernism?" (I think what he meant to ask was, "What's new about faith in a postmodern world?").

Sherri King, a Ph.D. candidate in literature at the University of Dallas, answered the question. "These things," she said, "are not so much new as they are a reaction against the modern, the era beginning with the Enlightenment that privileged rationality." With these words King pointed to the first conviction of the younger evangelicals: *Modernity with its emphasis on the finality of reason and science is a worldview that younger evangelicals reject.* Consequently, twentieth-century evangelicalism must also be deconstructed. Her statement continued: "So it [the new younger evangelical viewpoint] is not just postmodern but . . . also anti-modern and, for Christians, *a return to previous Orthodox theologies*"[2] (my emphasis). Here she suggests younger evangelical thinkers are not interested in deconstruction for its own sake but view deconstruction as necessary to *reconstruct* a historic life of the mind. Unlike the boomers of the sixties who wanted nothing to do with the past, the younger evangelicals have a love for the past and are convinced that the road to the future runs through the past.

This double theme of deconstructing twentieth-century evangelicalism and of returning to tradition is frequently found in comments made by the younger evangelical. Paul Jones, a student at Regent College, writes, "I grew up thinking that we have progressed so much over the past two thousand years that there really isn't much to gain from focusing on the past. In the last year I have begun to see how historic Christianity needs to be taken into serious account."[3] David Di Sabatino, editor of *Worship Leader*, says, "I was taught to believe that 'tradition' was a dirty word . . . [I now believe] the notion of tradition is a concept that Protestants need to revisit . . . we forgot that we owe a great debt to this process of consensus that has handed us traditions essential to our faith."[4] This return to tradition is a return to the foundational thought of the Nicene Creed, the insights of the Greek Fathers, of Augustine, of Thomas Aquinas, the Reformers, and John Wesley to name a few. These are the persons and schools of theological thought receiving the greatest attention in the thinking of the younger evangelicals.

Meet the Mind and Heart of a Younger Evangelical Thinker

I first met Joseph Clair in 1999 when he enrolled in my "Christian Thought" course at Wheaton College. He soon distinguished himself as a thoughtful future leader of the church. I asked him to write down his reflections as an evangelical facing the world of the twenty-first-century thought. Clair was twenty and a junior at Wheaton when he wrote the following. His comments serve as a helpful introduction to how younger evangelicals think about the twenty-first century:

> I have been involved in a small group of "struggling" evangelicals, a common disposition among evangelicals my age. The "struggle" regards the intellectual clothes evangelicalism has garbed itself with in the twentieth century.
>
> I break my journey and that of my peers into three different stages: precritical naivete; the critical-thinking desert; and postcritical naivete.

Precritical Naivete

For most of us the precritical naivete stage begins with birth and is an inherited faith. We take for granted that evangelical Christianity is true. This includes major historical-orthodox issues including Jesus' divinity, the virgin birth, the resurrection, and the ever-important doctrine of the Trinity. It also includes our acceptance of subcultural values such as how a person comes to find salvation, "holiness" issues concerning the explicit "no, no's" of the evangelical moral code, and evangelical practices of worship, evangelism, and spirituality.

The problem with precritical naivete is not the beautiful and childlike faith involved in accepting the orthodox-evangelical understanding of Christianity, rather it is the reality that *no one can justifiably stay there.* In our society today it is impossible to remain precritical in the face of such a mind-numbing multiplicity of worldviews. The questions don't come just from one's Hindu neighbor down the street but from within. For most of us there is an internal dialogue taking place continually. This is something like Dostoyevsky's wonderful exploration of "polyphonic dialogue" in his novel *The Brothers Karamazov.* Dostoyevsky uses different characters in his novel to represent the opposing liberal and conservative, atheist and Christian views that he finds circling within his very own head. Most of us swing between feeling like universalists who wish we could include everybody in the kingdom of God no matter how backwards they are and other times feeling like fiery fundamentalists who see the dire need for people to have their lives transformed through repentance and acceptance of Jesus Christ as their personal Lord and Savior.

The Critical-Thinking Desert

The first sign of transition from precritical naivete into the critical-thinking desert is an interest in apologetics. Apologetics is an important issue for evangelicals because of the emphasis placed on evangelism. We are told that Christians should be out sharing their faith with workers, neighbors, relatives, schoolmates, and so forth. While it is stressed that we are to share our "testimony," we are also encouraged to make a "convincing" presentation of the gospel. This leaves us groping. We know we live in an age of relativism and plurality like never experienced before. How are we to convince people that Jesus is "the way, the truth, and the life" (John 14:6)? Should we just read this passage from John's Gospel and a few other Scripture verses that make clear the uniqueness of Jesus Christ as the way of salvation? Should we press the results of unbelief? Yeah, that sounds about right, but ... not everyone trusts that Scripture verses from the Bible are some unique source of absolute truth and revelation that all humankind must heed. What to do then? Well, of course, we must find a way to prove that the Bible is the unique, authoritative words of divinity that spell out the absolute truth for humans to reckon with.

This is where the evangelical wanders into the realm of apologetics. How to prove this? This is a Pandora's box of endless historical analysis and critical debate from just about every direction you could imagine: science, history, philosophy, anthropology, sociology, and so forth. Just about every discipline has something to say about what this book, the Bible, is actually all about, or, even worse, how the

Bible should be interpreted! Evangelicals seem to be uniquely befuddled by this
notion of "interpretation." We are awkwardly caught between our fundamentalist
heritage of a safer, stauncher, "literal" interpretation of every jot and tittle in
Scripture and a more intellectual, capable, "contextual" type of interpretation that
listens sympathetically to the way in which these other disciplines, mentioned
above, inform our thinking about the words recorded in Scripture.

Postcritical Naivete

The internal dialogue builds and grows within the individual until the search
for some sort of solidarity reaches "crisis" stage. Issues that usually feed this tension in the younger evangelical center around unbelievers going to hell: how
many? And why is there so much chaos around the world? This is especially apparent today because of the media, the information age, and the war with terror
that stares us down from every side. The longing for solidarity climaxes in the step
or leap into postcritical naivete. This is what Paul Ricoeur calls the "post-critical
moment." This moment is so refreshing because it allows the Christian thinker to
recelebrate the "subjective" elements of faith without feeling intellectually dishon-
est or "not rational enough." This postcritical moment is a re-celebration, a re-appropriation, of the Christian faith in general, and in the different traditions expressed in history. In my own journey, historical theology put these issues into
perspective. I was no longer discouraged by the different ways Christians have related to their faith and the Scriptures over the past two thousand years. It was
rather encouraging to see how "contextual" God allows us to be in our relationship with him. Worship became a way to enter into a "participation" with faith
and was more necessary and important than rational theology. Biblical interpretation became a conversation between myself, my community, and the text where
we opened ourselves to the claims the text was making on our lives.

Many of the issues mentioned above like "community," "tradition," and "history" have sometimes been negative words around the evangelical camp. I am not
disparaging the wonderful work that has gone on, and continues to, in evangelical
Christianity. But we younger evangelicals recognize American evangelicalism was
founded in modernity. This is good and bad, but evangelicals need to stop pre-
tending to be a purely "scriptural," objective, and rational model of the Christian
Faith. It is not that. Evangelicalism is itself a particular tradition that needs to be
open to the Christian belief and practice expressed in different historical and communal contexts. We must overcome our exclusive self-understanding to maintain a
sane "postcritical" faith for today.

The way to overcome this is through intellectual and spiritual honesty and humility, which lets the tension of the critical thinking desert build until the leap forward into the postcritical moment. This moment seems very "ambiguous" to our
modern mindset at first. We, today, have trouble committing ourselves to something that is not easy to "convince" or "force" all other human beings to believe rationally. This is where we need the Holy Spirit to reinvigorate our "subjective" in-
tuitions, as expressed in our immediate communities and contexts, and bring some
wholeness back to what we think of as "knowledge." Then we can have a firm

postcritical faith, which hopefully will help us to lead lives that express a robust precritical faith as seen in Jesus' earliest followers.[5]

Clair has stated with clarity the goal of the younger evangelical thinker. How does one move beyond the morass of a rationally defended faith? How does one return to a faith that is as authentic, fresh, and passionate as the first love of a precritical faith? How does one speak an intelligible, defensible, and communicable faith to a world of philosophical relativism? *These are very practical questions that hold immense implication for a thoughtful Christian witness in a world marked by a new interest in the Christian faith and how it compares to the faith of Islam.*

The goal of part 2 is to reflect on this issue from the perspective of those trends and movements affecting the younger evangelical thinkers. This section looks at how the younger evangelicals are deconstructing evangelical reliance on modernity and how they are beginning to reconstruct an ancient-future faith.

This part develops the five major areas where the younger evangelical thinkers are challenging twentieth-century modern evangelicalism—the matter of communication (chap. 3); the return to tradition (chap. 4); the embrace of classical theology (chap. 5); the call to an embodied apologetic (chap. 6); and the recovery of the visible church (chap. 7).

In each of these areas is a deconstruction of modern twentieth-century evangelicalism and a reconstruction along more traditional lines of thought. While younger evangelicals are embracing tradition, Todd Johnson, an evangelical who teaches at Loyola University, made a point about which they are generally in agreement: "that no one tradition can completely encompass the whole."[6] The younger evangelical is returning to basics, to broad strokes and an eclectic Christianity held together by traditions that have lasted for centuries. The emphasis is more on "what does it mean to be Christian?" and less on the particulars that once defined what it meant to be a strict fundamentalist or traditionalist type of evangelical. This new shift toward basics affirmed by the whole church prepares the church for its twenty-first-century battle with postmodern relativism and for its comparison with world religions, especially the faith of Islam.

3

Communication
From Print to Cultural Transmission

It is impossible to understand the younger evangelicals and their differences with twentieth-century evangelicals unless they are placed within the communication revolution that has taken place since the sixties. Because younger evangelicals have been shaped by new forms of communication, they will hear and communicate the Christian faith in the twenty-first century in a new way. Younger evangelical Sydney Westrate puts it this way: "God seems bigger than words. There are times when words can't adequately express what we want to say . . . as we communicate with God, we should not disregard the nonverbal, but instead embrace it."[1]

It is probably safe to say that there has never been a major shift in culture without an observable shift in communication. Some would argue that the revolution in communication actually leads the cultural shift. Others prefer to see the rise of new communication forms as part of the complex and interrelated changes taking place during a time of cultural upheaval.

For example, a new book on the great fourth-century church historian Eusebius argues that his classic work *Ecclesiastical History*, which records the history of the Christian church in its first three centuries, is a media phenomenon. Doron Mendels argues "Eusebius of Caesarea describes the propagation of early Christianity by means of a media revolution." In this new and interesting interpretation of Eusebius, Mendels argues that Eusebius "presents Christianity as posing a serious competition—or rather threat—to the traditional media channels of the Roman Empire." The church, he claims, "constantly pursued the means and instruments of mediating its message to different audiences."[2] Like Eusebius of the ancient church, the younger evangelical is convinced that we face a new era in which the mediation of the faith into a new culture requires an approach different than that taken by the older evangelical. Because culture has changed, the method of communication must change.

All of us are keenly aware of the current communications revolution. Those of us who are over forty have watched it happen and many of us are baffled by it. But the younger evangelical was born during the height of the communications revolution and understands it from experience, not from mere observation as is the case for the leaders of twentieth-century evangelicalism. A brief review will put the current revolution in communications into perspective and help us grasp that *a vital key to understanding the younger evangelical is to perceive how much they are a part of the new communications revolution.*

It is necessary to place the younger evangelical in relation to the past as well as the future, so we begin with a brief overview of the history of communications. The shift is from the reliance on print communication, a discursive and analytical form, to cultural communication, a visual and more embodied form of communication.

Brief History of Communication

Oral Communication

Communication in biblical times was primarily oral. The primacy was on the spoken word, which was handed down in stories (patriarchs), parables (as in Proverbs), wisdom literature (as in Ecclesiastes), and in apocalyptic language (as in Daniel and Revelation). These were the oral traditions not of individuals but of communities. This ancient form of communication, which occurred in communities through oral means, is called "cultural transmission." For example, in Israel and the early church, one generation told and handed down stories to another generation. These stories communicated the meaning of the world—its origin, its meaning, its future. Because the community or tribe was shaped by these stories, people were involved in a tribal transmission of wisdom by simply living within the community and by sharing in its stories. Communication occurred through *immersion* in the stories and shared wisdom of the community, which conveyed the Christian vision of reality. Communication did not occur by some formal method of education but simply through lived experience, involvement and participation in the ongoing life of the community.

Oral communication reached its peak in the oral/visual society of the medieval era. Back then it was *par excellence*. Unfortunately, Protestants generally think of medieval Christianity negatively. We associate medieval Christianity with ritualism, dogmaticism, superstition, and idol and image worship—an external form of Christianity not internalized. While this image of medieval Christianity may have been true on the eve of the Reformation, it was not completely true of the thirteenth century, the golden era of medieval Christianity. Faith was quite alive not only in visual form but in the heart as well. Catholic historian Joseph Jungman argues that Catholics of that period learned "the Christian faith in the same way that they learned their mother tongue, without systematic teaching." It was a time of "extraordinarily religious practices."[3] Because culture was through and through shaped by a Christian consciousness, one became a Christian through lived experience.

For example, consider the following images of faith that permeated thirteenth-century Western culture: the emperor was consecrated by the church; the various orders of knighthood were all Christian; every working guild had its own patron saint and feasts; all apothecaries and druggists and such bore religious names; all the inns where weary travelers stayed were called by biblical names; numerous hospices were dedicated to the Holy Spirit; and cathedrals were visual images of the heavenlies, their spires pointing to the heavens, their liturgies recalling God's act of salvation and pointing to the new heaven and earth.

Everything proceeded from the church—architecture, art, music, literature, law, education, philosophy, town planning. In other words, "the whole of life was bathed in a religious climate." Think of the opposite: the whole of life bathed in a secular climate. The concept of immersion into culture as a form of communication is illustrated not only by the example of medieval culture but by the example of our current totally secularized culture. We are made secular not only by inculcation through teaching but most especially by breathing the air of a culture completely saturated with a secular, pagan outlook. This is the cultural-transmission form of communication.

The central feature of cultural transmission is participation, belonging, immersion. In the medieval period people participated in the Christian culture in their daily living. They ate, drank, worked, and slept in the rhythm of its feasts and fasts through the Christian year, in a visual environment of Christian images and in a symbolic atmosphere of Christian faith that communicated through all the senses.

Print Communication

This ancient cultural transmission was radically changed by the invention of the Gutenberg Press and the introduction of print media. The invention of print fueled the Protestant Reformation and accounts for the primary difference between premodern and modern forms of communication. Modernity shifted from communication through an immersion in culture to communication through didactic methods. Spiritual formation shifted from participating in the community to learning doctrine from printed material that could be examined analytically and affirmed intellectually.

Consequently, both the Reformation and the Catholic Counter-Reformation were characterized by the proliferation of written documents and treatises, the most famous being Luther's "Ninety-five Theses." Faith was now set forth not in great cathedrals, works of art, and images but in confessions, catechisms, hymns, and sermons that presented Christianity in written form—words to be studied, analyzed, believed, and confessed. In this way Christianity went through an enormous shift from the oral/visual/communal to the verbal/confessional/individual. Modern Christianity had been born and was to endure through the twentieth century. But by the sixties a reversal had begun taking culture back to the oral/visual/communal, back to cultural transmission. By 2000 this reversal was in full swing. Communication specialists did not deny the power of the word, but it was clear that the younger generation was persuaded by their immersion in culture. Cultural transmission has clearly made a comeback.

The Audiovisual Communications Revolution

The sixties revolution introduced radical reforms in communication, reforms which have taken us back to the communication insights of the oral/visual culture with modifications to account for the emergence of the electronic and technological society in which we now live.

The first thinker to see these changes was Marshall McLuhan, whose early impressions were reported in *The Gutenberg Galaxy*, published in the mid-sixties. Christian communication specialist Pierre Babin, a student of McLuhan's ideas and a pioneer in postmodern ways of communication, became convinced that "audiovisual-oriented people were being born, and we could no longer speak to them as we had spoken to them in the past." Consequently, Babin argued for "three characteristics of modern life that we must keep in mind in our approach to younger generations: the resurgence of the imagination, the importance of affective relationship and values, and the dissolution of national and cultural frontiers."[4]

Babin sees McLuhan as the central thinker of the new revolution: "He managed to make us understand how technology or, more specifically, the audiovisual medium of communication, is the key to interpreting our culture."[5] What McLuhan saw was "the complex interaction of technology with all aspects of our social and cultural reality."[6] What lies at the heart of the McLuhan revolution is the recognition that "the medium is the message."[7]

The idea that "the medium is the message" holds important ramifications for the communication of the Christian faith. First, the real message of Christianity is not rational propositions but the person of Jesus Christ with whom a personal relationship is possible. Second, this personal relationship is experienced and communicated in a community—the church, his body. Third, to communicate a relationship with Jesus Christ, the church must be an embodied presence, an authentic and real community in whom the Spirit dwells. Fourth, the primary concern of the church is to communicate not dogma, though it does have its place, but faith. Fifth, the primary way of communicating faith is through a combination of oral, visual, and print forms of participatory immersed communication (or cultural transmission).

Before I show how these principles relate to communication in the church, let me provide an illustration of how these principles relate to communication in general in our society, which is considerably more oral/visual than it was fifty years ago.

A conversation with my teenage daughter a few years ago illustrates the principle. "Dad," she said, "on Saturday I'm going to spend the day at the mall with my friends."

"What do you do there all day long?" I asked, curious as to why somebody would spend the day at the mall. "Hang out" was the answer. I noticed soon thereafter that my daughter began to express the values of the mall, mainly a commitment to consumerism, which lies at the heart of the entire ambiance and atmosphere of the mall. The mall, with its numerous goods and pictures of beautiful people wearing, eating, and drinking, makes a subliminal impression on the people who are there. This story illustrates the nature of cultural transmission. It is indirect rather than direct. It communicates a lifestyle. Most advertising is based on this principle: "Buy this product and it will change your life."

Considering the current shift in communications, Babin has translated the teaching of McLuhan into three basic principles:

1. The message of faith is primarily the effect it produces in me.
2. Faith is communicated through complex and variegated means.
3. The content of communication is the *listener* as he/she is affected by the message.[8]

A brief examination of each of the three principles noted above will create a better understanding of how the communications revolution has affected the younger evangelical approach to being Christian in a post-print world.

First, communication has to do with *the effect it produces in me*. It seems incontrovertible that an epistemological shift has taken place since the sixties. In the first half of the century the emphasis was on that which is known by rational means whereas the shift in the latter part of the century has been to emphasize the buyer, not the product. The accent is placed on the affective side of the person. Whether this shift is well received or not, the fact is that the role of imagination and affection is indisputable. The inner life has become the focus for good or for ill. This "inner" emphasis is a shift that has taken place both in the secular and in the religious world. It is less pronounced among fundamentalists and evangelicals who are still ruled by print. But clearly the younger evangelicals, who have been influenced by the communication revolution, look more to a cultural transmission of the faith than do their twentieth-century predecessors, who still view communication occurring primarily through print.

Second, the current media revolution has pointed to the need to *communicate faith through more complex and variegated means*. In the current media revolution, the emphasis is not only on "what" is being communicated but "how" it is being expressed. In an electronic age we communicate substance through images. Several images that are crucial for the communication of faith are sound, beauty, and symbol. For example, in our postmodern world we have learned to hear our environment. The places where we assemble, the sounds of the music or the people with whom we assemble send aural signals that make us feel at home or communicate indifferences or even rejection. Sound, in all its forms ranging from silence to piercingly loud, makes an effect on our receptors. Sound has the power to drive us to faith or away from faith.

Next, there is the complex nature of beauty or lack thereof. Plato declared, "Beauty makes truth splendid."[9] Beauty, whether it is that of an individual, a place, a landscape, or an environment, has the power to communicate a sense of well-being. Beauty is the eyesight of insight. The beauty of space, especially worship space, speaks of mystery, of transcendence, of the supernatural, of what Rudolf Otto refers to as "the numinous" or the *Mysterium Tremendum*, the otherness of the holy and infinite God. Beautiful space can speak of order, stability, and the absolute in a society of chaos and relativity, and bring quietness and peace to the inner person.

Finally, let's look at the symbolic. Modern print communications was primarily limited to cognitive activities such as reading, writing, clarity, analysis, ideas, explanations, linear sequence, and logic. But the symbolic forms of communication introduced since the sixties are concerned with image, experience, sound, such as vibrations, sense of environment through space and architecture, emotional knowledge (EQ), intuition and the unconscious, signs, spiritual sensitivity, ability to hold many seeming contradictions in creative tension, and above all knowing through participation and immersion in events. Symbolic forms of communication also include genuine and authentic friendship, *agape* love, a spirit of humility and openness, and an appreciation and support of the poor. All these forms of communication generate a reaction, a response. Where these forms are present, the receiver *feels* accepted, affirmed, and included. The receiver experiences the symbols of welcome, the welcoming nature of the God whom these images and actions signify.

Consequently, the third implication of "the medium is the message" is this: *communication occurs when a message takes up residence within the listener's life and heart*. When Christians live out and embody "the medium is the message," they disclose the Christian way of being and invite the listener to participate in a new way of life in the community of God's presence in the world, the church. The content of that which has been communicated is much more than an intellectual apprehension. It is a communication that has taken up residence within a person and transformed that person into the image of the content. This is much more than a person "accepting" the information. It is the person of Jesus Christ who grasps the listener. The listener in turn is made vulnerable to Christ and allows Christ to interpret life, and to provide meaning and purpose to life. This is a cultural transmission of the faith, an embodiment of faith that is a much deeper concept than print communication. The younger evangelicals understand and use this form of communication. It affects their whole approach to understanding and communicating the faith in the postmodern world.

Pragmatists and the Media Revolution

It is a fact that evangelicals have been the leaders in the use of new technology and communication media to spread the gospel. Evangelicals were the first to see the potential of radio. They quickly gravitated to television and are now moving to the internet. They also readily embraced the technology of the media revolution. First, the overhead projector, then slide projectors, and now Power-Point presentations. But the pragmatists, with their seeker-sensitive movement, missed the heart of the media revolution. They rejected symbol, sign, metaphor, imagination, and atmosphere, and failed to mine Christian symbolism in space, environment, Christian year, art, and most crucially the symbolic power of baptism and the Eucharist.

Instead, their energies were directed toward the new science of marketing. They became driven by the CEO model of the church, trying to plant big churches that offered a full smorgasbord of spiritual consumer goods. Pragmatists have been very successful at growing large churches and helping thousands of people. But the younger evangelical is not attracted to print communication wrapped in a slick consumer package. They want something else. That something else, to be described in this book, will be shaped by the cultural transmission of faith, an embodiment communication that produces a faith effect in the listener, communicated through numerous signs and symbols that become part and parcel to the very makeup of the person. Just as the ambiance of the mall affects our children and communicates values to them, so the church must create a counterculture that communicates the Christian faith through powerful indirect means.

The Communications Revolution and the Younger Evangelical

Adrian Riley gives us some insight into how cultural transmission and embodiment communication is likely to affect the younger evangelical. "Our basic sense apparatus," he writes, "is being used and shaped in ways that previous generations never experienced." Regarding the impact of sense on how we believe, he says, "Our senses are an important portal through which whatever there is to be believed must pass." Following in the tradition of the younger evangelical, he adds, "the multimedia culture that has developed around us does make it more difficult to appropriate belief systems that were developed and aimed at pre-multimedia cultures."[10] The question postmoderns must ask is, How do you communicate in an "image" society?

Twenty-three-year-old postmodern pastor David Hopkins has a suggestion. He claims Marshall McLuhan's *Understanding Media* is "one of the greatest books of this century." Commenting on "the medium is the message," he pleads for us to recognize that the "emerging culture desires something more narrative than information." In regard to sermons, Hopkins is convinced that the "spoken word should not just be a medium for communicating information to mass audiences." It must instead "express beauty and create space within worship for contemplation and initiate conversation." His goal in preaching, he says, is "not just to transfer information" but "to stimulate the mind." The use of media to communicate is, he says, for the sole purpose of "engaging a culture where we are." Reflecting on his use of media, he claims, "For my circumstance and setting, it creates a beautiful atmosphere." Recognizing that he cannot control the response of the people, he says, "They hear what they choose to hear. I cannot transfer meaning. I only give the setting in which people construct meaning. . . . I hope people walk away with a certain need to fill in the spaces with their own experience of the one true God."[11] In these words and images Hopkins has expressed the younger evangelicals' search for a new language of communication that goes beyond words alone.

According to Thomas Hohstadt, author of *Dying to Live: The 21ˢᵗ Century Church*, a new language is emerging "out of the dust of modernism." It is the "language of metaphor," and it will, he is convinced, "ride a wave of emotion." This new language, Hohstadt believes, "will revolutionize our senses." It will make "our emotions and feelings—especially touch—cognitive extensions of our minds. . . . We will know through our feelings." Metaphors, he argues, quoting Carl Hausman, are "active forces in the world" that have the power to bring "something into being."

The greatest of all metaphors is Jesus. He is, as Paul said, "the exact likeness of the unseen God."[12] He brings the invisible into visible form and his death and resurrection become the metaphors for our death to sin and our resurrection to a new life in him, the life of the Spirit. Our own life can be a metaphor, an embodied expression of how God can transform a life and create a person anew.

David Bunker argues in a similar way. "Media," says this fifty-year-old who thinks like a twenty-something, "has created a person that receives truth through a variety of mediums." He thinks that while modern churches are "sterile," postmodern churches "understand that ambiance, mood, and atmosphere all assist in holistically leading someone into an experience of repentance, worship, and joy." The symbols of the church, he insists, cannot be decided haphazardly but with purpose and intention. "Their location, size, and ability to create awe, wonder, and reverence is very important."[13] These symbols, he argues, should touch life and assist a person in Christlike growth.

Mark Filiatreau agrees. "God," he writes, "is a feast for the imagination," and "it is scandalous for Christians to have an imagination starved for God.

"Generation X grew up in a world that had the struts of enlightenment rationalism knocked out of it long before, and they are dropping in postmodern free fall. The nets of rational apologetics are too often too wide to catch them. But the story of Christ is not only a fishnet of truth; it is (like its creator) also a feast for the imagination. Why not serve it this way to those who are starving? . . . We need more than ever to practice the arts."[14]

The premise of this chapter is that the younger evangelical has embraced a more cultural form of communication and applied these communication principles to ministry. This has resulted in two significant factors that help to define and describe the new evangelical. First, younger evangelicals, by virtue of their embrace of the new audio and visual forms of communication, reject the restrictions of print communication with its emphasis on knowing primarily through rational means. Instead, they more readily embrace the more emotive, imaginative, and symbolic forms of communication (without rejecting the significance of the spoken word). Their embrace of the new means of knowing bears significant consequences in their approach to faith, as I will show. Because the current revolution in communication is a return to the oral and visual forms that dominated premodern Christianity, the younger evangelical is much more open to tradition and to the Catholic and Orthodox church and to their use of ceremony and symbolism. They are also very suspicious of propositionalism, rational apologetics, and the church invisible. Because of the influence of the oral and visual forms of communication, the younger evangelical is more apt to embrace story, the apologetics of embodied presence, and the church visible.

A second shift among younger evangelicals has to do with how they are different from their pragmatist predecessors. This matter is, I think, misunderstood by many people including people involved in various church-growth movements who helped to give rise to the market-driven church. Pragmatist Christianity is still closely connected with modernity and print. For this reason pragmatist Christianity may in a sense be regarded as the last gasp of modernity and the first breath of postmodernity. On the other hand, the younger evangelicals, who were born, reared, and educated within the new forms of communication and the postmodern world, more thoroughly embrace the implications of an embodied truth communicated through the cultural transmission of faith.

The church's shift from reliance on print communication to the recovery of the ancient concept of communication through immersion and participation in community is a distinct mark of the younger evangelicals. It provides insight into how they have distanced themselves from modern evangelicalism and why embracing tradition, narrative theology, communal apologetics, and the church visible is necessary for the survival, spread, and witness of the church within a world caught between the anarchy of postmodern relativistic thought and the fiery fundamentalism of Muslim extremism (see table 5).

Table 5
The Impact of Communication Theory

	Traditional Evangelicals	Pragmatic Evangelicals	Younger Evangelicals
Kind of Communication	Print communication	Broadcast communication	Internet communication
Style of Communication	Communication primarily through Word	Seeks instant communication	Communication is an interactive process in community
Impact on Theology	Propositional	Christianity 101	Communal faith
Impact on Apologetics	Evidential apologetic	"It Works" apologetic	Embodied apologetic
Impact in the Church	Established church	Market church	Incarnational church
Impact on Ministry	Knowing God	Experiencing God	Becoming a redeemed human in community

4

History

From Ahistorical to Tradition

David Ray Griffin reflects on the juxtaposition of modernity with tradition this way: "Modernity, rather than being regarded as the norm for human society toward which all history has been aiming and into which all society should be ushered—forcibly if necessary—is instead increasingly seen as an aberration. A new respect for the wisdom of traditional societies is growing as we realize that they have endured for thousands of years and that, by contrast, the existence of modern society for even another century seems doubtful."[1]

Griffin speaks to what younger evangelicals consider to be a constructive response to modernity. The younger evangelical, like Griffin, affirms that the modern era, with its reliance on reason and science, has come to an end. Consequently, the intellectual edifice of twentieth-century evangelicalism, which was integrated with modern science and reason, is now suspect. What is under suspicion is not the faith but the articulation of the faith through modern categories. For example, younger evangelical Michael Horton claims that modern evangelicalism owes its "view of the church more to American democratic (especially populist) sentiment" and that its "consciousness began with [its] own spiritual biography," as opposed to having a consciousness that connects with the church and God's people throughout history. No wonder, he muses, that "the postmodern emphasis on community and *tradition* make [*sic*] sense to the children of individualistic and privatized religion"[2] (my emphasis).

I will explore this return to tradition among three groups: first, among non-evangelicals; second, among evangelical spokespersons who are older but share the concern to return to tradition; and then, third, I'll cite several examples from the younger evangelicals.

The Return to Tradition among Nonevangelicals

A significant movement calling Christians back to the tradition of the church is "Radical Orthodoxy." This movement has attracted worldwide attention among nonevangelical Christians and is being read seriously by younger evangelicals. The primary spokesperson, John Milbank, is an Anglican who taught at Cambridge and now teaches at the University of Virginia.[3] His student Catherine Pickstock, a prolific author, is also a major leader of "the return to tradition" movement.[4] Also, a growing number of scholars around the world have joined the movement.[5] In their writings, which are highly complex and interdisciplinary, three recurrent themes strike a chord with evangelicals.

First, younger evangelicals are attracted to the assertion that theology is the "Queen of the Sciences." During the modern era, theology lost its place among the disciplines. There was a time when all the disciplines were interpreted through theology, but in modernity, reason, science, psychology, sociology, and other disciplines emerged as the independent disciplines of knowledge. Consequently, they became the disciplines through which Christianity was interpreted, defended, and then ultimately marginalized. Radical Orthodoxy proclaims the modern approach, which studied theology through these "secular disciplines," is bankrupt. The only hope to regain a Christian understanding of the world, the Radical Orthodox say, is to start with theology. Milbank argues that all secular forms of thought need to be interpreted by theology, not vice versa. Consequently, he claims that "Christian theology now offers a discourse able to position and overcome nihilism itself. This is why it is so important to reassert theology as a master discourse; theology, alone, remains the discourse of non-mastery."[6]

A second attractive aspect of Radical Orthodoxy is the ancient formulation of the faith as an "answer" to postmodern thought. For example, classical Christianity is not an "accommodation" to postmodernity, nor does it attempt to construct Christianity out of postmodern presuppositions. Instead, it is an "alternative" to postnihilism and includes a joyful affirmation that this is God's world rescued by the person and work of Jesus Christ. In *The Word Made Strange*, Milbank speaks of Jesus' work as "surprising" and says, "Perhaps the most surprise, the most shock, should arise when what is said is really most Orthodox and ancient, since the tradition is so rarely re-performed in practice today."[7]

Consistent with this commitment to Orthodoxy, Milbank works with the postmodern thought of Derrida, Foucault, Lyotard, and others and brings to bear on their philosophies the thinking of Clement, Athanasius, Basil of Caesarea, Cyril of Alexandria, Gregory of Nyssa, John Chrysostom, Augustine, and others. His commitment to historic Christianity leads him to the conviction that "any 'contemporary garb' for Christian truth is of course the most puerile form of betrayal."[8] His student Catherine Pickstock in *After Writing* follows in the same tradition. She writes that Radical Orthodoxy is a "third alternative" to modernity and postmodernity and that "while conceding, with postmodernism, the indeterminacy of all our knowledge and experience of selfhood, it construes this shifting flux as a sign of our dependency on a transcendent source which 'gives' all reality as a mystery, rather than as adducing our suspension over the void."[9]

The third theme of Radical Orthodoxy is the call to return to classical Christianity. Milbank writes, "Abandoning all scholastic attempts to graft faith onto a universal base of reason, it [referring to Radical Orthodoxy] instead turns to the church Fathers."[10] Milbank specifically goes back to the church Fathers' emphasis on the incarnation of God in history as the starting point for Christian reflection. Milbank writes, "All history before Christ can be narrated as 'anticipating' his story, and all history since as situated within it."[11] He speaks of the incarnation as "the 'finality' of God's appearance in a life involving suffering and violent death, and claims also that in a certain sense God 'has to' be like this, and has not just 'incidentally' chosen this path." He goes on to speak of this picture as a "joyful and suffering life" that "gives an active notion of divine love, and involvement in our destiny."[12]

In sum, younger evangelicals see Radical Orthodoxy as a promising theological movement. It "returns theology to the center of contemporary critical debate"; it argues "that it is no longer acceptable to accommodate theology to prevailing wisdom and fashion"; it rejects the secular humanism that was born out of the Enlightenment and prevailed during the twentieth century; it rejects postmodernism "in favor of a theological construal of the radically indeterminable"; it regards secular modernity as the "creation of a perverse theology"; it sees the opposition of reason to revelation as a "modern corruption"; it views "all thought which brackets out God" as "ultimately nihilistic"; and it argues that the "material and temporal realms of bodies, sex, art and sociality, which modernity claims to value, can truly be upheld only by acknowledgement of their participation in the transcendent." Consequently, Radical Orthodoxy "aims to reclaim the world by situating its concerns and activities within a theological framework."[13]

A second movement making an impact on the younger evangelical is associated with Robert Wilken. Wilken is not a member of the Radical Orthodoxy group and is not even a theologian. He is a believing historian who works in the field of patristic studies and is the highly respected William R. Kenan Jr. Professor of the History of Christianity at the University of Virginia in Charlottesville, Virginia (incidentally, where Milbank teaches). A number of younger evangelicals who have studied with Wilken have been influenced to ground their thinking in the early church.

Wilken's perspective on the early church is illustrated in his work, *Remembering the Christian Past*.[14] In the introduction Wilken writes, "The essays in this volume are a modest effort in remembering aspects of Christian tradition that have been forgotten. All touch on issues that are currently under discussion but in thinkers who lived long ago and in cultural settings distant from our own. Yet they address, if not directly, questions of our day. . . . All knowing begins with what we have received; before we become masters we must learn to be disciples, to allow others to form our words and guide our thought."[15]

Wilken observes that for many, "the ticket of admission to religious studies is a forfeiture of memory."[16] This approach he claims "is too high a price to pay."[17] "Without memory," he writes, "the language of scholarship is impoverished, barren and lifeless, a tottering scaffold of secondary creations."[18] He invites his reader to remember that "religious traditions of the world are not only communities of 'faith,' they are also traditions of learning."[19] Like Flannery O'Connor, he believes that "dogma is an instrument for penetrating reality."[20] This recovery of memory is a passion of the younger evangelicals. They have a burning desire to tap into the great Christian memory that starts with Scripture and the classical tradition.

A third group concerned with rediscovering the past are the postliberals. Evangelicals Timothy Phillips and Dennis Okholm refer approvingly of this group: *"Postliberalism,"* they write, "refers to a theological movement most commonly linked with Yale Divinity School. It seeks to reverse the trend in modern Christianity of accommodation to culture. . . . The originators of this movement are Hans Frei and George Lindbeck. Their students, creative and provocative theologians like William Placher, Stanley Hauerwas, and George Hunsinger, have further developed these key ideas."[21]

What lies at the heart of the postliberal agenda is a commitment, like that of Radical Orthodoxy, to a "classical" hermeneutic in "which the scriptural world structures the church cosmos and identity."[22] Phillips and Okholm write, "While the evangelical movement appears to be gaining ground, it is simultaneously suffering an acute identity crisis. . . . Ironically it is the postliberals, a confessional group from mainline denominational circles, that may provide the most help. They offer a theory for resisting the foreign extra-biblical assumptions of modernity while maintaining confessional identity within the church."[23] This is precisely the agenda of the younger evangelical: to (1) break the reliance of evangelical Christianity on its accommodation to modern culture and (2) to restore Christian memory by returning evangelical faith to its roots in classical Christianity.

The Return to Tradition among the Older Evangelicals

This concern to anchor faith in classical Christianity is also being espoused by some older, more seasoned evangelical leaders. For example, the new openness toward classical Christianity was captured in a conversation with Mike Brecht, a pastor in the Pentecostal side of the evangelical church. Brecht told me this: "I've tried every church renewal movement that has come down the pike— you name it, I've done it. Finally, after being tossed around like a cork on the sea, I decided there must be something that has staying power. I went back to the church fathers and found my home. I want a faith and Christian practice that has stability and isn't going to be changed by the next leader who reinvents the wheel."[24]

Pastor Brecht's response to current fads expresses the concern of a number of evangelicals. Like the Reformers of the sixteenth century, they want to reform the church. Like Luther and Calvin and Menno Simons, they want to peel away the extraneous cultural baggage that now encumbers the church and go back to the substance of the classical tradition. What is common to these writers is the conviction that an evangelicalism based on modern categories of thought will not survive in a postmodern world.

Because modern categories of science and reason have been deconstructed and are seriously questioned, many evangelicals are asking, "Why would you build a case for evangelical Christianity on these categories?" Two classes of older evangelical writers ask this question: (1) those who explicitly call for a return to classical Christianity and (2) those who call upon the church to recover Christian memory, which implicitly suggests a return to classical thought. Thomas Oden is an example of the first group. Years ago Oden was a committed liberal. Finding liberal theology to be vacuous, he turned to the study of the early fathers and became highly regarded among evangelicals. He speaks at evangelical conferences, publishes with evangelical publishers (Zondervan and InterVarsity Press), and writes on occasion for *Christianity Today*.

His main message to evangelicals is contained in his book *After Modernity . . . What?*[25] In the introduction Oden writes, "The sons and daughters of modernity are rediscovering the neglected beauty of classical Christian teaching. It is a moment of joy, of beholding anew what had been nearly forgotten, of hugging a lost child."[26]

Oden knows the evangelical situation and has some harsh words to say about the dumbing down of faith to this or that culture fad. He says, "Theological programs have come and gone at an embarrassing rate in the last two decades. . . .

Theology needs reforming but not in a new way, only in an old and familiar way."[27] He goes on to say, "What the ancient church *least* wished for a theology was that it would be 'fresh' or 'self-expressive' or an embellishment of purely private inspirations, as if these might stand as some 'decisive improvement' on the apostolic teaching."[28] Oden writes, *"The agenda for theology at the end of the twentieth century, following the steady deterioration of a hundred years and the disaster of the last few decades, is to begin to prepare the postmodern Christian community for its third millennium by returning again to the careful study and respectful following of the central tradition of classical Christian exegesis"*[29] (italics, his). It is of great interest to me that Thomas Oden is a Methodist, a member of the branch of Christianity that stems from John Wesley. Recent studies show Wesley himself was steeped in the thought of the early church, especially the Greek fathers. Randy Maddox concludes his study of the origins of Wesleyan theology by saying, "His general theological practice can best be described as a return to the early Christian approach of theology per se as practical."[30]

Another clarion call for the recovery of traditional Christianity is found in the writing of D. H. Williams. Williams is an evangelical who is an ordained Baptist minister. Formerly an assistant professor of patristics and historical theology at Loyola University in Chicago, he now teaches at Baylor University. His book *Retrieving the Tradition and Renewing Evangelicalism*[31] is a summons to recover Christian memory, especially that of classical Christianity. Williams is concerned about the lack of historical connection within evangelicalism and refers to "an acute problem of continuity affecting evangelical Christians."[32] Speaking of the rise of evangelical diversity in the latter part of the twentieth century and particularly the evangelical turn toward an accommodation with culture, Williams is concerned that "we have come to define evangelicalism by social and cultural factors as much as by theological or historical ones."[33] He expresses his antidote to culturally driven evangelicalism in this way: "An underlying purpose of this book is to integrate the serious study of patristics (study of the 'fathers,' or more broadly, the life and literature of early Christianity) into current theological reflections of evangelicalism, a task that has already begun though is very much in its infancy."[34] Williams concludes his introduction with a comment on how the movement continues to return to the early church. His comments are worth repeating to demonstrate that the younger evangelical return to Christian memory is not an isolated case here and there:

> Even as I write these words, there are other exciting attempts being made by evangelically sponsored or supported projects to foster an understanding of the church's Tradition through an encounter with the theological resources of the ancients. InterVarsity has just published the papers of a conference which dealt with Evangelical-Roman Catholic-Orthodox relations in light of the "great tradition" [he refers to James S. Cutsinger, ed., *Reclaiming the Great Tradition;* see below]. Larger undertakings include a series of volumes to be published by Wm. B. Eerd-

mans Publishing Company entitled *The Church's Bible* that will put at the fingertips of pastors and Christian leaders select extracts of patristic exegetical commentary on major passages of the Bible, all translated into English with annotation that guides the reader without smothering [the editor of this series is Robert Wilken, mentioned above]. Thomas Oden of Drew University is spearheading a similar project [he is referring here to the *Ancient Christian Commentary on Scripture* series (InterVarsity Press)]. All of this is in addition to the multiple editions of English translations of patristic texts that are continuing to be published such as fathers of the church, *Ancient Christian Writers*, and *Library of Christian Classics*, among others. An increasing wealth of resources for the ecumenically and historically minded Protestant (and Roman Catholic) is available as never before, providing for the working pastor, educator, seminarian, and diligent laity a critical foundation for the theological renewal of evangelicalism.[35]

Another writer among the older evangelicals is James S. Cutsinger. Cutsinger is professor of theology and religious thought at the University of South Carolina. His book, *Reclaiming the Great Tradition*, derived from a conference that brought evangelicals, Catholics, and Orthodox together for mutual conversation. Cutsinger describes the occasion for such a gathering with these words: "There seems to be a growing consensus that some larger, perhaps more definite, crisis is at hand, and that it is therefore time for serious Christians to join forces for a common task."[36] The goal of the conference was "to test whether an ecumenical Orthodoxy, solidly based on the classic Christian faith as expressed in the scriptures and ecumenical councils, could become the foundation for unified and transformative witness to the present age."[37]

A fourth writer, Rodney Clapp, has called the church to return to its classical memory. Clapp is the editorial director of Brazos Press, a division of Baker Book House, and a writer as well. In his book *Border Crossings*, Clapp writes, "There can, there must be, a re-appropriation of Christian tradition (and not just of its first three centuries), but it is necessarily a *re*-appropriation, not simply a rote imitation or repetition of the tradition as it was embodied centuries earlier. In God's providence, we are now witnessing marvelous demonstrations or at least hints toward such timely re-appropriations: deep Christian thinkers who are steeped in the tradition but also keenly aware of the unique challenges of postmodernity."[38]

While Oden, Williams, Cutsinger, and Clapp call for an explicit return to classical Christian thought, there are many other evangelical writers who call for a return to Christian memory. These writers want to end the reliance of evangelicalism on Enlightenment categories of thought and connect evangelical Christianity with a broader and more inclusive history of Christian thought. They call on evangelical writers to break with the ahistorical attitude of the twentieth century to find their place in the historical continuity of the church. I will refer here to only one evangelical, Stanley J. Grenz. Grenz is the Pioneer McDonald Professor of Baptist Heritage, Theology and Ethics at Carey Theological College and a professor at Regent College; both schools are in Vancouver, British Columbia. Grenz is a prolific writer and perhaps the most thoughtful author addressing the matter of rethinking evangelicalism for a postmodern world.

His recent books *Revisioning Evangelical Theology, Renewing the Center,* and *Beyond Foundationalism* address recovery of Christian heritage as a necessary ingredient for a viable evangelical faith in a postmodern world.[39] Grenz argues for an evangelicalism that returns to a spiritually centered faith like that of the pietists. The pietists were a post-Reformation group that, in response to seventeenth-century head-oriented Protestant Orthodoxy, called for the recovery of a heartfelt Christian faith.

Grenz adds, "The renewed emphasis on the practical understanding of theology marks a shift not only to the earlier Pietism but also, in a sense, a move back from modernity to the patristic era, or perhaps a move beyond modernity into the emerging postmodern era. The direct goal, if not the topic, of most patristic theological writers was the fostering of spirituality in the reader. . . . Above all, however, a theology rooted in spirituality will be cognizant of the centrality of the doctrine of the trinity. . . . The creation of the theology that both fosters and is demanded by this vision of faith is the task and challenge evangelicalism entrusts to those of us who are its theologians."[40] Grenz takes us back to the most significant creed of the Christian church, the Nicene Creed. This journey backward, he notes, as do Milbank, Pickstock, Hauerwas, Oden, and others, is necessary before we can move forward with confidence in a postmodern world.

Grenz tells us not only that we must return to the past to move into the future, he tells us why. It has to do with the story of God at work in biblical times, culminating in Jesus Christ and now handed down in the worship and spirituality of the church. This believing community is the true apology for faith in a postmodern setting. "Theology," writes Grenz, "becomes an intellectual enterprise by and for the Christian community, in which the community of those whom the God of the Bible has encountered in Jesus Christ seeks to understand, clarify, and determine the community's interpretive framework as informed by the narrative of the action of this God on behalf of all creation as revealed in the Bible."[41] For Grenz, the believing community does not just pick up the Bible and immediately discern what God is saying. Instead, "reading within community . . . means . . . that we approach the text conscious that we are participants in the one faith community that spans the ages."[42] This reading in community, Grenz says, is a "desire to be in hermeneutical fellowship with all the people of God." It is "our attempt to retain continuity of outlook with the church throughout the ages."[43] An argument similar to that of Grenz is found in the writings of other evangelicals who are calling for the reconstruction of evangelical faith after the breakdown of modernity and within the rise of postmodern thought. This is especially true of the works of Baptist theologians James William McClendon Jr.,[44] Gordon Lewis,[45] and Gregory Boyd.[46]

The Return to Tradition among the Younger Evangelicals

I have tried to show that there is a movement both outside the evangelical culture and within it that takes seriously the need for evangelicals to grow past their preoccupation with a Christianity enmeshed in modern categories of thought. This commitment to recover the past calls into question the ahistorical nature of the traditional evangelical articulation of the faith. It also sets into motion a search for evangelical roots and a desire to connect with the faith communicated in all the paradigms of history (e.g., ancient, medieval, Reformation, and modern). We look now at illustrations from the evangelicals who are younger in age. Because they are drawn to the entire Christian past, I will cite three examples: first the interest in Celtic tradition, then a fresh look at the Middle Ages, and finally a return to the catholic spirit of Wesley.

Younger evangelicals are drawn to the Celtic tradition. For example, Loren Wilkinson, in an article entitled "Saving Celtic Christianity," claims, "There's a wealth of Christian truth and devotion worth rediscovering."[47] Wilkinson speaks of being drawn to the Celtic tradition because it is a "rich source of recovering basic Christianity." Younger evangelicals are attracted to the emphasis Celts put on the triune God, especially on the relatedness of both the otherness and the nearness of God emphasized in the coinherence of the Trinity (called the doctrine of perichoresis). This ancient truth speaks specifically to the Western tendency to stress either the transcendence or the immanence of God without an appropriate balance. Younger evangelicals, like the Celts, affirm that God is wholly other and incomprehensible yet near and available. Younger evangelical thinkers see in a more ancient theology the potential for a language to help them affirm this paradox in God.

A second attraction to Celtic thought is its concept of creation. For Celts, creation "is not so much a process that God began and occasionally intervenes in. Rather, creation involves a relationship in which the whole cosmos is at every point dependent on the self-giving God whose very nature is love involving community and relatedness."[48] This attitude toward God's presence in creation shifts attention away from the more modern attitude of evangelicalism (of the fundamentalist sort) that presupposes science to be the crucial issue and argues for a young earth and a seven-day act of creation. Instead, younger evangelicals find in Celtic faith an understanding of creation and God's role within it that is more spiritual in nature. God, the one who gives meaning to creation, can be known and experienced through creation. This view puts the emphasis on the meaning of creation, not on a particular intellectual theory about how or when God created.

A third value of Celtic Christianity for younger evangelicals is on how the Celts viewed Christian practice. Celts were characterized by "availability, vulnerability and hospitality"[49] and offered a unique ray of hope in a dark period of history. The way they merged faith and practice is a model for younger evangelicals today. They have become keenly aware of the unity that exists between believing and doing—another modern separation that younger evangelicals seek to overcome.

A second example of the younger evangelical embrace of the past is found in the new interest in the Middle Ages. For example, Joseph Huffman, associate professor of history at Messiah College, has written an interesting article on faith and practice entitled "Faith, Reason, and the Text: The Return of the Middle Ages in Postmodern Scholarship."[50] He argues that "postmodernism has in some significant respects returned to the Middle Ages for its deconstruction of modern epistemology." He concludes that "medieval and postmodern approaches to textual authority in particular reveal the epistemological limitations of modernism." He therefore encourages Christians to cease privileging modernism and to "recover their neglected medieval Christian legacy as a valuable resource for speaking with relevance to the postmodern spirit."[51] The modern notion that meaning and morality can be ascertained through reason apart from God have become increasingly empty. The concept of progress and the notion that history is moving civilization to higher levels of consciousness is no longer valid. The idea that growth in knowledge will save civilization, that science always has an answer, and that we can depend on it to solve our problems, has been shattered by the frightening nature of our technological future. Medieval thought acts as a critique of these Enlightenment notions. Medieval thought puts God at the center and shows how a world built on Enlightenment presuppositions of independence from God will come to ruin. During the Enlightenment, thinkers used their enlightened notions to critique medievalism. Now we return to the medieval era as a postmodern method of critiquing modernity. What goes around, comes around.

For a third example, I turn to the republication of John Wesley's sermon 34 on the catholic spirit, published in *Regeneration Quarterly*. The editors state, "We commend to you the full text of this challenging sermon." They point to a question posed by Wesley, a question that has emerged once again in the pluralism of postmodernity: "Although a difference in opinions or modes of worship may prevent an entire external union, yet need it prevent our union in affection?" This "union in affection" is the catholic spirit that Wesley was all about, a spirit that pervades the *Regeneration Quarterly* as a plethora of younger evangelical writers freely borrow from Catholic and Byzantine sources as well as the writings of the Reformers, John Wesley, and others. Learning from Wesley, these new younger evangelicals do not affirm a wishy-washy latitudinarianism. For them all opinions, practices, and congregations are not equally right. They agree with Wesley that the catholic spirit is not relativism but is embodied by one who knows how "to value, and praise God for, all the advantages he enjoys, with regard to the knowledge of the things of God, the true manner of worshiping Him, and above all, his union with a congregation fearing God and working righteousness: one who, retaining these blessings with the strictest care, keeping them as the apple of his eye, at the same time loves—as friends, as brethren in the Lord, as members of Christ and children of God, as joint partakers now of the present kingdom of God, and fellow heirs of His eternal kingdom—all, of whatever opinion or worship, or congregation, who believe in the Lord Jesus Christ; who love God and man; who, rejoicing to please, and fearing to offend God, are careful to abstain from evil, and zealous of good works. *He is the man of a truly Catholic Spirit*" (my emphasis).[52]

We may ask what impact the new interest in recovering a historical perspective has made on younger evangelicals. It has made them more zealous for truth, for Christian life and action. Yet they are humbled by the complexity of truth, and they are gentle and generous toward those who differ. The younger evangelicals are not fighters intent on splitting churches. They are not dogmatic zealots or mean-spirited close-minded bigots. They seek to hold that which has always been held by all and affirm affection for those with whom they differ. Their love of the ancient and their return to tradition has given them this "catholic spirit."

These three illustrations are by no means exhaustive, but they do show a new evangelical propensity to embrace the past, an earnest desire on the part of some to move beyond fixation with the Enlightenment. Younger evangelicals have begun a trend to "get out of the box" and to enrich evangelical articulation of the faith with insights from significant movements of the past.

This love for the ancient past, for classical Christian thought articulated by the fathers of the church and the ancient creeds, puts the younger evangelical at odds with traditional and with pragmatic evangelicals. Traditionalists hearken back to the theology of fundamentalism, particularly the Reformed development of it in the Princeton school of thought established at the turn of the century and affirmed by Carl F. H. Henry and those under his influence. These traditionalists will go back as far as the Reformation and speak warmly of Thomas Aquinas and Augustine. But generally they dismiss the fifteen hundred years of theological thought prior to the Reformation and care little about the fathers of the church and the formation of classical Christianity. Pragmatic evangelicals are bold and assertive regarding their ahistorical stance. They are innovators, who, while affirming historic Christianity, care little about exploring it or building their theology around it. They advocate a break with tradition, a fresh start, a new and creative face that primarily looks forward.

In this context the younger evangelical emerges with a new love for the past and a commitment to the notion that the road to the future runs through the past. In this attitude they express their involvement in the cultural transmission of the faith. They want to immerse themselves in the past and form a culture that is connected to the past, a culture that remembers its tradition as it moves into the future. Consequently, the younger evangelical is attracted to theology as narrative as we observe in the next chapter (see table 6).

Table 6
Attitude toward History and Tradition

	Traditional Evangelicals	Pragmatic Evangelicals	Younger Evangelicals
Approach	Retain Reformation distinction	Start something new; innovate	The future runs through the past
Attitude toward Ancient Church	The true church began with the Reformation	Best form of Christianity begins with twentieth-century seeker movement	Restore the ancient church Connect with the entire church
Attitude toward Catholics	Anti-Catholic	Evangelicals and Catholics together	Work, worship, and evangelize with Catholics
Interpreting Scripture	Authorial intent (Inerrant)	Bible in one hand, culture in the other	Scripture interpreted within community of church throughout history
Worship	Maintain tradition of your denomination	Break with the past to introduce chorus-driven worship	Converge all traditions of worship
Spirituality	Read Bible, pray, church, witness	Small-group accountability	Restore ancient traditions

5

Theology

From Propositionalism to Narrative

A few years ago I was asked to debate the question of God's existence with an atheist. I knew my opponent would come ready to use his rational arguments against the existence of God to destroy my rational arguments for the existence of God. In order to shift the discussion away from arguments for or against God's existence, I used my opening comments to inform my opponent and the listening audience that I would not discuss traditional arguments for the existence of God. When asked, "Well, how then shall we proceed?" I answered, "Let's talk about the reality of the communities of Israel and Jesus. Let's probe those stories to uncover what they tell us about the origin, meaning, and destiny of the world." In this way I shifted the discussion from propositions based on evidence to stories based on faith.

During the modern period the primacy of reason gave rise to arguments for or against the existence of God. Both believers and nonbelievers followed the rules of evidence to arrive at statements to support or deny the propositional statement, "God is."

Both believers and nonbelievers thought they had good *reason* to believe or disbelieve this proposition. Those who believed were convinced that they knew something about God through God's revelation of himself which they could interpret with the use of reason. Those who did not believe were quite confident that their knowledge of the origin and working of the world was based on reason and science. Consequently, the believer and the unbeliever were at a standstill. Both thought they had good reason to believe or not to believe.

In the twenty-first-century world, the attitude toward the use of reason has shifted rather significantly. The new attitude, born out of cultural shifts, is that the use of reason and science to prove or disprove a fact is questionable. This conclusion is no argument for irrationalism. It points rather to the postmodern conclusion that we deal with "interpreted facts." The believer looks at creation and speaks of God as the Creator. That's an "interpreted fact." The nonbeliever looks at creation and assumes the world derived from chance. That, too, is an "interpreted fact." Thus in the postmodern world, both believers and nonbelievers are people of faith. One has faith in the story of the Bible; the other has faith in the story of reason, science, some other religion, or the god of his or her own making. The case for the Christian faith is no longer reason against reason but faith against faith in opposing stories.

For example, modern science has a story about the world. It says in brief that the world originated by chance, is impersonal, runs like a machine, and that man must determine his own future. The dream of modernity is that humanity aided by reason and science will be able to move the world and its inhabitants toward the goal of perfection. Christianity also has a story. It says God created the world, made man in his image, and gave him the responsibility to care for the world. Because of sin and rebellion, humanity has fallen away from God. But God became involved in our history, in Israel and in the incarnation of God in Jesus, to rescue the world through his death and resurrection. The church is his new people who point to the ultimate reign of God over all things.

We call these stories metanarratives ("meta" meaning "with," "narrative" meaning "story," so by derivation metanarrative means "with story"). Metanarratives are comprehensive stories for the whole world. We Christians say that the biblical story is not one story that runs alongside other stories. It is not a relative story. It is an all-encompassing story for all people in all places and in all time. Postmodern philosophy disagrees. It says there is no such thing; there are many stories and each one is as valid as the next.

The Christian Metanarrative

Classical Christianity knew nothing of the concept of propositionalism as held by Christians after the Enlightenment. Classical Christianity interpreted the faith more as a story that swept from creation through the fall to the rescue by God through Jesus Christ and to the final outcome in the new heavens and the new earth. Let's look at the story, the metanarrative, of faith as it was presented in the early church.

The common hermeneutic of the early church fathers was to interpret the Bible through the story of creation, incarnation, and re-creation. This approach is found in second-century theologians Tertullian and Irenaeus; in the third-century work of Origen (with some fanciful aspects not accepted by the church); and in the work of fourth-century theologians such as Athanasius, the Cappadocian Fathers, and Cyril of Alexandria.

The metanarrative begins with creation. Creation is an act of God bringing something into being out of nothing *(ex nihilo)*. Once there was nothing. Now there is time, space, and history. As Gregory of Nyssa states, "The very subsistence of creation owed its beginning to change."[1] But it was not a change in God. Creation is not an "extension of God" as New Agers teach. Creation is something outside of God and different than God. For example, Athanasius wrote creation "is not in the least like its creator in substance, but is *outside* Him."[2] For the early fathers, creation was endowed with freedom and choice. St. Gregory the theologian wrote, "God legislates human self-determination."[3] Thus creation has the power to choose to be in union with God, to work in harmony and in concert with God, or to break away from God and to move in a direction that asserts its own independence.

The metanarrative continues with the fall. The fathers of the church interpreted Scripture as saying the choice for rebellion and separation from God is the way of death. This is the choice of the powers of evil who, in rebellion against God, became anti-God and chose by their influence to move God's creatures and creation away from God. Evil is, as Georges Florovsky states, "a force, a violent energy. And the opposition of evil to God is very active. The good is seriously limited and oppressed by the insurrection of evil. God himself is engaged in a struggle with these powers of darkness. And in this struggle there are very real losses, there is a perpetual domination of the good. Evil is an ontological danger."[4] There is in creation and throughout history a "struggle between divine goodness and evil."[5]

Because of the sins of the creatures, the world lies under the curse of death. As Paul stated, "Just as sin entered the world through one man, and death through sin, . . . death came to all" (Rom. 5:12). Evil is "a radical opposition to God, a revolt, a disobedience, a resistance."[6] The original sin of Adam and Eve was not "just an erroneous choice, not just an option for the wrong direction, but rather a refusal to ascend toward God, a desertion from the service of God."[7] According to St. Athanasius, the human fall consists "precisely in the fact that man limits himself to himself, that man becomes, as it were, in love with himself."[8] In this sense the fall represents a "de-spiritualization of human existence."[9] The fall has resulted not only in our loss of relationship with God but also of a deliberate, intentional, and violent rejection of our former union with God in the garden and thus a "death and decomposition of human structure."[10] The spirit of God, which had been united with the human structure of personhood, was wrenched from humanness, and man, void of any relation to the transcendent, was turned loose to his own arrogant self-assured confidence that he could "go it alone" without God. Now "the dark tide . . . envelops all creatures and the entire cosmos." The fallen world is "decentralized, or rather it is oriented around an imaginary fictitious center. One could say perhaps that the circle (with a unique center) is deformed, becoming an ellipse with two points of reference—God and anti-God. Being, in any case, is dynamically divided in two."

True freedom, which is the choice to be in union with God and with God's will, is now lost. Man has become a slave of his passion, free only to sin. The image of God in man is "paralyzed" and unable to choose the good for salvation. This is the picture of the human condition and the state of the entire creation. The entire cosmos is, as Paul says, "subject to decay."

This story of the fall and its disastrous cosmic effect must be told as a central piece of the story before we speak of salvation, redemption, and re-creation. The issue is, How does God restore his creation now infected by sin and by its own choice subject to death?

The salvation story centers on the incarnation and subsequent events. God entered our history and became incarnate in Jesus. In the union of the divine with the human in the person of Jesus Christ came the "lifting up of human nature into an everlasting communion with the divine life."[11] This union of the divine and the human is crucial, for it affirms the two axioms that "only God can save" and that "that is saved which is united to God."[12] The first axiom was affirmed in the Nicene Creed of A.D. 325. The creed confesses the son of God to be "eternally begotten of the Father, God from God, light from light, true God from true God, begotten not made, of one being with the Father."[13] The second axiom was established in the Chalcedon Creed of A.D. 451, which confesses that Jesus is "of one substance with us as regards his manhood; like us in all respects, apart from sin." Salvation is from above and below. In the union between God and man in the person of Jesus, Divine Action is united to human response. He, the God-man, alone is able to save.

The union of the divine occurred, the creed continues, "in two natures, without confusion, without change, without division, without separation; the distinction of natures being in no way annulled by the union."[14] What happened in the incarnation is a reversal of what happened in the garden. In the garden, Adam and Eve were called into union with God, but their rebellion against God affected all people as well as the created order. Sin put them under death, broke their relationship with God, and prevented their union with him. But this union with God, which Adam and Eve could not achieve, was accomplished by God's initiative to unite himself with man through the incarnation. The incarnation began the process of re-creation; the mission of God to restore the world was taking place. The incarnation, however, was not an event that stood alone.

Rather, it was inextricably linked to the death of Christ. For by his death, death has been vanquished and life has been restored to creature and creation. By the death of Jesus Christ, God has become the victor over sin and death. All that is evil in the world is conquered by Jesus, who overcame death by his death and will destroy all the powers of evil at the end of history.[15]

In this biblical vision of the world, death is not the natural result of life but life's enemy. Death is "a painful metaphysical catastrophe . . . a mysterious failure of human destiny."[16] Death is the work of the evil one, a work which had to be overcome to release creatures and creation from its hold so that all might be restored to God. Jesus, by his death, took upon himself the wages of sin, and his voluntary sacrifice for sin prepared the way to overcome death. By death he destroyed death and by his resurrection he opened the way to heaven. For "by death God not only punishes but also heals fallen and ruined human nature."[17] The fathers saw the resurrection as the "true renewal, the transfiguration, the reformation of the whole creation. Jesus' death is not just a return of what has passed away, but a heightening, a fulfillment of something better and more perfect."[18] His death is the "cleansing of the whole world," the "baptism by blood of all creation," the "cleansing of the cosmos through the cleansing of the microcosm."[19]

This story captures the view of history revealed in the Bible. History, brought under ruin by the first Adam, is now brought into redemption by the second Adam. Therefore Christ is our eschatological hope. Because of the incarnation, death, and resurrection, we live in the hope of the new heavens and the new earth. In him the *Missio Dei* has been accomplished. Creation will be restored when he returns to put evil away forever and to reign over his redeemed world, throughout eternity.

New Questions

Because the younger evangelical is turning away from theology as ruled by reason and the scientific method toward theology as a reflection of the community on the narrative of Israel and Jesus, three new questions are emerging.

1. How are we to interpret the Genesis account?
2. How are we to view the stewardship of creation?
3. How is truth known?

Interpreting the Creation Story

Christians have held four different interpretations of the Genesis story. The first is that Adam and Eve were made at once and that God created the world in seven literal days. This view is held by fundamentalists. A second view is that the origin of creation is a mystery and that the creation accounts are to be read doxo-logically. This view is held by most new evangelicals and those within evangelical diversity. A third view, theistic evolution (evolution caused by God), is held by many evangelicals who work in the field of science. A fourth view, that the creation story is a myth, is generally not held by evangelicals. Perhaps the view most widely held by the younger evangelical is articulated by John C. Polkinghorne.

Polkinghorne's book *Science and Creation: The Search for Understanding* won the *Christianity Today* Book of the Year Award in 1998.[20] The author spent most of his vocational life as professor of mathematical physics at Cambridge University where his work was acclaimed worldwide. In a midlife career change, he studied theology in an Anglican seminary, subsequently became ordained as a priest, and is now dean and chaplain of Trinity Hall, Cambridge. He brings theology and science together to speak with an authoritative voice, and many younger evangelicals find he articulates a view with which they feel quite comfortable.

Polkinghorne, like the early church fathers, embraces the biblical imagery of a cosmic Christ who made all things, became flesh to save all things, and in the end of history will restore all things. The "incarnation," he says, "testifies to God's deepest possible involvement with his creation," and the empty tomb "holds forth the hope of a destiny for matter as well as for men."[21] The doctrine of creation is therefore not a static issue standing on its own and answering to a specific literal historical or scientific investigation. Instead, the Christian view of creation is a theological issue intricately intertwined with the matter of incarnation, re-creation, and the purposes of God for the world. Creation, Polkinghorne insists, finds its meaning in the completed work of God to restore and renew the created order.

This theological vision of creation points to the issue of *telos* (the purposes of God in creation) and to the understanding that "the creation of the physical world is not a merely transient episode but matter must have its destiny too, along with men. What this means is clearly beyond our powers to anticipate."[22] What Polkinghorne alludes to here is that salvation is not the salvation only of people but of the whole world, the rescue of the created order. And this is not a salvation of determinism but one involving risk and freedom.

For example, Polkinghorne says, God created "a world in which chance has a role to play, thereby both being responsible for the consequences accruing and also accepting limitation of his power to control."[23] This view, espoused in creation science, has more recently been discussed in the openness-of-God debate raised by Clark Pinnock, John Sanders, Gregory Boyd, and others.[24] These writers reject the more predestinarian view of a God who controls the minutiae of history. For them, predestination of every detail of life is an interpretation that plays into the science of modernity, the Newtonian view of the world as machine, a view called into question by quantum physics.

Polkinghorne affirms that God is not "the unchangeable ultimate ground of the phenomenal order" but "the free origin of the contingent events of the world, whose interrelations are contingent and constitute no eternal order but a history moving from event to event."[25] But Polkinghorne adds, "I would want to say that he is revealed in *both* these models, as 'ground of the phenomenal order' and as 'free origin of contingent events,' the God of necessity and the God of chance, the ground of both being and becoming, the one who is at once reliable and vulnerable. Though God was under no compulsion to undertake the risk of creation, by that free act the world has become necessary to him and he is intimately involved with its fate."[26] Polkinghorne affirms that the world as observed by science is "characterized by both order and design" and theology "asserts . . . process is the expression of the Creator's purpose."[27]

Polkinghorne brings theology and science together in a way that does not see them in opposite corners fighting for two different interpretations.[28] The theological interpretation of the world presents the "why," the purpose, the *telos*, even as science investigates the "how" of the inner working of God's creation. Many younger evangelicals find this "both-and" view to be significantly more attractive than the "either-or" view of fundamentalism. It allows for God's interaction with the world and the process of history, and it lays a foundation for Christians to think and act responsibly within the world. The view of an open world leads to the second current issue, the matter of ecology.

Ecology and the Stewardship of Creation

The ecological issue is one of the foremost issues of our time. Some older evangelicals have dismissed ecology as a nonissue because they believe the world and its history will soon end in the second coming. The unfortunate consequence of this approach to eschatology, reflected in Hal Lindsey's *The Late Great Planet Earth* and the more recent Left Behind series by Tim LaHaye and Jerry Jenkins, is a focus on prophetic schedules and timetables at the expense of environmental stewardship. This eschatology generates the opinion that says, "Let the earth run out of resources and don't worry about ecological balance or survival. The world is going to end anyway, so let it happen."

For younger evangelicals who affirm a cosmic salvation, ecology and the stewardship of creation is a central issue related to the story of creation, incarnation, and re-creation.[29] The Reformed side of evangelical faith has always spoken of the "cultural mandate" given to Adam and Eve to "rule over" (Gen. 1:26) creation and "to work it and take care of it" (Gen. 2:15). Humanity's calling in life is to be a steward of God's good creation and to unfold the inner workings of God's creation according to God's will. The fall results in the wrong unfolding process. In our time in history, we have lived to see the destructive nature of technology on the created order. We have seen the negative results of the "domination" of the created order, the conviction that we can do anything we want with creation. This destructive approach has resulted in an ecological imbalance that has "hurt" the creation and "prevented" it from functioning according to God's redemption.

We Christians who know the theological meaning and purpose of creation are called to function in creation in a "redemptive way." We know that God loves the creation, that in the incarnation God became a part of creation, and that God's work on the cross was not only a sacrifice for personal sin but a sacrifice that "won the battle with the enemy." This victory released creatures and creation from their "bondage to decay" so that the whole world is "in the pains of childbirth right up to the present time" (Rom. 8:18–22). Our care of God's creation is therefore not mere humanitarian effort but participation in the process of redemption as we anticipate the ultimate reign of God over the entire creation.

Knowing the Truth

A third question of younger evangelicals is, How do we know this story is the truth? In order to shed light on this matter, we need to explore how this question was answered in the modern world.

Truth in the modern world was based on reason and the scientific method. Both liberals and fundamentalists used the same method to arrive at truth. The difference between liberals and fundamentalists was their attitude toward the Bible. Liberals argued for the Bible as the result of "man's search for God." For them, the Bible was subject to human error and to fabrication. Consequently, they demythologized the Bible to find a universal truth that could be affirmed by reason. They concluded that the one thing true about the Christian faith was that God is love, and we ought to love our neighbors as God loves us.[30]

Fundamentalists, on the other hand, viewed the Bible as "God's revelation to man." For them, the Bible was without error in its message and in all references it made to historical or scientific matters. The positive feature of this view is that the fundamentalist evangelicalism has always affirmed the historic doctrines of Christianity to be true. The weakness of the fundamentalist argument is that it attempted to prove its view of the Bible through reason and science. This made Christianity subject to the scrutiny of reason and science. Consequently, the way to Christianity for the fundamentalist was not by faith merely but first proof which in turn generated faith.[31]

However, the transition from modernity to postmodernity has eroded our confidence in reason and science as the method of bringing us to the truth. Consequently, we must ask again, How do we approach the question of truth?

The most fertile ground for rethinking the question of truth is to return to the tradition of the story. We do not understand or verify a story by standing outside it and seeking to analyze or defend it. Rather, we understand stories by becoming a part of them, experiencing them as participants.[32]

For example, the website for the Mars Hill Fellowship in Seattle, pastored by Mark Driscoll, contains an essay on meaning. It begins, "The Gospel is the story of God told from His perspective, to His glory. Only God is bigger than the Gospel. At first it sounds like a foolish paradoxical mystery. And so we try to make it sound more believable and sane. It is not. The Gospel is neither rational nor irrational, but trans-rational."[33]

Author David Mills writes that believing the Christian story is "seeing the cosmos truly." He tells the story of Bishop Terry Kelshaw visiting in the home of a very wealthy and highly educated family for lunch. In a time of chatter before lunch, the host made it very clear to Bishop Kelshaw that he considered the Christian story to be nonsense. He couldn't believe in the story of the virgin birth or the resurrection. These were absurd stories outside the bounds of reason. But just before lunch the host stepped to the dining-room table and stood before a crystal hanging over the table. He spun it and stared into it until it stopped spinning. Then calling to his wife he said, "It's okay." When Bishop Kelshaw asked about the spinning crystal, the host told him it was a spiritual exercise, a prayer that put him in touch with the universe. This illustration speaks to the influential role of faith. Faith steps into a story and sees the world through the story. This man regarded the Christian story as absurd yet by faith saw the world through the story of a crystal.[34]

"The story," writes David Taylor, "has become the chief unifying principle in contemporary evangelism. It is now," he says, "an important epistemological force binding a group or community or society together. No longer is it simply a brute concept, whether political or economic, or in the form of universal reason, or brute force, whether military or ideological—all of which functioned as an external entity imposing itself upon the community. It is now the story, the narrative that provides the cohesion and thus meaning to the community. Truth comes from the story; it is both organic and dynamic, and in an unexpected way very substantial, not experiential, meaning. Furthermore, it is only humans who can and do write stories. Hence truth is fundamentally personal, involving and legitimizing both the subject and the object, both the I and the Thou." His point is "that what we have here is a magnificent coincidence: a coinciding of postmodernity and orthodox Christian faith. For it is Christianity that declares the essential truth that reality is personal and relational because God himself, revealed in Jesus of Nazareth, was a person in an intimate union with God and humanity. Postmodernity in this sense reflects greater than modernity the biblical perspective on life."[35]

The younger evangelical is at odds with the traditional and pragmatic evangelical when it comes to theological method. The method of the traditionalists is to treat theology as a science, subject, as all other sciences are, to the empirical method. Through an analysis of the data of revelation, one could be brought to propositional truth. Theology, the traditionalist says, is a system of objective truth understood by the mind. The pragmatists, on the other hand, are not theologians and care little for the nuances of theological thinking. They tend to reduce theology to Christianity 101 to make it clear and understandable to the seeker.

The younger evangelical sees theology as the way to understand the world. It is an understanding based on the biblical narrative. This is the approach to faith that has captured the postmodern mind. Postmoderns have abandoned the modern worldview in which the supremacy of interpretation is given to science. In this context younger evangelicals are calling on us to see the world primarily through the Christian story. They believe in the God revealed in the great events of creation, incarnation, and re-creation, interpreted first by the prophets and apostles in Scripture, protected in creeds, and handed down to us in the worship of the church. This is the growing vision of the younger evangelical, a vision that stands within the historic confession of faith. Theology is not a science but a reflection of God's community on the narrative of God's involvement in history as found in the story of Israel and Jesus. But how does one defend the communal reflection on this particular story as universally true? To gain perspective on this question, we turn in the next chapter to the younger evangelical approach to apologetics (see table 7).

Table 7
Approach to Theology

	Traditional Evangelicals	Pragmatic Evangelicals	Younger Evangelicals
Approach	Systematic	Christianity 101	Ancient-Future
Type	Propositional	Contextual	Narrative/contextual
Theologian	Carl F. H. Henry	Gilbert Bilezikian	Stanley J. Grenz
Creation	Seven days or seven lengthy periods of time	Mystery	Creation and science brought together in interactive view
Hermeneutics	Grammatical Historical Reformed	Internal Consistency	Typological Communal What does it say to us?
Biblical Theology	Dispensational Reformed	Internal Consistency	Covenantal Metanarrative
Historical Theology	Post-Reformation history is valuable	Not a helpful discipline	An essential feature of theological thinking
Eschatology	Premillennial	Not a matter of great import	An essential feature of cosmic salvation

Theology

Table 7
Approach to Theology

	Traditional Evangelicals	Pragmatic Evangelicals	Younger Evangelicals
Salvation	Concentrate on the individual	Individual in community	Cosmic salvation God saves individuals and the created order
Sin	Depravity	Brokenness	Rebellion
Redemption	Sacrificial Substitutional	Sacrificial Substitutional	Recovery of *Christus Victor* By his sacrifice Christ won a victory over the powers of evil and left an example for us to follow
Sacraments	Ordinances	Ordinances	Return to more sacramental understanding

6

Apologetics
From Rationalism to Embodiment

My coming to faith was not deep and philosophical but rather a simple encounter prompted by a question. My dad approached me about being baptized, and I immediately walked out on the back porch of the parsonage where we lived and looked up into the sky. I asked, "Are you there, God?" The only answer was the inaudible witness of the stars and the mystery of the visible creation itself. I don't remember thinking of creation as evidence. What I do remember is that I felt a need to make a choice, a commitment. That night I made a conscious intentional decision to acknowledge God and to follow Jesus in baptism. I have always considered my baptism to be my first real conscious choice to affirm God's reality and to live in the pattern of Jesus' death and resurrection. This commitment was real, authentic, and actually radical, even though it was not the result of knowledge and certainly was not based on rational arguments or evidence that "demanded a verdict."

In seminary and graduate school, I was challenged to prove faith through reason. I was taught rational arguments for the existence of God, archeological proof for the accuracy of Scripture. I was given exegetical tools to dig into Scripture and find the authorial intent.

For some reason I cannot fully explain, this evidential approach to the Christian faith had a negative effect on me. It made faith an object to be proven.

My head became filled with arguments, proof texts, distinctions, and a kind of intellectual arrogance. In the meantime God became an object; faith became a system; and my heart grew cold. My commitment to faith as intellectually verifiable did not strengthen my resolve to live in the pattern of Jesus' death and resurrection.

I am not alone in this conflict. I have talked to numerous younger evangelicals who feel the same way. They, like myself, have been told that Christianity is an intellectually defensible worldview, that an understanding of the arguments will bring them to truth, deepen their commitment, and compel them to be effective witnesses. But for many, it doesn't work that way.

The question of this chapter is, What does Christian apologetics in the postmodern world look like? This chapter (1) surveys the history of apologetics, (2) looks at the foundationalism of twentieth-century evangelicalism, (3) shows the shift away from rational apologetics toward a nonfoundationalist approach to faith, and (4) presents embodied faith as a way of life, an alternative to the evidential apologetics of modernity.

Historical Background

The ancient and more biblical approach to apologetics was initially associated with the people of God, who embody faith and live out a communal life in obedience to God's will. Thus the story of Israel and Jesus enacted in the daily, weekly, and yearly rituals of worship and the individual and communal life of the believing community is the primary historic apologetic for the Christian faith. For example, Tertullian, a church father of the late second century, declared that the pagans were astonished by how Christians related to each other and to those outside of their community. In a pagan world where every person "lives for himself," the pagans don't cry, "Look at the power of their rational arguments" but "See how they love one another!"[1]

This early church apologetic may be rightly called an "incarnational apology." The church is the continuation of the incarnation. It is the earthed reality of the presence of Jesus in and to the world. Herein lies the ancient apologetic. The church by its very existence is a witness to the presence of God in history (Eph. 3:10). There is only one actual incarnation of God and that is in Jesus Christ, but the church, being his body, sustains an incarnational dimension. The church is a witness to the presence of Jesus in the world as it embodies and lives out the faith.

The church gradually moved away from an embodied and incarnational apologetic to emphasize the written revelation as evidence for God's existence. This shift occurred in the context of the rise of modern epistemology, which asserted truth was available through reason (Descartes), experience (Locke), and science

(Bacon). The empirical methodology, it was asserted, could arrive at truth through observation and analysis of the raw data.

During the Enlightenment, Christian leaders, instead of remaining faithful to an embodied apologetic through the life of the Christian community, turned to a new apologetic that followed the secular empirical method. The raw data of the Christian apologetic was the revelation of God put to the test of reason. The liberals put reason above revelation and proceeded to "demythologize" Scripture to find the truth, which stood behind the myths, namely love. On the other hand, the conservatives placed reason under and in the service of revelation, seeking to "prove" revelation and then to systematize and analyze it to arrive at propositional truth.

In this way the emphasis on truth as embodied by a people was replaced by truth as objective and observable fact. This became the primary apologetic that shaped the fundamentalism and evangelicalism of the twentieth century and is known as foundationalism. This apologetic dominated college and seminary education in evangelical circles throughout the twentieth century. It is now being called into question by the younger evangelicals. A brief look at foundationalism will help us understand its intellectualized version of the Christian faith.

Foundationalism

Modern epistemology asserted that truth could be attained by the autonomous mind at work with the empirical method. Truth was derived from observation, reason, and science. This view resulted in propositional knowledge. It created a wedge between the Christians who claimed they could gain knowledge through God's revelation and the non-Christians who claimed they could arrive at truth through the empirical method without the use of revelation. Truth was separated from an embodied reality and given independent existence. Postmodern philosopher Michel Foucault faults Descartes with this bifurcation.

> Descartes broke this when he said, "To accede to truth, it suffices that I be any subject that can see what is evident." Evidence is substituted for askesis at the point where the relationship to the self intersects the relationship to others and the world. The relationship to the self no longer needs to be ascetic to get into relation to the truth. It suffices that the relationship to the self reveals to me the obvious truth of what I see for me to apprehend the truth definitively. Thus, I can be immoral and know the truth. I believe this is an idea that, more or less explicitly, was rejected by all previous cultures. Before Descartes, one could not be impure, immoral, and know the truth. With Descartes, direct evidence is enough. After Descartes, we have a nonascetic subject of knowledge. This change makes possible the institutionalization of modern science.[2]

The key to understanding evangelical foundationalism lies in this separation of truth from embodiment. This separation can be illustrated from the writings of Carl F. H. Henry. In volume 2 of *God, Revelation and Authority* are fifteen theses regarding revelation. While many of them are compatible with historic Christianity, three demonstrate Henry's capitulation to a modern epistemology which elevates reason as an apologetic for Christian truth, theses 10, 11, and 12:

10. God's revelation is rational communication conveyed in intelligible ideas and meaningful words, that is, conceptual verbal form.
11. The Bible is the reservoir and conduit of divine truth.
12. The Holy Spirit superintends the communication of divine revelation, first, by inspiring the prophetic apostolic writings, and, second, by illuminating and interpreting the scripturally given Word of God.[3]

In this work and that of other evangelical apologists of the twentieth century, the emphasis is on a defense of Christianity based on God's revelation in an inerrant Bible. The Bible, being the "raw data," had to be without error to result in propositional truth.

Many twentieth-century evangelicals continue to teach and defend a form of foundationalism.[4] For them, the inerrancy of the Bible and the commitment to propositional truth as objective statements which can be known and defended by reason is the means of knowing all truth. For them, this literal interpretation of the Bible yields truth not only in matters of faith and practice but also in matters of history and science. There are also liberal foundationalists who continue to interpret Christianity through the use of reason. David Tracy of the University of Chicago still wants to pursue Christian understanding through a modified nineteenth-century liberal theology. He feels that Christianity must "speak in a manner that can be disclosive and transformative for any intelligent, reasonable, responsible human being."[5] In spite of the collapse of modern science and reason, foundationalism that uses reason to defend an inerrant Bible and the notion that reason can bring reasonable people to a commonly shared truth will continue to persist in our postmodern world.

The Challenge to Foundationalism

The first challenge to the twentieth-century notion of propositional truth came in the seventies with the rise of contextual understanding. Contextualism argued that theology is done in dialogue between Scripture and a particular cultural context. People read Scripture differently in a third-world context than in a Western technological context. Third-world Christians bring to the reading of Scripture their background in demonism, sorcery, witchcraft, and ancestor worship, whereas the Western world reads the Bible out of their background of science and reason.[6]

This recognition of the contextual dimension of truth led to a shift in the use of the word *inerrant*. For example, Millard Erickson writes, "Our doctrine of inerrancy maintains merely that whatever statements the Bible affirms are fully truthful when they are correctly interpreted in terms of their meaning in their cultural setting and the purpose for which they were written."[7] This statement is a clear shift away from the hard-line "propositional inerrancy" set forth by Henry and Lindsell. The older view of inerrancy is purely objective. It says, "Here in the Bible are the cold hard facts that anyone, whether from America, Asia, or Africa, can plainly see. Reason is the same everywhere and brings all under any circumstance or cultural situation to the same objective knowledge." Erickson, by saying "in their cultural setting," allows inerrancy to contain a subjective side. This view created confusion among evangelicals over the use of the word *inerrant*. With the admission that scriptural interpretation is in some measure a personal and subjective enterprise, *inerrant* lost its meaning and has never recovered.

Furthermore, the rise of contextual interpretation made a crack in the strict propositionalism of the evangelical who had demanded uniformity of interpretation. Now a clear allowance for the different cultural interpretations of Scripture was fully accepted. Because contextualism made the defense of Scripture through reason more difficult to maintain, more general approaches to Scripture were presented, such as "Scripture is inerrant in all that it *intends*," or "Scripture is inerrant in matters of faith and practice but not in matters of history and science."

In sum the issue of modernity has revolved around reason. Does reason show the Christianity of the New Testament documents and the early Christian tradition to be true? Do we affirm Christianity because reason validates it?

The rise of postmodern thought in the nineties has changed the entire discussion. Postmodern philosophy has challenged the use of reason as a test for truth. For postmoderns, reason has no power to bring a person to truth. Neither the liberal nor the conservative arguments are valid, because the world of modernity no longer exists. In the postmodern world, truth cannot be known. It is completely relative. This new point of view, which is now widespread throughout the Western world and spreading into the rest of the world, is based on revolutions (in science, philosophy, communications, and other fields) that have swept us into postmodernity. These revolutions have led to the postmodern view that says, "There is no single unifying truth. Truth is personal, subjective, and belonging only to each individual." The entire infrastructure of modernity, built on the notion that truth is attainable through reason and the use of the empirical method, has collapsed. And while many evangelicals continue to insist on an apologetic based on reason, a new postfoundational apologetic has emerged.[8]

Postfoundationalism

Postfoundationalism asserts that Christianity can stand on its own; it needs no rational defense. For example, the new thinkers of Radical Orthodoxy argue that reason has been made the interpreter of the Christian faith. Therefore, modernity looked to the social sciences to come to the aid of Christianity, to prove it or to add arguments that made Christianity plausible. Radical Orthodoxy begins with the assumption that Christianity is truth. Because it is true, everything in the world—the world itself, its history, its religions, its social sciences, its ethics, and its behaviors—should be interpreted and understood through the Christian faith.

John Milbank, the primary spokesperson for Radical Orthodoxy, writes, "I wish to challenge the idea that there is a significant sociological reading of religion and Christianity, which theology must take into account."[9] Milbank wants to reverse the method of modernity. Modern evangelicals said, "Truth lies in reason. Reason has been used in the social sciences to arrive at common truths. Let's bring the truth uncovered by reason in the social sciences to support the Christian faith."

Milbank faults liberalism for the current irrelevancy of theology. "The story of faith," he claims, "is a complex theological statement that none of us fully understands. The idea that it's nonsense if it doesn't fit scientific principles, is in itself a secular form of knowledge." Milbank traces the origin of secular knowledge back to John Duns Scotus, the thirteenth-century theologian who was a "metaphysician" and his talk of "reality as if it consisted of discrete objects, atoms and facts . . . things we can talk about without any values." Milbank argues that Scotus shaped the Enlightenment, with its faith in "natural laws." Then came the "social sciences" to shore up those beliefs—and send God into exile. These assumptions ultimately moved God out of the equation. But now in the postmodern world Milbank wants us to return to the unknown, invisible reality that stands behind all things, through which all things are understood. Therefore philosophy finds its origin within theology. "Today," says Milbank, "the discrete realm of philosophy is collapsing. Today, the logic of secularism is imploding."[10]

This radical reversal of the starting point for truth is now the approach of postliberal theologians like Hans Frei and William Placher. In *Unapologetic Christianity*, Placher gives his own summary of Frei and expresses the essence of an unapologetic nonfoundational Christianity with these words:

> Frei proposes a radical solution. Suppose we do not start with the modern world. Suppose we start with the biblical world, and let those narratives decide what's real, so that our lives have meaning to the extent that we fit them into that framework. That is, after all, the way a great many Christians—Augustine, Aquinas, Luther, Calvin—read the Bible for a long time. If we do that, then the truth of the

biblical narratives does not depend on connecting them to some other real world. They describe the real world.[11]

Placher advocates getting out of the apologetic stance because "Christianity cannot criticize our culture very effectively if it has already accepted many of the assumptions of that culture as the price of intellectual respectability."[12]

The theme that Christianity needs no external verification is presented by George Lindbeck in the *Nature of Doctrine*. He calls the apologetics approach the "extratextual" method and emphasizes how it "locates religious meaning outside the text or semiotic system either in objective realities to which it refers or in the experiences it symbolizes."[13] In evangelical circles the extratextual method is used by those who speak of "evidence that demands a verdict." Lindbeck and other postmodern nonfoundationalists reject extratextual apologetics and advocate an "intertextual" view of the Christian faith that looks out at the world and interprets the world through Christian eyes. This is the opposite of modernity, where the critic assumed the world as interpreted by a social science was truth and looked at Scripture or Christian faith with the eyes of the world in an attempt either to legitimize the Christian faith or to critique it in light of their "worldly knowledge." This "Scripture first" hermeneutic has become attractive to postmodern evangelicals.

A younger evangelical and postfoundational writer, Rodney Clapp, writes, "If we quit foundationalist rhetoric, we can more easily perceive and draw attention to liberalism itself as a tradition."[14] Clapp believes that liberalism is the view based on Descartes' dictum that he will believe only what can be tested by reason. This is the liberal foundation of all who seek to affirm the validity of the Christian faith on the basis of reason, whether liberal or conservative. For such people reason has become the determiner of truth, not revelation. Faith is determined by reason, not by the witness of the Holy Spirit.

To show how these two approaches work out, Clapp compares traditionalist evangelical Kenneth Kantzer, a foundationalist who wants reason to shore up truth, with postmodern Stanley Hauerwas, who insists Christianity can stand on its own as truth without the support of reason. Kantzer commends Christianity as truth because "it fosters a sense of life on a higher plane of human existence than is provided by other examples,"[15] whereas Stanley Hauerwas declares that God has entrusted the church with "the best damn story in the world."[16] Clapp continues to argue that "in the pluralized, postmodern world in which we now live, few if any careful thinkers actually rely on foundationalist reasoning. I am now arguing that it is time to leave foundational rhetoric because it is, in the beginning and the end, liberal rhetoric."[17] Clapp insists that "if we quit foundationalist rhetoric we can claim the specifics of the Christian tradition and forthrightly speak the name of Christ in any public forum. We can admit that our argument is contestable, as are the arguments of Marxists, Hindus, free-market capitalists, and every other party, then speak unapologetically as Christians."[18] Clapp speaks for many younger evangelicals.

Theologians Stanley J. Grenz and John Franke offer us the most substantial younger evangelical argument to get beyond foundationalism. In their book *Beyond Foundationalism*, they set forth a methodology of nonfoundational thought. They suggest "a theology that seeks to take seriously postmodern sensitivities views itself as conversation . . . this constructive theological conversation requires the interplay, or perichoretic dance, of three sources of insight of types of conversation partners."[19] They pose these three conversational partners to be (1) the Bible as "the norming norm," (2) tradition as an "indispensable source for theology," and (3) culture as the "embedding context for the theological talk."[20] Assuming all theology is "local" or "specific" as postmoderns insist, the authors pose three "focal motifs that give coherence to Christian theology." They argue that all Christian thought is "Trinitarian in structure (or content), communitarian in focus, and eschatological in orientation." This theological method, they argue, "lies beyond the demise of fundamentalism" and "explicates the Christian belief—a mosaic in accordance with the ecumenical faith of the church throughout its history and on behalf of the church throughout the world."[21] In other words, truth is not proven, it is embodied by individuals and by the community known as church.

There is a general agreement among younger evangelicals that the emphasis in apologetics has shifted from reason to embodiment. Twenty-eight-year-old David Clark, a student at Regent College in Vancouver, puts it succinctly: "Reasons by themselves don't motivate too many people to become Christ followers. I don't think evidence is absolute one way or another, so both the acceptance and the rejection of God can be to some degree justified."[22] Paul Jones, another twenty-something seminary student, agrees: "Not everything can be defined in arguments and with evidence," he says. "People are becoming more and more aware of the fact that we are spiritual beings, that *believing*—not knowing everything empirically—is at the heart of our humanity."[23] David Di Sabatino, editor of *Worship Leader*, speaks for many younger evangelicals when he states, "I lean to the fideist side of the argument over against rationalists or evidentialists simply because I see so many people coming to God in such weird and bizarre ways."[24] Kyle Roberts, graduate student at Trinity Evangelical Divinity School (TEDS), agrees and says, "At some point there is a gap that can only be bridged by a Leap of Faith."[25] Dawn Haglund, a recent graduate of TEDS, suggests that reason "may have had a greater purpose to earlier generations that were more concerned about proving the existence of God . . . but I think postmoderns are more concerned about seeing the real impact of what this means on life."[26] What she refers to is the power of embodied experience to communicate the reality of the gospel. This is the heart of a younger evangelical apologetic.

This younger evangelical viewpoint is clearly expressed by Charles Moore, a member of the Spring Valley Bruderhof, in Farmington, Pennsylvania. He tells the story of a seminary friend who had all the right answers but was derailed because he did not have a surrendered heart. "Apologetics," he writes, "as we thought of it back then, only let that condition flourish." Moore turns to another kind of apologetic which, "simply put, . . . lies not in discursive, conceptual argument for the truth but in becoming the truth. Or, to put it in another way, the only interesting apologetic question concerns the existence and fidelity of the church." Truth, he says, is not defended by reason but by the individual and the community that embodies it and lives it out. As Stanley Hauerwas has written in *An Alien People*, truth is found in "a new *polis* called church."[27] What Moore presents here is Christianity as a way of life. It is interesting that the general shift in postmodernity is away from systems to a search for wisdom and a way of living.

The emphasis on truth as an embodied experience is returning to the table of philosophical thought. Pierre Hadot, in *Philosophy as a Way of Life*, writes:

> For the ancients, the mere word *philo-sophia*—the love of wisdom—was enough to express this conception of philosophy. . . . Philosophy thus took on the form of an exercise of the thought, will, and the totality of one's being, the goal of which was to achieve a state practically inaccessible to mankind: wisdom. Philosophy was a method of spiritual progress which demanded a radical conversion and transformation of the individual's way of being.
>
> Thus, philosophy was a way of life, both in its exercise and effort to achieve wisdom, and in its goal, wisdom itself. For real wisdom does not merely cause us to know: it makes us to "be" in a different way. Both the grandeur and the paradox of ancient philosophy are that it was, at one and the same time, conscious of the fact that wisdom is inaccessible, and convinced of the necessity of pursuing spiritual progress.
>
> First and foremost, philosophy presented itself as a therapeutic, intended to cure mankind's anguish.[28]

Younger evangelical Joseph Clair, reflecting on the shift from technical philosophical analysis to the art of living, writes:

> Disillusionment with Rationalism is obviously promoting a recovery of Wisdom. And by "wisdom," instead of "rationality," we intend to understand knowledge as part of a more holistic schema that culminates in the task of "living well," not merely "thinking well." We are surely still concerned with rigorous training in "thinking well," or "thinking rationally," but we are sensitively aware to the limitations of looking at life through a rationalistic lens. This lens keeps you away from, and many times cuts you off from, avenues of knowledge about the "Truth" that we are no longer willing to miss out on. [We're seeking] avenues of truth that come through a broad swathe of human experience that include things like emotions (i.e., listening to music, watching a film, or seeing a beautiful moment in nature). "Truth" hits you here at somewhere like the "gut level." Here you don't "think" out the truth, or conceptualize it, the truth captures you in its unspoken look. Another avenue reconsidered is religious or "spiritual" experiences, which used to be considered epiphenom-

enal froth, or maybe just wishful thinking, by the Rationalist philosophers. The younger evangelical takes all these things into account and considers them soberly.[29]

Younger evangelical Joel Handy, a Wheaton College student, also thinks the problem of evidential apologetics is its division between head and heart, and he finds that an embodied apologetic brings head and heart together, which results in wisdom, a way of life that is transforming. He reports the following incident:

> I recently had a conversation with a depressed student. During lunch she told me of how tired, empty, hopeless, anxious, hurting and lonely she had become. It turned out that she had been clinically depressed for years, but it had started early on in her family. Her little brother had died and the struggle his death created for her parents resulted in them neglecting her. The combination of losing her brother and the neglect of her parents wounded her deeply. When she talked to me, she had not started to deal with either of those past hurts.
>
> I explained how her pain could find healing. When I told her that Jesus died on the cross in order that all effects of sin and death, including depression, loneliness, hurt, and rejection, might die as well, it shocked her. "What do you mean?" she asked.
>
> Jesus, I explained, died and rose from the dead to conquer death and all the effects death has on us. By believing in that power, and by taking up our own cross and dying to self, we are allowing Christ to take us through that same transformation. That is what happens in baptism: we die and are raised to new life. I directed her to let the death of her brother and the rejection of her parents go into Christ's wounds as he hung on the cross, and allow the risen Christ to heal and restore her suffering through his suffering.
>
> When I finished, she looked at me and said, "I'm a Bible major, but why haven't I ever heard this before?" She had to see how what Jesus did on the cross had everything to do with not only her salvation but her living. That split between her head and heart resulted from growing up in a church where saying and believing the right things was all-important. She had to learn that truth is embodied and lived. It's not a theory abstracted from life.
>
> If we cannot connect the power of the Gospel to our own lives and hearts, then we personally miss its transforming power. The truth of the Gospel is that God gave us what we could never have ourselves: life. The Christian world has to embody that life in order to preach an apologetic that is both contagious and convincing. Unfortunately, for many rational apologetics does not bring transformation. It is only in an embodied faith that the life Christ died to give brings healing, and life.[30]

Younger evangelical Joseph Clair wrote a paper for one of my classes dealing with the theme of communal embodiment. His arguments deserve consideration for they speak to the larger movement among the young to find faith not through rational argument but through communal embodiment. His paper is long and complex and deserving of a lengthy treatment. However, I can refer here only to its main thrust. He first rejects the modern notion that "what can be known must be validated with scientific objectivity." He suggests a postmodern apologetic must return to the ancient tradition where "faith was found by an individual in connection to the church." Historically, because the church was the guardian and chief interpreter of Scripture and because it was guided by leaders in apostolic succession, a person was regarded as Christian because of his or her "participation in the community of faith." In other words, faith is participation in truth embodied by the community. To "know" truth, one needs to step inside the community and into the stream of its interpretation and experience of reality.

However, this approach to truth changed when scriptural texts were separated from the church. The texts were perceived to stand "outside" the church and were therefore subject to the interpretation of the individual. Students of the text, ignoring the communal interpretation of scriptural texts, sought through reason and historical criticism to understand authorial intent. Subsequently, reason, not the text, became authoritative. This separation of Scripture from the church forced Christianity into a rationalistic apologetic, which in the end put reason over the church and its interpretation of the text, thus modern apologetics was born.

The goal of postmodern apologetics is to recover the role of the church as the interpreter and the embodiment of truth. Thus faith is not born outside the church but within the church as individuals see themselves and their world through the eyes of God's earthed community. This, in essence, is the "communal epistemology," which Joseph Clair suggests "needs to be revalidated and rediscovered in the Christian church today." But the individual does not merely acquiesce to communal truth in an intellectual way. "The correct interpretation of the narrative is *response* to it." This "true interpretation then becomes transformation, transformation into a new existence of virtue (e.g., love, peace, joy) within the faith community." In sum the community embodies the Christian narrative, the unchurched "step into" the narrative, the narrative grasps them even as they grasp it, and eventually the individual embodies the reality of the church's story as he chooses to live his life from the standpoint of the community of faith.[31]

Joseph Clair has articulated in this concept of "communal epistemology" what I have heard from numerous young people; they are moved more by an authentic lived-out faith than they are by internally flawless, logically coherent, and evidently consistent argument.

The question "How do we know Christianity is true?" will continue in the postmodern world to be a matter for discussion. But the rules for the conversation have changed. The issue revolves around the new suspicion of reason and science. If reason and science are no longer able to bring us to truth, what will? Does the continuation of modern foundationalism, which uses reason in defense of Christianity, have any validity at all in a postmodern world? Is the recovery of a "radical orthodoxy," which dismisses rational foundationalism as irrelevant and opts for a nonfoundational presentation of Christianity, the best option?

It seems clear that in a postmodern world, many younger evangelicals have shifted to the "communal affirmations" of faith which are rooted in the early consciousness of the Christian church and which have been handed down in the life of the church and its worship. The modern distortion of this focus has now been exposed and rejected as an aberration shaped by the secular notion that truth can be determined by reason outside of the Christian community. The future of evangelicalism lies in the rejection of this modernist notion and in the affirmation of the historic tradition that truth is embodied in the incarnate Christ, revealed in the narrative of Israel and Jesus, interpreted in the writings of Scripture, and embodied and handed down in the local church as a living experience of truth in a particular time in history, in a particular geographical place, and, might we even say, "in a particular person."

How the younger evangelicals differ with the traditionalists is quite clear. They reject the rational and evidential apologetics of the traditionalists. The pragmatist evangelicals, as I have indicated, represent a transitional moment from the modern traditionalists to the postmodern evangelicals. As such they straddle the fence. Their primary apologist is Lee Strobel, and his defense and arguments for Christianity have been made in *The Case for Faith* and *The Case for Christ*. But pragmatists also have a strong sense of embodied apologetics. They advocate living a life and a kind of friendship evangelism that brings people to the community where they see and experience faith in action. The difference between the pragmatist evangelical and the younger evangelical lies perhaps in the younger evangelical's more radical view of the church as a visible community united with the entire history of the church and in union with the global community of Christians. The church is not just an invisible community of people known in the mind of God but a local yet universal body of people who live in countercultural witness to the reality of God. We turn in the next chapter to understand more fully the nature of the visible church as affirmed by the younger evangelical (see table 8).

Table 8
Approach to Apologetics

	Traditional Evangelicals	Pragmatic Evangelicals	Younger Evangelicals
Place of Reason in Faith	The evidence demands a verdict	Rational Experiential	Mystery, but Christianity is intelligible
Worldview	Truth can be separated from an experience so that a worldview can stand on its own	Truth and experience go hand in hand	Truth must be embodied Truth is known only by those who live it

(continued)

Table 8
Approach to Apologetics

	Traditional Evangelicals	Pragmatic Evangelicals	Younger Evangelicals
Type of Apologetic	Rational apologetics It stands the test of reason	Success apologetics It works	Incarnational apologetics The community lives it
Revelation	An inerrant Bible is the foundation upon which truth is based	The Bible is the foundation of our knowledge Christianity starts with an authoritative Bible Inerrancy held, but not an issue	Knowledge is incarnate in the person of Jesus Christ The Bible infallibly takes us to Jesus, the living embodiment of truth
Christian Theory and the Social Sciences	Social sciences are used to support Christianity	The social sciences are points of contact	Theology is the queen of sciences Sciences are interpreted by theology, not the other way around
Christianity and Philosophy	Philosophy is used to support a Christian worldview	Attention is given to Christianity as a philosophy of meaning	Philosophy returns to a way of life: wisdom and guidance
Christianity and World Religions	Christianity is right; world religions are wrong	Little attention is paid to other religions	New interest in comparing Christianity with Islam

7

Ecclesiology
From Invisible to Visible

Like most evangelicals my age, I grew up with a highly individualistic view of Christianity. It was Jesus and me, I thought. It wasn't until I was at Concordia Seminary, working on my doctorate, that anyone challenged the individualistic view of faith I held. An Old Testament professor introduced me to the corporate concept of faith in the Old Testament—the faith of Israel. At first I balked at such an idea. Doesn't God save individuals—this one and that one, here and there? When I finally saw how Israel was God's corporate community, called to be God's witness in the world to God's salvation for the world, I realized I had been reading my Bible through the lens of Enlightenment individualism. The concept of a visible community in this world, a community that belongs to God and witnesses to God's presence in history, to God's reign over all things, and to the Isaianic and Revelational vision of God's peace, spread over all God's creation opened the door to a glorious vision of history.

The younger evangelicals are moving into this cosmic vision of the new heavens and the new earth. And the conviction is emerging that it is the visible corporate church that witnesses now to the reality that is to come—the reign of God over all things.

Modern evangelicalism has never had a very strong view of the corporate church. It has suffered from the individualism of modernity and from the impact of both the rationalism of the Enlightenment and the experientialism of the romantic era. For example, the early fundamentalist view of the church was shaped by the battle with the modernists. They withdrew into a separatistic theology which was defined primarily by doctrinal purity. The true church was found where Christians gathered around what Francis Schaeffer called "true truth." Any deviation from this truth was a fall into apostasy. This attitude still persists among fundamentalist groups who are convinced that their theology stands in absolute continuity with the doctrines of the early church. This fundamentalist attempt to identify the meaning of the church as a "depository of the truth" is, as I will show, partially consistent with the ancient view of the church but is incomplete and reductionistic.

The move by Billy Graham and others of the new evangelicals to include the mainline church in evangelistic efforts was rightly understood by the fundamentalist as a shift in ecclesiology. Evangelistic ecumenism shifted ecclesiology from the "purity of the church" to a view of the church shaped by its commitment to fulfill the Great Commission. This Great Commission ecclesiology is much less doctrinally specific than the fundamentalist view. It adheres to the historic doctrines of the faith but allows for greater diversity of interpretation. Consequently, this shift into Great Commission ecclesiology laid the groundwork for the emergence of evangelical diversity. The evangelical church by the end of the twentieth century was a "saving station." Its primary purpose and mission in the world was to proclaim the saving message of Jesus to individuals, to get individuals saved, to rescue their broken lives, and to repair their relationship to God.

Like the fundamentalist desire for purity of doctrine, the commitment of the broader evangelical church to the Great Commission is indeed *part* of what the church is all about. But to reduce ecclesiology to the Great Commission alone is not adequately biblical. The younger evangelical intuitively knows this and is in search of a deeper grasp of what it means to be the church. Consequently, this chapter focuses on the younger evangelical commitment to the church visible. The first part of the chapter will explore the development of this new interest in the church visible and the second will explore specific examples of this interest among younger evangelical leaders.

Convictions of the Church Visible

The Return to an Ancient Theology of Church

While the younger evangelicals question the modern notions of ecclesiastical purity and Great Commission ecclesiology, they continue to insist that the church should be concerned with doctrine and committed to evangelism. Contrary to modern evangelicalism, however, the younger evangelical sees the church as *more* than a community that holds right doctrine and engages in evangelism. Younger evangelicals want to go beyond the reductionism of twentieth-century evangelicals to recover a more full understanding and experience of the church.[1]

The younger evangelicals' concern about the visible church is quite understandable. They want, as I have shown in previous chapters, to return to the cultural transmission of faith; to recover the story of the Christian faith rooted in historical events and handed down in the traditions of creeds and confessions; and to recover an apologetic that is expressed in an embodied presence of God's reign in an earthed community. Therefore, it follows that they long for a new, visible, and tangible expression of the church.

Historic Christianity is a visible and earthed faith, not a Gnostic esoteric spiritualization of faith. Because God became incarnate in a visible and tangible person, the church has acknowledged from its very beginning that the divine is communicated to us in concrete earthed realities. The younger evangelical is recovering this truth and its implications for the church. How did this recovery of the visible church come about? What are the sources for this recovery? What are the implications of the return to a strong sense of the visible church? These are the questions I'll take up in what follows.

The Recovery of the Visible Church

The concern to move toward a more visible concept of the church derives from cultural, religious, and theological factors of the latter part of the twentieth century.

The rise of secularism, pluralism, globalization, and the communication revolution all nudge the church toward a recovery of its visible unity. Secularism with its emphasis on the self, repudiation of values, and the rejection of the sanctity of life, is an enemy common to the whole church. Pluralism, with its assertion of the equality of all religions, has forced the church to emphasize what it has in common rather than its differences. The communication revolution, with its power to make information available, has created new channels for relationship. Globalization, with its emphasis on the village nature of the world, has resulted in a breakdown of the previous isolation in which Christians have lived and worked. The communication and global revolutions have worked together to create a new awareness and appreciation of a global community and of the worldwide church in its many facets. While some evangelicals choose to remain in isolation, the younger in particular have been shaped by a more open view of the world and of the unity they share with all Christians of other cultures and geographical areas.

Numerous religious factors have moved younger evangelicals toward an affirmation of the church visible. These include the influence of the pope, the inter-Christian dialogue, movements such as that of charismatic Christianity, the restoration of spirituality, the worship movement, and the current demise of denominational boundaries. All these movements point to the restoration of interest in premodern Christianity. Courses in the early church and in medieval Christianity have proliferated in evangelical colleges; the spirituality movement is largely a return to the spirituality of Catholic and Orthodox sources among the monastics. Widespread is the rise of spiritual retreats based on *Lectio Divina* (an ancient way of praying Scripture), Celtic Christianity, and the reading of contemporary Catholics like Thomas Merton and Henri Nouwen. The young are attracted to the liturgy of the hours, to ancient prayers, and to cathedral worship. Catholic and Protestant men and women gather together in conferences on worship and spirituality where they pray and fellowship together. All these movements have occurred in recent decades. The younger evangelicals have grown up conscious of these movements and participating in them.

Significant theological factors have moved the younger evangelical toward the visible church. They include the impact of Vatican II; the theological writings of Orthodox, Catholics, and Protestants; and the new concordat between Lutherans and Catholics. For example, in the "constitution on the church" promulgated at the ecumenical council called Vatican II, the primary image of the church does not involve hierarchy but the biblical emphasis of the church as *the people of God*. Catholic writers like Avery Dulles in *Models of the Church* help us see various models of the church that have reflected to some extent the church situation in culture. As we enter the twenty-first century, a new Catholic-Protestant rapport is emerging, a new resolve to work together. And new hopes that the division between the three main bodies of Christianity have begun a process of healing, albeit ever so slight.

Then there is the influence of postliberal ecclesiology on the younger evangelical. The most influential book is *Resident Aliens* by Stanley Hauerwas and William Willimon. Their basic argument is captured in a comparison of two theologians: Tillich and Barth. For Tillich, the purpose of theological thinking is "how to make old Christianity credible to a new modern world." Tillich's concern is to change a person's *belief system*. But Barth "knew that the theological problem was the creation of a new and better church."[2] Barth's understanding of the church was based on the cosmic salvation accomplished by Christ, and Barth saw discipleship from this perspective. Christians are called to be a distinct people who live out of an understanding of God's victory over the powers of evil. Furthermore, Christians are "a new people who have aligned themselves with the seismic shift that has occurred in the world since Christ."[3]

This pre-Constantinian view of the church calls Christians into a visible demonstration of what it means to be a disciple of Jesus. In this view, the primary issue of the church is not to have all the theological issues settled but to be characterized by a commitment to be a disciple. Commitment stands at the heart of younger evangelical faith.

The Recovery of the Visible Church among Older Evangelicals

In recent years the older evangelicals have been moving toward a more thoughtful ecclesiology, nudged by movements that seek to bridge the gap between evangelicals and Catholics, the recovery of incarnational theology, and recent influential books on the church. Perhaps the most significant move toward the visible unity of the church has been made by the document "Evangelicals and Catholics Together," also known as ECT.

The document "Evangelicals and Catholics Together: The Christian Mission in the Third Millennium" was issued by an *ad hoc* committee of evangelical and Catholic leaders in May of 1994. According to Chuck Colson and Richard John Neuhaus, the two organizers and leading lights of the document, "it became evident that Christian engagement in the great cultural, social and political tasks of our time would be largely futile, even counterproductive, unless that engagement was grounded in shared spiritual commitment and gospel truth."[4] The document itself was divided into five sections: we *affirm* together; we *hope* together; we *search* together; we *contend* together; and we *witness* together. The "we *contend* together" section has to do with what Francis Schaeffer called "cobelligerence." It calls for joining forces in contending together for religious freedom, against abortion, for good public education, against pornography, for a "renewed spirit of acceptance, understanding, and cooperation across lines of religion, race, ethnicity, sex and class," for a free society, for a renewed appreciation of Western culture, for renewed respect for the "family, churches, and myriad voluntary associations," and for a realistic understanding of America's part in world affairs.[5]

The concept of "contending together" over shared moral, social, political, and economic values has been hailed as a step in the right direction. It shows that the animosity between Catholics and evangelicals that endured during most of the twentieth century is apt to change in the twenty-first century. ECT was, however, vigorously opposed by leaders within a conservative branch of the Reformed faith, especially by R. C. Sproul, D. James Kennedy, and John MacArthur. They declared the Roman church apostate, argued that Catholics represented "another gospel," and insisted that evangelicals should not be unequally yoked with them.

This criticism prompted a heated discussion among the drafters of ECT, which in October 1997 resulted in the document "The Gift of Salvation," also known as ECT II. ECT II affirmed the "substance of historic Christian orthodoxy against the ideology of theological pluralism that marks much mainline Protestant thought as well as avant-garde Catholic theology."[6] The document affirmed matters that seemed ambiguous to the opponents of ECT, "the doctrine of justification by faith alone and the biblical mandate for world missions and world evangelization."[7] But the opponents to ECT were still critical. R. C. Sproul referred to both documents as "seriously flawed" and wrote, "The effort to seek unity and accord with Roman Catholics had the negative effect of driving a wedge between Evangelicals who formerly were closely allied."[8] Evangelical supporters and opponents of ECT and ECT II met to reconstitute their unity in the gospel by composing a third document, "The Gospel of Jesus Christ: An Evangelical Celebration."[9]

Despite the criticism ECT and ECT II incurred, already a genuine appreciation for Catholic (and Orthodox) Christianity and a longing to find points of contact for contending and witnessing together have emerged as markers of the significance of these documents.

While younger evangelicals are impressed with the older evangelicals' call for a new kind of relationship with Catholics, they are not particularly impressed by the overall agenda. ECT still reflects a "Constantine agenda" for the church. It calls for the church to support civil good for the sake of society. It does not call for the kind of alternative culture envisioned by Hauerwas and Willimon and based on an incarnational understanding of the church.

Incarnational Understanding of the Church

The church, Peter tells us, is like Israel. It is "a chosen people, a royal priesthood, a holy nation, a people belonging to God" (1 Peter 2:9a). In this sense the church is like Israel, created by God to be God's people, but yet more than Israel because it is the "body" of Christ.

The image of the church as the "body" of Christ has resulted in a new awareness that the church is the continuation of the presence of Jesus in and to the world. Even though there is only one actual incarnation of God, and that is in Jesus Christ, the church as the "body" participates in the incarnation as an "extension of God's presence in the world." God continues by the power of the Spirit within and through the church to have a special presence in the world. This presence is understood as a pneumatological, christological, soteriological, and eschatological presence of the new creation.

The pneumatologial dimension of the Spirit in the church is expressed by Nicholas Cabasilas: "[God] does not create anew out of the same matter which he created in the beginning. Then he made use of the dust of the earth; today he calls upon his own body. He restores life to us, not by forming anew a vital principle which he formerly maintained in the natural order, but by shedding his blood in the hearts of communicants so that he may cause his own life to spring in them. Of old he breathed a breath of life; now he imparts to us his own spirit."[10]

This "Spirit-formed community" is characterized by a christological dimension. The younger evangelicals view the church as both human and divine. The divine presence is expressed in the visible and tangible signs of the assembled people gathered around the ministry, the Word, and the sacrament. In this gathering the church is actualized. It comes into being as an organism of people through whom the presence of the divine is communicated. The human side of the church is that God's people gather in a particular geographical place in a particular time and culture.

This divine/human expression of God's presence in the world bears a soteriological dimension. Cyprian expressed this in the third century when he wrote, "He who hath not the church for his mother hath not God for his father."[11] By this he meant that those who are in Christ are also in the church. Like Cyprian, the younger evangelical sees the church as much more than an association of like-minded people. The church is where the Spirit of God is forming a people who are the expression of God's redeeming work in the world. They are the people in whom the dwelling of God is forming a new creation. They are God's witnesses in the world; they witness to God's victory over the powers of evil (Eph. 3:10) and are a sign of the ultimate reconciliation of all things (Rom. 8:18–22).

For this reason the church does not *have* an eschatology, it *is* an eschatological people. This explains the younger evangelical indifference to the new eschatological series, Left Behind, by Tim LaHaye and Jerry Jenkins. This series grew out of the old view of "having an eschatology," a dispensational premillennial eschatology in the case of LaHaye and Jenkins. The younger evangelicals want to *be* an eschatological community. They want to be a people formed by a theological understanding of the world and the presence of the Spirit, who makes this people a community that prefigures the future and expresses a foretaste of the kingdom to come.

In sum, to say the church is the body of Christ is to affirm the church is the continuation of the presence of Jesus in the world; its life is sustained by the energy of the Spirit who is "the Lord and giver of life"; there is a divine side and a human side to the church; the church is a witness to the drama of salvation; and the church is the presence of the eschatological future in the world. In this sense the church does not "have" a mission, it is mission, by its very existence in the world.

Recent Influential Books on the Church

In recent years a plethora of books have been written by evangelicals on the new understanding of the church as mission. Rodney Clapp, a younger evangelical leader, calls on evangelicals to return to a more pre-Constantinian understanding and experience of the church. "Now that the long Constantinian age has passed," he writes, "we Christians find ourselves in a situation much more analogous to that of New Testament Christians than to the Christendom for which some nostalgically long." Clapp, like Willimon and Hauerwas, calls upon Christians "to reclaim, and present again to the church, the politics of Jesus."[12]

Clapp calls for the recovery of the church *visible* along the lines of the early church. He calls Christians to be more like early Christians for they were "not merely devotees" but "members of Christ's body, the people of God." This community of people sees the Christian faith as "a new and unique culture." Clapp quotes postliberal George Lindbeck to the effect that the church is "more Jewish than anything else. . . . It is above all by the character of its communal life that it witnesses, that it proclaims the gospel and serves the world." Consequently, "an invisible church is as biblically odd as an invisible Israel."[13] Clapp concludes that the biblical narrative demands a specific, visible people, a society or societal remnant, a *"polis."* My research suggests the younger evangelicals also believe in this biblical vision of a visible, tangible, enfleshed group of disciples of Jesus.

Another evangelical, Miroslav Volf, teaches "that an appropriate understanding of the trinity suggests a more nuanced and promising model of the relationship between person and community in the church." He writes, "The goal of my efforts is an ecumenical ecclesiology—not in the sense of a construct that draws on all traditions, but is rooted in none, but in the sense that all the great themes of this unmistakably Protestant ecclesiological melody are enriched by Catholic and Orthodox voices."[14]

Brian McLaren, pastor of Cedar Ridge Community Church in Maryland and clearly the guru of younger evangelical pastors, expresses the same sentiment. Writing about the need to break out of the small ecclesial world in which most evangelicals have lived, he says, "We will trade in our private histories for one grand, shared history. Over the horizon of the new world, we will cherish not the memories of our little splintered clans, but the story of the whole tribe."[15]

We turn now to an examination of the concept and practice of the church visible among the younger evangelicals. Is a new movement of the church visible really being born? If so, what are the characteristics of this new movement?

Church Visible among the Younger Evangelicals

Younger evangelical Gary Goodell, a young pastor in San Diego, compares the present renewal of the church with the Reformation of the sixteenth century. He argues that the Protestant Reformation "brought a reform of theology but failed to affect the practices of the church." He thinks this new revolution, brought about by the younger evangelicals, will "affect how the church functions, both in its life and in its mission." The result, he is convinced, will narrow "the gap between Orthodoxy (what we believe) and Orthopraxy (how we live or how we act)."[16]

Not everyone agrees that we are in such a radical shift of paradigms. According to Brian McLaren, some believe "that the postmodern transition . . . is just a mirage . . . a phase . . . a media event."[17] But Brian McLaren speaks for the younger

evangelical when he writes that "while philosophers often get balls rolling, popular culture, the arts, and even religion often turn the rolling snowball into an
avalanche that takes on a life of its own." Convinced that a vast cultural change is
under way, McLaren calls on the younger evangelical to "engage . . . with rare
passion and purpose during this time of transition." He fears that the "guardians
of modernity will not want to accept this." They are committed to "conserve the
modern foundations . . . and preserve the modern atmosphere, which they
breathe." But because cataclysmic changes are occurring, the younger evangelical is no longer bound by the rules of modernity. A new world is emerging
where "we can talk about spirituality. We can talk about mystery." We can say
there is "more to life than what science delivers or explains." Instead of being
"obsessed by analysis . . . we can explore synthesis and systems thinking." And
we can recognize "there's something better than control, power, and certainty
out there. Maybe that something is love, stewardship and faith."[18]

A good example of a younger evangelical church is Mars Hill Fellowship in
Seattle. Mark Driscoll, a twenty-something pastor, describes how they planted a
church "for the emerging postmodern generation in one of the least churched
cities in the U.S." From its very beginning, Mars Hill has emphasized four "Core
Values." To follow is a list of the values and explanations of each taken directly
from the Mars Hill Fellowship website:

> *Meaning:* God is eternal and therefore gives meaning to every age, culture and
> worldview. For this reason, Mars Hill seeks to continually understand cul-
> tural and worldview shifts to effectively minister to new generations.
>
> *Beauty:* God is beautiful and His creation reflects His beauty. God created
> man and woman in His image and likeness to also create works of beauty.
> For this reason, Mars Hill values the arts, expression, and creativity.
>
> *Truth:* God is True and has made His Truth known in His Word and the per-
> son of Jesus Christ. For this reason, Mars Hill seeks to know, live, and pro-
> claim Truth out of a love for God.
>
> *Community:* God exists in a perfect community of Father, Son and Holy Spirit
> and created men and women to also live in community. For this reason,
> Mars Hill seeks to model deep and personal faith by serving others in a lov-
> ing and authentic community.[19]

Mark Driscoll and others working with him through the Acts 29 Network
have begun an initiative to found one thousand churches that share these values.
Churches characterized by the Mars Hill values are being founded in major cities throughout the world.

These churches are committed to the notion that "Christianity never changes
its core beliefs from age to age." But they are also committed to "contextualization"; they seek to contextualize historic Christianity within postmodern cul-

ture. Mark Driscoll writes, "A church must be missional and seek to make that gospel its central focus . . . so, to do ministry in a postmodern world is not to fully embrace or fight postmodernity, but rather to seek the windfalls and pitfalls it provides for the gospel."[20]

Mars Hill is only one example of numerous churches that are being planted and raised up by younger evangelicals around the world. Some of these churches are well known and reach out through their websites. Most, however, are not known and cannot be readily identified. But they are doing church and ministry in a way that differs significantly from traditional and pragmatic evangelicals. These churches, writes younger evangelical Dan Lee, a professor of practical theology at Northern Seminary, are "less about logic and apologetics or theological propositions than about the dynamics of experiencing Christian Spirituality, less about the laws and tradition of the institutional church than about creating niches for a growing number of spiritual seekers, and less about denominational boundaries than about the network effects of pastors and churches with common ministry visions, values and approaches."[21]

Eric Stanford, a younger evangelical, writes of six ways the new postmodern church differs from the pragmatic seeker church:

- First, while Boomer churches tend to be highly structured and organized, Xer churches tend to operate by what you might call charismatic leading. Church staffs are smaller and less hierarchical. There's a strong emphasis on all church members helping out in the activities of the church. These churches take seriously the idea that God is the leader of the church, moving mysteriously and powerfully in individuals' lives, and so church ministries are not always planned by the church leadership but instead are instigated by church members who feel led by God to start a ministry.
- Second, while Baby Boomer churches tend to rely heavily on programs, Xer churches put their emphasis on relationships. There's a very clear understanding in Xer congregations that programs are means and not ends. Their purpose is the lacing together of souls. Church events, as well as spontaneous gatherings of church members, are less about learning or doing than about just being together. Xers seem willing to take the time that is required for developing relationships; that's where their priority lies.
- Third, while Boomer churches emphasize "excellence" in church ministries, Xer churches emphasize "realness." Xers don't seem to care much if the preacher stumbles over his words or the singer is of merely karaoke quality or the small-group leader doesn't know much about the Bible. But they insist that people be authentic. Don't pretend you've got it all together, spiritually or otherwise. Admit your mistakes and struggles, for then we can work on them together. No posers allowed.

- Fourth, while Boomer churches often tout themselves as "contemporary," Xer churches are typically "ancient-future." That is, the Xer churches have a dual orientation when it comes to time: they are naturally and comfortably up-to-date with a high degree of respect for the traditions of the Christian past. It's not unusual for an Xer pastor to refer meaningfully to Thomas á Kempis and Bill Gates in the same sermon. More than one hip Xer Web designer practices the *Lectio Divina*.

- Fifth, while Boomer churches are basically rationalist, Xer churches are more holistic, honoring intellect and emotions, doctrine and intuition. You can see this in Xer preaching, which is highly narrative, emphasizing both the stories of the Bible and the stories of Christians of today. You see it as well in worship, which involves an apologetics which is not a matter of presenting evidence and demanding a verdict but rather of urging people to say yes to Jesus on a daily basis.

- Sixth, while Boomer churches often have a competitive streak, Xer churches are more cooperative. It's not us-them; it's all us. Xers see, on the one hand, that God is working in the lives of non-Christians and that, on the other hand, Christians are not too different from nonbelievers in a lot of ways. Xers note things of value in other congregations and don't care for the walls put up between denominations. To many Xers, even the walls between the big three—Orthodoxy, Catholicism, and Protestantism—seem as ready for demolition as was the Berlin Wall.[22]

Convictions of the Emerging Postmodern Church

The values of the postmodern church more clearly reflect the values prior to Constantine than those of the modern era. In the next few pages my concern is to show the distinction between premodernism and modernism, and to clarify what it means to be a premodern church in a postmodern world.

The Return to an "Ecclesial" Paradigm

The younger evangelical makes a distinction between the established church of Constantinianism and the "ecclesial" church of premodern times. The Constantinian church joined the political arm of its society to shore up values and to achieve the good life. As secularization occurred, Christianity retreated into an inward and personal faith. In recent years the established church has become a place for privatized "me" religion, a therapeutic religion of "feel good" Christianity.

The younger evangelicals assert the church is not a private but a public faith. It is a community of people who represent the "new creation." They live and act as a witness to the overthrow of evil, to the kingdom that is to come and thus point to the vision of a new heaven and a new earth where God's *shalom* will rest over the whole world. Jim Belcher, cofounder and facilitator of a twenty-something fellowship at Lake Avenue Congregational Church in Pasadena, California, writes, "When we understand the gospel rightly we begin to realize that fulfilling felt needs is not the first step in the process at all." Instead, he argues, "The way to reach our generation is by living and proclaiming the gospel." New converts are to "begin to view life as a biblical drama in which they are called to be a part. They are called to be part of God's unfolding kingdom." The "ecclesial" church is a public, visible community of people, not a private individualized faith.[23]

The "Ecclesial" Church Is an Alternative Community

The Constantinian church became so enmeshed with society that it soon served as the "caretaker" or the "chaplain" of society. By being enmeshed with society and by offering prayer at its various societal functions, the church created a kind of "civil religion" that legitimated the social order. It became the moral teacher for all citizens, calling upon them to live good, moral, and upright lives. This relationship of the church to society in the twentieth century was particularly seen in the liberal agenda of social action in the first half of the century and the conservative agenda in politics in the latter part of the century. The younger evangelical wants to break away from the church as the servant of civil religion.

John Green, founder of a ministry to gay and lesbian street prostitutes in Chicago, writes, "The Christian church is so enmeshed with the American culture that it cannot see that that same culture is frighteningly anti-Christian . . . we are made to be a light in the darkness—calling people to the road less traveled, to a costly discipleship that rejects the materialism, nationalism, militarism, classism, racism, and sexism of the American culture for the cross of Christ."[24]

Green points to the "ecclesial community of premodern and postmodern times as an alternative community, a contrast culture and society of people. He writes that "the church is not called to be a business marketing itself to meet the needs of consumers who wrongly believe they know exactly what they need. Instead, the church is a family." This family is "intended to be a local and organic garden planted in the soil of a greater community and as such is rooted *in that time and place*"[25] (my emphasis).

The younger evangelical is interested in building organic Christian communities, not huge Wal-Mart churches that deliver a full range of Christian consumer goods. Steve Ibbotson, who teaches at Prairie Bible College, believes postmoderns have "an incredible thirst for real community, real love and care."[26]

This is why, as Tory Baucum, a young professor at Asbury Seminary, says, "We honeycomb the parish with small groups (of all kinds) and create a culture of honest conversation."[27] Church isn't just a "Sunday morning experience." Instead, as Mark Driscoll writes, "It is a family with members of all ages . . . a family with members who are students and software designers and retail clerks and parents and construction workers . . . a family with members who have an intimate relationship with God, others who desire to know him better and still others who don't know him at all . . . a family who gather to worship God, to pray, to learn, and for some to just hang out."[28]

In addition to being an alternative society that points to the ultimate kingdom of God, a people under the reign of God, younger evangelicals are distinguished by several features.

First, they have no desire to develop the big church. They want to grow through the multiplication of smaller groups and avoid the larger consumer-driven church. Dawn Haglund, a recent Trinity Evangelical Divinity School graduate, writes that the primary goal of the church is to "make disciples." Generally, Haglund claims, disciple-making "doesn't happen in the larger context—it is in smaller contexts where we are pushed and challenged to live our lives in ways that actually reflect what we believe."[29] Younger evangelicals Andrew Black and Sarah Sarrott, writing for postmodern magazine *Faithworks*, claim there is "apathy toward big programs, big ministries, big ideologies, and big solutions." They say the only way "you can make a difference or make an investment is in individual lives—not in things or institutions, but in people." They quote a new survey of eighteen- to thirty-year-olds conducted by Washington-based Public Allies that shows these young people put "people before programs, place value in direct action, and appreciate diversity."[30]

The fact that younger evangelicals appreciate diversity points to three very distinct features of their smaller, community-based churches. They are committed to being intergenerational, intercultural, and postdenominational—three convictions that fly in the face of church-growth principles. For example, Dieter Zander, a younger evangelical church planter in San Francisco, was hired to begin a Generation X church within Willow Creek Community Church near Chicago but was uneasy with the "church within a church" approach. This younger generation wants the wisdom of other generations; they don't want to be separated out as a group with characteristics they "will grow out of and graduate from." Instead, writes Zander, Xers have "the very characteristics that the church ought to grow into,"[31] one of them being their commitment to the intergenerational church, another their love of intercultural communities. Demographer Barbara Parsole from Atlanta reminds us that numbers of "ethnic people are growing at six times the rate of the U.S. as a whole."[32] Demographer William Frey writes, "Historically Christians responded to America's growing diversity by starting churches aimed at distinct ethnic groups. But as intermarriage and assimilation blur those ethnic lines, perhaps a new kind of multicultural church will emerge."[33] It will. And it will be led by the younger evangelicals who know that God has called out a people from "every tribe and nation" and that the church here on earth needs to be a sign and foretaste of the kingdom that is to come.

This lack of distinction between people is carried over into the younger evangelical attitude toward denominations, including Catholic and Orthodox. Mark Driscoll describes the postmodern world as a "postmodern network." The day of "central hierarchy," at least in denominations, is a thing of the past. The trend, he claims, is toward "local, connected churches from various traditions bringing their gift to the larger body and celebrating the other gifts that are brought to the party." What he sees are "partnerships" that will be developed among people who "share a common heart and ministry."[34] This will, of course, depend on the spread and maintenance of servant leadership, the kind of leadership the younger evangelical is committed to live out.

The "Ecclesial" Church Is a People of Ministry

The Constantinian church is characterized by its *professional* clergy who have been trained in acceptable seminaries and passed through examinations conducted by their peers. If their education is adequate, their theology in keeping with the group's convictions, and their abilities at least somewhat compatible with denominational expectations, they are ordained and appointed or elected to a church. Their job is to deliver the goods (e.g., sermons, education, baptisms, care of the sick, and various services). Lay people, for whom the clergy work, are the consumers of the clerical services. If they don't like what their money buys, the deliverer is expendable and they go on a search to find the person who will deliver the goods they want.

The pre-Constantinian view of ministry, recovered by the Reformers but since lost in most Protestant churches, is the priesthood of all believers. Every man and woman is a minister. Everyone has a gift and is to use that gift for the good of the body. At Mars Hill, for example, everyone who becomes a member of the church makes a covenant with the body that includes the statement, "I commit to using the spiritual gift(s) God has given me for the building up of the church, both at MH and universally."[35]

In a postmodern church it's not "everyone for herself" but "everyone for each other." The world's agenda of individualism or of CEO hierarchy is exchanged for relationship with various functions of service for each other. An excellent example of the tension between individualism and community was expressed in the television hit *Survivor*, for it "represented the perfect postmodern paradox." The participants were told to "work together to build shelter, find food, and survive the island, but ultimately it is everyone for themselves."[36] People long for community. They want to use their talents to help each other, but in the end, says our culture, it is individual survival that counts. In the church, of course, things should be different. In the true church everyone is a provider and everyone is a recipient.

The "Ecclesial" Church Is about Mission

In the Constantinian church the local church *sent* missionaries. The church was an agency committed to provide money. Christian workers, teachers, evangelists, and missionaries were sent into the world to carry out the mission of the church. The church provided all the resources to make missions happen. It brought back its missionaries for mission conferences. The people gathered in masses to hear what their missionaries had done with their money and prayer support. Missionaries traveled to churches to gain support to go back to the mission field and "do" missions.

In the pre-Constantinian and now postmodern paradigms, the church does not "send" missionaries nor does it have "a missionary program." Instead it is mission, no matter where it is geographically. The postmodern church invites people in its neighborhood into the new alternative community of people who embody the kingdom, and it promises them an experience of the kingdom that is to come.

David Clark, professor at Bethel Seminary in St. Paul, Minnesota, writes, "The best way to be effective is to care little for success. The best way to be a transforming leader is to care more about what's in your own hearts than what we accomplish. When we give up this need to be successful or powerful for purposes of inward validation, we are free to be truly effective in fulfilling our callings. I long to see the church led by people who care so little about being successful as the world sees it and care so much about being in touch with God and in community with the people that the reality of God's power is powerfully unleashed." Speaking the same message but more bluntly, he says, "I'm turned off by religious professionals who are filled with pretense. . . . I feel more connected with people who have been damaged by theology than those who love it."[37]

Erwin McManus, younger evangelical and pastor of Mosaic Church in Los Angeles, regards mission to be the first priority of the church. In Mosaic's "Five Core Values," mission is first. "It is why the church exists." This doesn't mean Mosaic affirms church-growth principles. "In our time in history," writes McManus, "we talk with an incredible sense of insight about church growth as if we know where the Spirit's coming from and where it is going. The truth of the matter is that any strategy for growth that isn't based on an intimate relationship with Jesus Christ will not prevail in the long run." McManus eschews "methodologies that help you grow your church faster, or programs that you could establish in your cultural context." The key to the missional church is "to love more profoundly and more deeply." This is what makes the missional church "effective in bringing people to Christ." It is not "having" a mission, but "being" God's mission, God's alternative people who signify God's reign over all that lies at the heart of the missional church.[38]

It is interesting that for the most part younger evangelicals are committed to start-up churches. Many existing churches, most perhaps, still function in the modern established pattern and are fearful to take the kind of risks it takes to become a post-Constantinian church. This may explain why so many of the younger evangelicals are church planters. They feel the investment of time it takes to change an existing institutional church is hardly worth it. Like the fundamentalists of the early part of the twentieth century, they have turned toward new soil, especially in the inner cities and among the poor. Here, among people who have no tradition to uphold and no denominational battles to fight, the younger evangelicals find open minds and hearts to the fresh winds of the gospel.

In sum the younger evangelicals differ with the traditionalists and the pragmatists. They reject the traditionalist notion of the "purity of the church" or the "Great Commission ecclesiology" as too reductionistic. And they have turned away from the megachurch movement to find a visible smaller fellowship of believers drawn from all the traditions that affirms the whole church and seeks to embody Christ's presence in a particular neighborhood, often in the city (see table 9).

Table 9
Approach to Ecclesiology

	Traditional Evangelicals	Pragmatic Evangelicals	Younger Evangelicals
Approach	Invisible	Invisible	Visible
Theological Understanding	Mostly affirm the purity of the church	Great Commission ecclesiology	Incarnational ecclesiology
Attitude toward the Church Worldwide	Separatist	Interdenominational	Intentionally ecumenical
Historical Attachment	Constantinian	Not attached to any historical tradition	Pre-Constantinian
Church Polity	Mostly denominational	Mostly congregational but creating new fellowships	Mostly congregational but networking with all Christians
Style of Operation	Church board	CEO model	Servant ministry of all God's people

Table 9
Approach to Ecclesiology

	Traditional Evangelicals	Pragmatic Evangelicals	Younger Evangelicals
Church and State	Mostly Republican	Mostly Republican	Resident aliens
Paradigm	Established	Creative	Missional
Church and Eschatology	Has an eschatological view Mostly premillennial	Indifferent to eschatological views	Seeks to be an eschatological community living out the future in the present

Conclusion

In part 2, "The Younger Evangelical Thinkers," I have attempted to set forth the theology and philosophy of the younger evangelical leaders. I should note that their theology shares the same overriding themes of the theology of twentieth-century evangelicals. They are committed to a supernatural view of the world. They profess a personal loving God who created the world, who grieves over its fallen condition, and who resolved to save it through Jesus Christ. They believe God became incarnate in our history in the person of Jesus Christ, who was sacrificed for our sin, conquered the powers of evil, and ascended to heaven where he now rules over the church, which is a witness to his ultimate rule over all the world. It is from this theological context that the younger evangelical believes the church is to call people toward repentance, faith in Christ, life in a community under the reign of Christ, and hope for the new heavens and the new earth.

As I have shown, however, the *ethos* of the younger evangelicals is shaped by their setting in a postmodern world. Consequently, they differ *methodologically* with their twentieth-century predecessors. They are skeptical of theological innovation; they value tradition; they are wary of propositional systems and prefer narrative theology; they shy away from arguments and intellectual persuasion in favor of a witness of the Holy Spirit and truth verified by embodiment; they believe in the power of the written and spoken word but feel a need to restore visual and symbolic forms of communicating the gospel; and they have turned their backs on the established Constantinian form of the church in favor of the early-church ecclesial paradigm of an authentic visible community of disciples that witnesses to God's reign over the entire creation.

We turn now to see how these commitments of the younger evangelical thinkers shape and form their practice of ministry.

The Younger
Evangelical
Practitioners

In part 3, "The Younger Evangelical Practitioners," the principal question I'll be addressing is, What kind of impact are these new paradigm shifts making on the church and its practice? The emphasis of the younger evangelicals, as I will show in every chapter of this section, is a shift toward embodiment. They want not only to *do*, they want to *be*. Wheaton College student Joel Handy puts it succinctly:

> So many churches and Christians separate what they know to be true theologically from their deepest being. But, it is only by knowing Christ *in us* that we learn to take up the cross. By our union with Jesus we are healed, and we become a Church that heals in the promise of the resurrected Savior. I am so hungry for churches that teach new life, instead of unbreakable logic and propositional doctrine. I want a church that teaches me how to know Jesus, and not to just think rightly. I want to know how to reveal the healing power of our Savior, as well as His true Character to a world so desperate for something real.[1]

Joel has put his finger on the real issues: personal existential knowledge of Jesus, an incarnational embodiment of Jesus in every aspect of life, and the healing presence of Jesus made real to others through lives lived out of a radical, if not extreme, commitment to discipleship and ministry.

I frequently receive correspondence from people who think about the church and its life in the postmodern world. Most of the correspondence I receive is from twenty-somethings. This book reflects such correspondence, some of it solicited, some unsolicited. As I came to the writing of this last section, an unsolicited essay arrived from Tullian Tchividjian.

Tullian is the thirty-year-old grandson of Ruth and Billy Graham and a minister to young adults and families at the historic Cedar Springs Presbyterian Church in Knoxville, Tennessee. The paper is titled "A Cry for Difference from the Culturally Weary." It provides a fitting introduction to this part of the book:

A Cry for Difference from the Culturally Weary

In recent years many books and articles have appeared concerning the appropriate role of the church in our present cultural milieu. This, of course, has included an analysis of contemporary cultural trends and how we as the church, God's "alternative society," are supposed to respond to the challenges and opportunities these trends present. The proposed solutions to these challenges and opportunities vary widely, but as yet no consensus has emerged. And while I do not claim to have the final answer, I would like to offer a perspective that, I hope, might stir us to think about this subject, which we, as disciples in the twenty-first century, cannot afford to ignore.

I was blessed to grow up in a solid Christian home. The middle of seven children (4 brothers and 2 sisters), I was raised in an environment where authentic faith was lived out before my very eyes. I have always known who God is and I have always known that He sent His Son to die on a cross for sinners like me. As far back as I can trace, strong Christian conviction and devotion to Jesus Christ have been defining marks of my family heritage. My dad, who was born and reared in Switzerland, is a well-known and respected psychologist who has always put his family before anybody or anything. My mom, the eldest daughter of Billy and Ruth Graham, is an award-winning author and speaker whose commitment to discipling her children surpassed any other competing ambition. They have been married for thirty-eight years and counting. Growing up, my other brothers and sisters walked the straight and narrow, for the most part, rarely giving my parents any real trouble. Then there was me . . . a different story!

It's certainly not an excuse, but I found it difficult growing up as a middle child. At times I was bunched with the "older ones," and at other times I was bunched with the "younger ones." I ended up, it seemed, bearing the responsibilities of both and enjoying the privileges of neither. I wasn't sure where I fit in (still don't at times), and I wanted to be heard, to be distinct. But instead of "casting all of my anxiety on Him," I turned to the world. At sixteen I dropped out of high school, was kicked out of my house (actually escorted off our property by the police), and began living in a manner I thought would satisfy. I craved freedom more than anything. So, committing myself to a lifestyle with "no boundaries," I became a promiscuous, drug-using club hopper, living in South Florida, who pursued pleasure harder than most. It wasn't, however, until after I had lived this way for six years that I began to realize my so-called freedom had made me a slave to desires and habits that were quickly destroying me. I had been seeking satisfaction so vigorously that I was unconscious of just how unsatisfied I had become. I was hungrier for meaning at twenty-one than I had been at sixteen. I found the Enlightenment promise that all things, including satisfaction and contentment, could be found "this side of the ceiling," was a lie. The world had not satisfied me the way it had promised, the way I had anticipated. The world's message and the world's methods had hung me out to dry. I hungered desperately for something, someone, "out of this world." Broken and longing for something transcendent, I began going back to church with my parents.

I was very thankful that I walked into a church that was *different*—a church where the otherness of God was sensed immediately. In the music, in the message, and in the mingling afterward, it was clear that God was the guest of honor there, not I. I had suffered the consequences of the modern world's emphasis on the individual, and I was unbelievably refreshed to discover a place that took the focus off me and put it on Him. He was the one being "lifted up for all men to see," not the pastor or the "praise team." He was the difference I longed for, not some carefully orchestrated performance that, believe me, I would have been able to see right through. And I am glad He was not communicated in the distasteful ways, whether musically or otherwise, that I had grown weary of. Whether or not I understood everything the preacher said that morning didn't matter. I was the recipient of something more powerful than a "user-friendly" service with its "seeker-sensitive" sermon. I was observing the people of God honoring God as God, and I was drawn in by the glorious mystery of it all. I was being evangelized, not by a *man-centered show*, but by a *God-centered atmosphere*. I was experiencing what Dr. Ed Clowney calls "Doxological Evangelism." It was, quite literally, out of this world!

The people like me, whom the church is trying to reach in the modern world, live their lives in a "world without windows."[2] Traditionally, according to sociologist Peter Berger, human life was lived with "windows to other worlds." In other words, *ordinary reality* was not the *only reality*. People acknowledged that there was much more to reality than the world in which they lived. They recognized that there was someone bigger than their capabilities, someone to appeal to beyond themselves, a larger purpose to life reaching beyond the immediate, beyond this world. Prior to the Enlightenment, all cultures and societies recognized the "superior power of some kind of supernatural."[3] "The deepest experiences of all," says Os Guinness, "were held to be 'religious,' 'sacred,' 'other,' or 'transcendent,' however these terms were defined."[4] But modernity has been shutting the windows and closing the blinds. "The Enlightenment's development of science and reason," says Marva Dawn, "turned the center of societies from the supernatural to the natural,"[5] creating a "world without windows." In a world without windows, God, transcendence, and mystery become less and less imaginable, and as a result, all of life becomes, as Max Weber put it, "rationalized." Everything becomes a matter of human classification, calculation, and control. "What counts in a rationalized world," says Guinness, "is efficiency, predictability, quantifiability, productivity, the substitution of technology for the human, and—from first to last—control over uncertainty."[6] Everything is produced, managed, and solved "this side of the ceiling," which explains why so many people are restless and yearning, as I was, for meaning which transcends *this world*.

Many who live in this world know what the church is trying to do when we "accommodate" them, and they are disappointed. Because, they are, as I was, hungry for something and someone different. There is a reason why television shows such as *Unsolved Mysteries, Touched by an Angel,* and *X-Files* return season after season to a waiting audience, why the song "Higher" by the rock band Creed stayed at the top of the charts all of last year, and why Ecstasy is the dominant drug of choice, not only in the rave culture, but in youth culture as a whole. The increasing fascination with Eastern religions, angels, aliens, psychics, the afterlife, metaphysical healing, etc., indicates that our culture is crying out for something different, something higher, something out of this world. They long for mystery, transcendence, and a deep sense of wonder, awe, and belonging: elements that the modern world disallows.

Because the modern world is in a constant state of flux, always changing and never staying the same, people are craving constancy and depth, as well as something "higher" and out of this world. The modern "virtues" of choice and change have become for many people burdens to carry, not privileges to cherish. And this painful impermanence makes people in the modern world open to, and desirous for, things traditional and historical, ancient and proven. "From the historic preservation movement to the nostalgia of popular culture with its TV reruns, historical fiction, and 'retro' fashions," says cultural critic Gene Veith, "contemporary people are fascinated and attracted to the past."[7] They are desperately reaching not just *upwards* but *backwards.* They yearn for a day gone by when things seemed more constant and less shallow. They want to tap into the treasures of the past as they search for staying power that seems unattainable in the present. They are weary of the pressure to *become,* while they long for the privilege to *be.* Therefore, they want different music (not just words but style) and different people with their sights set on a different world. They long for someone to speak to them with authority about someone other than themselves and about a time other than their own. They are not as interested in what they can become as in who they are and where they came from, historically speaking.

To be sure, "there are none who seek God, no not one," according to the Bible, but it seems apparent that our world is becoming weary with the message and the methods of modern culture. If you stop and listen to the cry of our culture, you will hear people crying out for an *otherworldly dynamism,* not a *this-worldly solution.* They are up to their necks in "up-to-date" structures and "cutting-edge" methodologies. They are beginning to understand that life's meaning extends beyond the "bottom line" and that modern capabilities are neither able to make us better, more satisfied people, nor able to make this world a better, more satisfying place.

I have talked to many people who are becoming increasingly wary of the latest "techno-trend" and complain of how impersonal and disenchanted modern life has become. The influx of secularization has left many yearning for an otherworldliness *and* a historical connection that modernity cannot provide. They seem desperate to recover a world that once was, a world that allows for mystery, miracle, and wonder, a world with "windows to other worlds." Their cry is for something completely unique to this world, something otherworldly, something only the Church can truly offer.

"The world," says Richard John Neuhaus, "desperately needs the Church to *be* the Church," not to *do* church differently.[8] The difference that people are longing for, in other words, is a difference in *being,* not *doing.* So while many church "strategists" are locating reformation and revival in structural renovation, we must remember that the deepest needs of the Church today are *spiritual*, not *structural*. And yet, "church-growth" advocates are constantly telling us that the Church's cultural relevance depends *ultimately* on its ability to keep up with the changing structures, on its ability to *do* church differently.

I have good news for all of us who are becoming weary of this type of pressure: We don't have to keep up the way we think we do; the world doesn't want us to! So how do we compete? We don't! We must come to see that God has established His Church as an "alternative society," not to compete with this world but rather to offer a home to those who realize the homelessness of life in this world without Him. It is the calling and the privilege of the Church to be "*against* the world *for* the world." We should be encouraged and challenged by the historical reminder that the church has always served the world best when it has been most countercultural, most distinctively different from the world. My fear, however, is that the modern church's emphasis on "structural renovation" and "doing church," has inadvertently communicated to our culture that we have nothing unique to offer them, nothing that is deeply spiritual and profoundly *other*-worldly. And as a result, they have looked elsewhere.

We have so emphasized the modern notion of *doing* (techniques, methods, programs, marketing strategies, etc.) that we have missed the opportunity to *be* who we're called to *be*. "Bigger is better and newer is truer" seems to be the banner under which church-growth conferences all over the country are organized and advertised. We have mastered the program, while eclipsing altogether the Master Himself. Our focus on doing church has certainly overshadowed the biblical focus of being *church,* and this comes at a time when our culture is growing weary of slick production, while growing hungry for authentic presence. They do not want *entertainment from* the Church; they want *engagement by* the Church: engagement with historical and cultural solidity that facilitates meaningful interaction with transcendent reality. It is ironic that just when our culture is getting vertical, the Church is spending most of its time and energy getting horizontal. Just when our culture is yearning for difference *from the world,* the Church is looking for creative ways to develop similarities *to the world.* Just when our culture is looking to the past, the Church is pronouncing the "irrelevance" of the past.

In order for the Church to establish its voice in our postmodern culture, we must remember who we are, where we have come from, and where we are going. We must avoid the modern tendency towards "chronological snobbery," believing that *our time* is the most important time while expressing little regard for history, tradition, and all those who have gone before us. We must *remember* that we are the people of the future, formed by the past, and living in the present. We must *remember* that our citizenship lies in "the city with foundations, whose architect and builder is God," not man. We must *remember* in our worship that while contemporists operate with their heads fixed frontwards, never looking over their shoulder at the stock from which they have come, and traditionalists operate with their heads on backwards, romanticizing about the past and always wanting to go back, the Church, in contrast from both extremes, is called upon to be a people with spinning heads: learning from the past, living in the present, and looking to the future. We must *remember* that it is our unique privilege and responsibility to remind our culture that this world is not all that there is, and that they are not left to the resources of *this world* to satisfy their *other* worldly longings. For, as Lauren Winner notes, "[People today] are not so much wary of institutions as they are wary of institu-tions that don't do what they're supposed to do."[9] As the Church, we are *supposed* to provide this world with that transcendent difference they long for because only the Christian Gospel offers a true spirituality, an otherworldliness, that is grounded in reality and history. It is only *our story*, the Christian story, that fuses past, present, and future with meaning from above and beyond, and we are *supposed* to tell it.

The old saying that we should "not be so heavenly-minded that we are of no earthly good" is true, as far as it goes. But it seems that in the modern world, our earthly good *depends* on our heavenly-mindedness. In our present cultural climate, it becomes neces-sary for the Church to remember the words of C. S. Lewis who maintained that Christians who "did the most for the present world were precisely those who thought the most of the next."[10] The late Henri Nouwen, too, points us in the right direction saying, "I am deeply convinced that the Christian leader of the future is called to be completely 'irrele-vant' . . . That is the way Jesus came to reveal God's love."[11] And speaking of relevance in the same way that Nouwen spoke of irrelevance, John Seel said, "The *timeless* is finally that which is most relevant, and we dare not forget this fact in our pursuit of rele-vance."[12] All good and wise reminders that we have been entrusted with a timeless truth that can transform any weary culture and open their eyes to a world beyond their own: the story of a simple Jew who made a difference *because* He was different.

This entire section, "The Younger Evangelical Practitioners," is an unfolding and expansion of the concerns registered by Tullian. His is not an isolated voice in our postmodern, post–September 11 world. His voice represents the heart, the cry, and the direction of the younger evangelical.[13]

8

Being Church

From Market to Mission

Northern Seminary, where I teach, is located in the suburbs of Chicago. We are not that far from Willow Creek Community Church, so whenever I teach a one-week class, I always take my students to Willow Creek. "It's an experience," I say. "As you drive down the long, winding, and beautiful road that leads to the church campus, you are experiencing the gathering. As we eat in the mall-like dining area, you are experiencing each other, the environment, the ethos of the place. As we go to the service, you are experiencing a contemporary presentation of faith through music, the arts, and preaching."

Ask anyone and they will tell you that the genius of Willow Creek, in part at least, is its sensitivity to the market. B. Joseph Pine and James Gilmore, in *The Experience Economy*, argue that the marketing of an experience is making a fundamental change in the way companies do business.[1] For example, you can buy a cup of coffee in a restaurant for one dollar but pay two or three dollars for a cup of coffee in a Starbucks café. Why? You pay for the experience. Starbucks is more than a coffee drink, it's a cool experience in an environment rich with atmosphere and yuppie-like people. The megachurch is not only church, it's an experience of a megamovement—an environment much like a theatre, a worship that is much like a presentation, a show in some cases. It fits the ethos of a

131

crowd gathered for a sport event or concert. People can dress casual, eat on the premises, remain anonymous, come and go as they please.

There is no question that this market-driven and experience-oriented approach to doing church "sells." Since 1980 the phenomena of the megachurch and of church-growth principles have been the number one topic of conversation. Christians have stood by and watched the traditional church shrink as the contemporary church has grown beyond the wildest dreams of its leaders.

But will it last?

New books on the church of the future point away from the megachurch and its market-driven success to the recovery of the missional nature of the church. George Barna, a strong advocate of the market-driven church, writes, "For several decades, the church has relied upon greater sums of money, better techniques, bigger numbers and facilities, and more impressive credentials as the means to influence society at large. These elements have failed us; in our efforts to serve God, we have crowded out God Himself."[2]

A major problem of the market-driven church is that it is so immersed with the culture that it has become enmeshed with it. The younger evangelicals, on the other hand, are recovering the church as a *counterculture*. The church, this view argues, should not seek to integrate itself with culture or to baptize culture. Instead, the church should see itself as a mission to culture. The church as the instrument of God is called to carry out God's mission in culture, calling people to come under the reign of God through Jesus Christ.

Responsible for this new model of the church are Lesslie Newbigin, David Bosch, and a new cadre of leaders who see the church as the servant of the *Missio Dei* (Mission of God). This understanding of the church has captured the minds and hearts of the younger evangelicals. Their commitment is not to fill the church with people through marketing techniques but to be an authentic and radical presence of God in a countercultural way.

Church as Mission

Lesslie Newbigin, missionary to India in the middle of the twentieth century, threw down the gauntlet and shifted the spotlight to domestic missions. His call, George Hunsberger writes, was to "challenge the churches of the West to look to our own contexts as missionary settings and to be as rigorous about what that may mean for our own missionary life as we have been about doing missions elsewhere."[3]

Newbigin's call to question the modern method of doing missions was a response to a ministry shaped by a mindset that ignored North America as a mission field and viewed Europe, Africa, Asia, and Latin America as places to "send" missionaries. The first feature of Newbigin's missional church is to recognize that the calling of the church in every culture is to be mission. That is, the work of the church is not to be an agent or servant of the culture. The church's business is not to maintain freedom or to promote wealth or to help a political party or to serve as the moral guide to culture. The church's mission is to be the presence of the kingdom. As Newbigin has written, "In every culture Jesus is introduced as one who bursts open the culture's models with the power of a wholly new fact."[4] The fact is God's reign over the whole world through Jesus Christ. The church is now the "sign, instrument, and foretaste" of the coming kingdom. The church's mission is to *show the world what it looks like when a community of people live under the reign of God.* The true gospel is portrayed best by the community that believes it, embodies it, and testifies to it in the midst of any given culture in all places and at all times. The church is not the same as the predominant culture. It is an alternative culture that points to the kingdom of God and the reality of the new heavens and the new earth. In this way, "The church's style of life becomes a missionary dialogue."[5]

A second feature of Newbigin's gauntlet is his recovery of a more biblical sense of conversion. Faith stands in the traditional pattern of *metanoia*, a turning from sin to come to Jesus and to be under his reign. But salvation also "involves membership in a community and decision to act in certain ways."[6] So conversion touches the heart and mind and includes a new ethical direction and a new communal dimension. The apologetic of the faith is based on the corporate witness to this *metanoia*. Apologetics is no longer primarily about a reasoned faith but a demonstrated faith. By entering into the community of faith, which embodies what it means to be a Christ community, a person is grasped by the embodied faith and brought to conversion, membership, and a new life "within" the body. In this way "the local congregation is the essential hermeneutic of the gospel, the lens through which it may become known and by which it can be rightly interpreted."[7]

This missional position of the church is best expressed in the image of "exile." The church, in its exilic condition, stands against the "secular salvations" of the world and calls attention to God's claim to reign over the world through its community *(koinonia)*, its service to the world *(diakonia)*, and the message it proclaims to all cultures *(kerygma)*. In this way the exilic missional church will "seek the welfare of the city, but not from any impulse that they must somehow seize control of its policies and dictate its ideology."[8] This mission will be accomplished by the growth of the church and its pervasive influence in society.

The third crucial issue presented by Newbigin is that of evangelism. How do we tell the story? How do we call people into Christ and the church? In our postmodern world we must abandon our "guilt-ridden motivational strategies" and develop an evangelism that is "grounded in a credible demonstration that life lived by the pattern of commitment to Jesus is imaginable, possible, and relevant in the modern and postmodern age." In this model the local church living its mission in the world is the most crucial form of evangelism. In this ancient and now new model, people are not asked to "come to Christ and go to the church of your choice." Instead, people are drawn into the church out of relationship and there, finding the community that embodies the faith, live under the reign of God. Evangelism is not "come to Christ and then to church" but "come to church and then to Christ."

The influence of Newbigin and his colleague and successor David Bosch has set into motion a very old understanding of doing church in a postmodern world. An increasing number of traditional evangelicals have been at work presenting and applying the principles of the missional church to North America.

In a recent publication, *The Church between Gospel and Culture*, the editors flatly state, "The social function the churches once fulfilled in American life is gone." The modern model of church has resulted in "a lack of focus in the midst of a proliferation of church programs, a loss of meaning in the work of the clergy and laity alike and an uneasiness that our faith does not really fit into the world where we live."[9] Today's church is caught in the middle of two paradigms. The paradigm of modernity is collapsing, but some fear the future and tenaciously hang on to the sinking ship. The new paradigm for a postmodern world is not clearly in sight. Grasped by fear, many pastors who know the old paradigm has collapsed are unable to move into the new paradigm. "The present crisis for the churches is not a matter of regaining lost ground or turf. It is not about asserting the claim that we should again hold the privileged position for America's moral and spiritual guidance. Rather, it has to do with our need to encourage the encounter of the gospel with our culture. It will mean learning how to be a church that by its nature lives always *between gospel and culture*, recognizing, on the one hand, the cultural dynamics that shape us as well as everyone else in this society and, on the other hand, hearing the gospel that calls us to know and value and intend things in a very different way."[10]

The younger evangelicals are in a unique position to offer leadership to the missional church as it lives fully in the gospel and fully in the culture. They were born and raised with the church during the years of the collapse of the modern model. As they came of thinking age, they found themselves at odds with the modern church and its assimilation into culture. The leaders of these younger evangelicals are thinking their way into the missional understanding of the church and are in a position to offer a new kind of leadership for the church of the twenty-first century.

The Missional Church among the Younger Evangelicals

What I have found among the younger evangelicals is (1) the rejection of the modern Western model of the church and its relationship to culture and (2) the widespread commitment to lead small, growing, start-up churches.

Rejection of the Modern Model of Church

Younger evangelicals are very critical of the way the American church has embraced and Christianized the values of the West. For example, James Stump, professor of philosophy at Bethel College in Minneapolis, agrees with Tom Sine's claim that "most American Christianity is just the good life as defined by the American dream (acquire more stuff, scale the corporate ladder, go to the "in" schools, etc.) with a thin 'Jesus-overlay.'"[11] What Stump finds is that Christians are really not distinguished in any significant way from secular culture, for "they do the same things as our secular counterparts, but the Christian version of these."[12] Dawn Haglund agrees. "Do we have a Christian faith that *doesn't* reflect American values?" she asks. "Marketing, promotion, advertising, consumerism, selfish materialism. I'm not sure the church is much different than the American culture. I find that sad, disappointing, and disturbing. Church has become a place of consumerism. People come to get their needs met. The church is about giving people what they want—making them comfortable. Maybe we've reached more people, but I'm skeptical if we've participated in transforming lives."[13]

These younger evangelicals are equally skeptical about the form of apologetics they have seen. For example, pastor David Taylor reports on a lecture on "Islam" presented by an evangelical on a secular campus: "The room was full of both Christians and Muslims and electric with tension and fear. By the end of the Q and A, it had turned into a shouting match, the Muslims grumbling that the fellow had dishonored and misrepresented Islam with his ten reasons 'Why Islam Is Not True' apology and Christians clapping when the apologist answered well. The problem: it was 'us' vs. 'them,' it was theoretical, abstracted from life, one man vs. the rest. There was nothing warm or personal about it. The style was embarrassing to Christians, even if the content may have been true."[14]

Tim Erdell, a missionary, questions the value of some "sent" missionaries. Speaking of his own observations, he writes, "You can't imagine how offensive many U.S. missionary enterprises are. . . . People on short-term trips can do outlandish harm in a brief period of time."[15]

So what does the younger evangelical want from the church as mission? Dawn Haglund hopes that "we will eventually want to be a church that is missional in nature. That calls people around a mission—of becoming like Jesus and participating with Him in bringing on His kingdom for the benefit of the entire world."[16] James Stump and his family are doing what many younger evangelicals are doing to make this kind of missional church a reality. "My family and several others," he writes, "are attempting to purchase an old school building right now, and convert it into housing for our families with some big common rooms left over to foster more intentional community."[17] Jonathan Nelms, minister of music and worship at First Baptist Church in Cookeville, Tennessee, approves of this kind of missional church. He thinks Americans "have little or no concept of suffering. . . . Sacrifices are being made by Christians around the world . . . yet we Americans have elevated the status of the individual far beyond our value of the corporate good. Consequently many Christians determine the strength of the Christian faith on how it serves their own needs."[18] James Stump agrees: "Giving up some of your private space in favor of purposely interacting with your neighbors cuts against the grain of American culture."[19] But this is exactly where the younger evangelical is ready to go. They have turned their backs on the big, market-driven, consumer-oriented, something-for-everybody church and turned toward the smaller, more sacrificial, missional church that embodies the faith in community and seeks to serve its immediate neighborhood.

The Small Growing Start-Up Church

Via email, Scott Gornto, young pastor of Journey Missional Church, asked, "What is the place of the church in the postmodern culture?" He wants to know what it looks like for people "to be missionaries in this postmodern context."

He and a "team" of others started Journey Missional Community in the spring of 1999. "They knew," he writes, "that the old bag of tricks such as tracts, mailers, street evangelism, etc., was not the answer to be missional." Instead, a missional church is "something you embody and live out." The example he cites is the early church. "They were," he writes, "living out the gospel. They were establishing God's kingdom on earth."[20]

John Graham, an older and experienced pastor who is characterized by a younger spirit, sees his future in the church start-up movement. He compares his choice to leave the established church and begin a start-up church to his former experience as a home builder. "Remodeling a house," he writes, "costs twice as much as new construction because there is twice the work involved: and even when it was done, it was never as good as new construction because so many compromises were required to adapt the old with the new work. The same is true of the church. I have been trying to spiritually remodel my congregation for twelve years. . . . While I have had moderate success, on the whole it has been a difficult and costly experience. Now, however, I am planning a new construction project, from the ground up with no old work to do."[21]

What are the issues that John Graham and other younger evangelicals face as they go about being the missional church from the ground up? Dann Pantoja addresses these issues in an article entitled "Please Don't Start Another Postmodern Ministry." He has issues with people who want to start up a new church because it's the trend, a cool thing to do. He cites a conversation with a young enthusiast. "I'm ticked off about our traditional church," this earnest person stated, "so I'm seriously considering to be a church planter . . . I think this postmodern model is the right method for our generation . . . I've attended a *Willow Creek* conference and a *Purpose-Driven* conference. But I think the postmodern approach is the most relevant."[22]

Pantoja thinks there's "no such thing as a postmodern strategy." God's actions, he says, "don't fit with spreadsheet plans." Church planting in the context of a postmodern world "could mean being a spiritual community who actually experiences the spiritual reality of God in our world. It could mean building up a spiritual community who would honestly testify of the brokenness and sufferings of this world. It could mean building a serving community who would do ministries of justice and compassion as a testimony that God is present in this broken world."[23]

Next he pleads with his readers: "Please don't buy multimedia stuff or other digital toys believing that they will postmodernize your ministry." He then tells the story of his involvement in quiet nondigital worship in an Anglican chapel. This traditional service, he says, with its traditional hymns, with the sight and scent of the candles, with its mystical aura, brought him "to a sacred level of consciousness beyond time and space." During the traditional passing of the peace, he said, "I felt Jesus touching and hugging me." This was, he said, "a nondigital, multisensory, spiritual, communal experience." He concludes, "You can now buy your digital toys. But you don't have to."[24] For younger evangelicals authenticity is what matters. Pantoja supports the use of digital forms of communication but only if they are not used as gimmicks; they should be ways of merely *assisting* an authentic and holistic worship of God.

Third, Pantoja wants us to know that start-up churches shouldn't "discriminate based on age." He observes that postmoderns are frequently called generation X or Y, but postmoderns "hate these market segmentations." He goes on to say, "Many young people today have come from divorced families. Many of them do not know what it means to have a mom, or a dad, or a grandfather, or a grandmother. A multigenerational church can provide the spiritual family that is missing in the experience of many people who belong to the new generation. This generation needs spiritual moms and dads who would embrace a wounded and hurting generation."[25]

Finally, Pantoja challenges church planters by saying, "Don't worry too much whether your ministry is postmodern or not." He advocates instead that "your ministry connect a real God to real people." Just be, he says, "a broken vessel," a "wounded healer," and "admit that life sucks, but let your life shine! . . . Whatever your ministry style is, be sure that . . . God is there!"[26]

Examples of Start-Up Churches

Numerous younger evangelicals in their twenties have committed themselves to start-up churches, most of them in cities throughout North America and even around the world.

I once commented on this phenomena in a workshop in Toronto. I said, "I find that twenty-somethings are unwilling to become pastors of traditional churches where a handful of people resist change. They turn their backs on fairly good jobs in churches that won't change, so they can do tent-making ministries with a start-up church without the hassle of dealing with change resistors." After the workshop a twenty-five-year-old male asked, "Do you know why we won't serve in those traditional churches that resist change?"

"No," I said, "I know that you won't, but I'm not sure I know why."

"We're surfers," he said. "We surf TV, we surf eating places, we surf everything. If you don't like this, go there. If you don't like there, go here. Our lives are full of choices. Our parents were fighters, we're not, we're survivors. So, rather than fight a battle that can't be won, we start our own thing. That's why we are attracted to start-up ministries."

I am aware of many start-up churches begun by younger evangelicals. Three examples will give insight into the variety of start-up churches that have a missional focus.

First, the pastor of Mosaic Church in Los Angeles writes, "My job was to pray and seek the future of the vision of God. . . . We needed to discover the core essence of who we are as a church . . . a vision to be a spiritual reference point throughout Los Angeles and a sending base to the ends of the earth." After much prayer and discussion, this community came to realize that their vision was "to live by faith, be known by love and be a voice of hope."[27] To fulfill this mission, Mosaic Church developed five core values:

1. Mission is why the church exists.
2. Love is the context for all mission.
3. Structure must always submit to spirit.
4. Relevance to culture is not optional.
5. Creativity is the natural result of spirituality.[28]

First, mission is why the church exists. In this younger evangelical community the church is "not a social organization, a political organization, or a health club." The church does not even have multiple purposes, it exists for one purpose alone and that is to "join God in His purpose for the world." Consequently the church has strict membership standards. It requires members to make four commitments: "to honor God with your life; to participate in the life of the church and be involved with a small group; to commit to an evangelistic lifestyle; and tithe a minimum of 10 percent." Our goal, the pastor writes, is to "have a community of life transformation that honors, glorifies and serves God."[29]

The second value is that love is the context for all mission. The pastor writes that for a long time he wanted to be known "by faith, not love." It took God, he said, "about ten years of keeping me among the urban poor before he could drive into me that He wanted me to be known by love. . . . If you take just one idea from my words here, it shouldn't be about methodologies that help you grow your church faster, or programs that you could establish in your cultural context, but it should be that a commitment to love more profoundly and more deeply will make you far more effective in bringing people to Christ."[30]

The third value of Mosaic is that structure must submit to spirit. Structures are often very rigid and thus controlling. "We talk with an incredible sense of insight about church growth as if we know where the spirit's coming from and where it is going," but all strategies for growth "that are not based on an intimate relationship with Jesus Christ will not prevail in the long run." Submitting to the Spirit is not an alternative for "when the structure doesn't seem to work, rather it's the primary option that waits upon God to work."[31]

A fourth value is that relevance to culture is not optional. It is God's calling. The purpose for change is not so "we don't die as a church" but so "God can speak in the culture in the most effective way possible."[32] This requires a willingness on the part of the church to die to the old even as it is called to live to the new.

This spirit of dying in order to live is expressed in the fifth core value: creativity is the natural result of spirituality. "Imagination," writes the pastor, "is where God can meet you. It's the only place where you can be everywhere at one time, the only place where you have unlimited resources, power and potential." Imagination is fueled by an intimate relationship that "both your uniqueness and the unique contribution that God wants to make through you" is discovered and ignited.[33]

The example of Mosaic Church is only one of thousands of younger churches. It points to the radical uniqueness of new start-up churches headed by the younger evangelicals. They have turned their backs on marketing techniques and programs to allow a unique unfolding of the church by the Holy Spirit through those who choose to be the missional church in the postmodern world.

The second illustration of a missional start-up church comes from a major Midwestern city. The church has asked me not to refer to it by name, so I'll call it YEC (Younger Evangelical Church). These younger evangelical leaders along with about fifty people from a suburban church have moved into a city area to be a missional church. To give a sense of their approach, I will draw from an introductory publication they give out to interested visitors.

Like other start-up churches, YEC's first commitment is to the gospel. They write, "The gospel defines our commitments. It calls us to careful study of the Bible as the story of God in history. It calls us to open our homes to share the abundance that God has given us. It calls us to conversation with others on the most serious questions of life—and to the proclamation of hope for the desperate situation of the world."

Unlike the boomer market-driven church, which is primarily suburban, the younger evangelical churches are primarily neighborhood churches, often in the worst part of the inner city. This is the other side of the commitment of YEC. They write, "We have a particular commitment to neighborhood church life. We want to stay rooted in neighborhoods. We desire to reflect the cultural and ethnic makeup of the local community."

A third feature of YEC is its recognition that it is a church that stands in the historic tradition. "There really is," their pamphlet states, "only one church of Jesus Christ. . . . This church includes people from every walk of life and is scattered across all five continents of the world."

A fourth feature of YEC is its commitment to community. "We believe," they write, "community is best fostered when it is intergenerational. We like the idea of a university student and a four-year-old sitting in the same living room with a married couple and a single parent. We like the idea of people connecting who are different from one another, people accepting one another for the bond they have in Christ."

Another commitment of YEC is to justice. They write, "Pursuing Christ means actively engaging the world." For them this means that "we must seek justice in this world: feed the poor; clothe the naked; help widows and orphans; minister to the stranger and alien."

Finally, while YEC is committed to growth, it is not committed to being bigger. Their idea and that of most churches pastored by the younger evangelical is to multiply by planting more small start-up churches. They write that they are asking God to allow them "to plant 100 churches in this generation." For them, church is people, not buildings. They want to reach the *nations*, but they want to do it as a missional church, starting in their own neighborhood and spreading to "unreached people groups." They are committed to "cross-cultural ministry."[34]

For many younger evangelicals, the missional church is no longer an option but a mandate. For them, the traditional church is frequently too difficult to change because, as John Graham writes, "The consistent reaction of the people in all the congregations I have served has been spiritual lethargy."[35]

Younger evangelicals seem more ready and willing to pay the price. Jeff Bailey, the editor of *Cutting Edge*, a magazine dedicated to help start-up churches and pastors, writes, "As I reflect on the spirit of consumerism and the worship of success that dominates our culture, I am convinced we are to aim at church health, not growth."[36]

Not all younger evangelical churches are small or committed to growing a number of smaller groups. Mars Hill Bible Church in Grand Rapids, Michigan, is one example. Mars Hill has grown to ten thousand in three years without marketing. When I asked Rob Bell, Mars Hill's thirty-one-year-old pastor, to reflect on his ministry, he responded with the following:

> We started Mars Hill in February of 1999 out of a desperate desire to build a new church that speaks a new language for a new world. While we could endlessly discuss the challenges that come from being a witnessing community in the midst of this new world, I simply want to share what we have learned so far.

Words

We actually believe that the biblical text is a living and breathing Word. For the first year or so of our existence as a church, I preached through the Book of Leviticus, verse by verse.

Yes, that's right.

Menstrual blood, goat sacrifice, and no shell fish, please.

Every verse.

Now if you at this moment are smiling or laughing or thinking that is crazy, what have you just said about the biblical text? Do you have a canon within a canon? Either you believe that God speaks through his entire text, or you stick within the evangelically approved texts that are tamed down enough for the local congregation.

We have no desire to tame the text. We want to let it out of its cage and we want to see it prowl around our lives, devouring us and spitting out the bones. We don't want to be detached, methodical scientists who stand over the subject and apply the proper rules, methods, and procedures so that we can achieve favorable results. The modern impulse is always to reduce it to simple principles and clever maxims. To continually insist that with enough work, it will all make sense and line up.

Life doesn't always line up.

We love the Scriptures and we want them to sweep us off our feet.

In the new world, much of what is currently considered preaching and study will be rendered totally irrelevant. The Bible is not a nice book. It is not a clean book. It is not a guide to proper behavior. It does not even seem to care whether it is "relevant" or not.

I have asked the congregation to please never tell me that my message was "nice."

The Bible is a revolutionary manifesto that could get you killed in many parts of the world. It is living, it is breathing, and it demands that we surrender to it unconditionally so that it can transform us.

There are several things about Leviticus that make it the ultimate postmodern book for preaching. The first thing is that it is visual—it is essentially a book of props and images. Instead of trying to describe an abstract concept like substitutionary atonement, God instructs the worshiper to slit the throat of a lamb and place it on the altar.

This innocent, perfect lamb is getting what I deserve.

Instead of a philosophical treatise on the nature of the kingdom of death, God gives detailed instructions on how contact with a corpse will affect your ability to come into his presence.

God understands how we are wired and how we learn and what stirs us—images and metaphors and pictures. So in communicating to us the deepest spiritual truths about what it means to relate to him, he speaks to us in a visual language that we can understand.

Second, Leviticus is communal. What is the worst punishment you can receive? Having to live outside the community.

Everything revolves around the life of this assembly who belong to God. The Day of Atonement is a fascinating exercise in dealing with communal sin—a totally foreign concept in the modern world, this strikes a chord deep within postmoderns.

Thirdly, Leviticus is experiential. You butchered the bull. You handled the intestines. You said the prayers. You went through the procedures. It is visceral, bloody, and participatory. Rarely are they commanded to watch anything passively because most of the teachings center around what a person was to do.

Here's a fourth theme: metanarrative. Much of Leviticus appears so random at first reading, one has to ask probing questions about context:

What is *this* doing in the Bible?

What we discovered is that every single chapter brought us to Jesus. It is almost as though there is a magnetic pull towards the cross in every chapter. Perhaps it should be retitled: The Gospel According to Leviticus. The confidence and faith that this inspired in our congregation was amazing. If that totally bizarre passage is a picture of Christ in some way, seemingly against all odds, then what does that say about the rest of Scripture? Is there more going on with the minor prophets than perhaps we are aware of? How about Lamentations? And what is the deal with the Book of Judges?

We have learned that the Scriptures speak and they speak now and they speak to all of us. It is not our responsibility to prove its relevance or usefulness. It is our privilege to enter into them and to be transformed by them.

To absorb them, and to let them absorb us.

To read them, and to let them read us.

To devour them, and to let them devour us.

By the way, I'm getting ready to preach through Numbers. Have you read 5:11–31? Oh, man.

Mystery

We believe that the goal of the church is to celebrate mystery, not conquer it. One of the greatest diseases to have infected the church in the modern era is the desire to reduce.

Seven steps to prayer.

Four steps to prayer.

Three ways to . . .

Methods, steps, programs—in a couple of sessions we can give you all of the answers to . . .

And yet we serve a God who constantly reminds us that his thoughts are not our thoughts.

We were baptizing believers in a nearby lake soon after the church began, and we came to the end of the list of those who had signed up. I had this sense that God wanted to do something more. So I asked if there was anybody in the crowd who had witnessed this event and as a follower of Christ knew that they needed to come down to the water right now in their street clothes and be baptized. A second later a woman in a dress came charging into the water. She had tears streaming down her face and she looked me square in the eyes and said, "I want to get baptized right now and I'm not even a part of this church." After her countless people came streaming into the water. Families, single moms, drug addicts, spouses standing on shore sobbing while their lovers entered the water.

Can you figure that out?

How does that happen?

What is it that moves people to those defining moments in their spiritual journey?

At our last baptism celebration, I stood on the shore and talked with each person or family before they entered the water. I asked almost all of them why they were doing what they were about to do; 109 people later I was mystified. Every single one of them told me about promptings to follow Jesus in a variety of ways, yet none of them came from some nice, neat programs that the church offered.

We don't do anything to promote or persuade people about baptism.

We just announce when and where the celebration will be. People are drawn to these symbols in deep and profound ways. This cannot be programmed. A glossy brochure simply does not work in this case.

I need to be honest here. Hanging around a local church, I hear and see amazing stories all the time, literally every week, every day. Marriages healed, addicts cleaned up, people falling to their knees and confessing sins held inside for years. You cannot explain it outside of the working of God's Spirit through his bride.

Honesty

We had an issue in the first few months of our existence as a church with people being rude in the parking lot. The traffic jams were causing people long delays . . . you know the drill. So I told the church that if you were not a follower of Jesus and you had been joining us, we were thrilled to have you in our midst. But if you were a follower of Jesus and you were being rude and mean in the parking lot, you needed to stop this behavior. And if you continued, then we would get your license plate number and treat this as an issue of church discipline. I made it clear that if we could not live up to our high calling in the parking lot, then we had no business going into the world. And besides, we could use your seat.

The place erupted in applause.

My spanking of the congregation, or at least some members of it, was met with such affirmation it was unnerving.

Why?

We have learned that people are starved for honesty. They want to be told the truth regarding money, leadership, sin, challenges facing the church—whatever it is they are desperate to know they are being given a straight dose. Even if it's ugly.

When we outgrew our first building, we bought a nearby mall. After moving in we discovered that the roof leaked almost everywhere. There were buckets hanging from the ceiling and kiddie pools rigged into the beams in many rooms. We pointed out the buckets and told the body that we needed a new roof.

And if they got wet during a service or a meeting or a class, perhaps they could pay for that section of roof to be fixed.

Whether it is money, the personal weaknesses of the lead pastor, the struggles of the elders and staff in leadership, or people yelling at each other in the parking lot, we have discovered that in the new world people want to hear the truth no matter what it is.

I literally announced one Sunday that a particular message I recently preached wasn't as faithful to the text as it could have been so I was going to preach it again.

So I preached the same exact text over again.

People still remind me of that Sunday.

Numbers

Our gatherings on Sundays are huge. Somewhere around ten thousand people gather in the mall on any given Sunday. How in the world do you call people to lay down their lives in the midst of that kind of circus? It takes somewhere between seven hundred and a thousand VOLUNTEERS to run the children's ministry, birth to fifth grade. How do you have any sense of sanity and mission when the church is bigger than many small towns?

The harder we push, the more clear we make the demands of the cross, the more we teach about self-denial and service and commitment and losing your life, the more people come. The higher we try and raise the bar, the more people join us. The greater emphasis we place on the fact that Jesus calls us to lay down our lives, the bigger the numbers.

We are learning that deep down people were wired for revolution. Nobody in the culture is calling them to anything worth dying for. They were created to live for massive, global purposes, and yet all day long they are bombarded with messages about how their life would be better with more products.

I know our church has a huge back door. I know that thousands have visited, felt lost in the crowd, not gotten connected, and left. I know that many have found our message to be irrelevant or boring or even offensive. I know that some are spectators at heart. I know that we have dropped the ball in a multitude of ways in being the authentic church that Jesus has called us to be. I know that we have reacted to abuses of the modern church by swinging the pendulum the other way too far. I know that anybody could observe our community for a period of time and make a huge list of the things that were ineffective, destructive, or missing altogether.

What we have learned time and time again is that we are students.

Learners.

Figuring it out.

The spirit of God is messy.
And that is not heresy.
The Spirit moves in wild and unrestrained ways and demands that we run as
fast as we can to keep up.
The most dangerous place to be in the universe is the center of God's will.
That is where we want to be.
I hope we never think we've nailed it.
I hope we never believe that we have arrived.
I hope it is always dangerous.
Always chaotic.
Always flying by the seat of our pants.
Never settled.
Messy.
I hope the struggles keep us begging God for guidance.
I often hear Christian leaders tell what God has been saying to them in their
times of meditation and study and prayer and I'm often amazed. He tells them the
most profound, eloquent things.
All I seem to ever hear is: "Rob, get out of my way."[37]

My research suggests that there are hundreds of these kinds of churches being started all over North America and around the world. They are in a sense
bubbling under the surface of visibility. In a few years they will burst forth with
a new visibility and leadership that will mark the twenty-first century with a
new kind of evangelical missional church.

In the remaining chapters of this book, I will explore this new kind of church
and ministry to show the new kind of leadership that is coming from these
younger evangelicals (see table 10).

Table 10
Approach to the Missional Church

	Traditional Evangelicals	Pragmatic Evangelicals	Younger Evangelicals
What Is the Church?	Church is a place for private faith	Church is a place to meet everyone's needs	Church witnesses to the *Missio Dei* by word and deed
What Does the Church Do?	The church serves culture as its religious voice	The church reaches out to the seeker	The church is a new creation, a vision of the *eschaton* in a broken world
How Does the Church Function?	The church is a guide for moral behavior	The church is a place to repair humanity	The church functions as a countercultural community

(continued)

Table 10
Approach to the Missional Church

	Traditional Evangelicals	Pragmatic Evangelicals	Younger Evangelicals
Who Runs the Church?	Professional clergy	A business model of hierarchical leadership	Clergy and people are united in common ministry
How Does the Church Help People Connect with the World?	Provides resources to enable people to minister to others	Consumer mentality There is something for everybody Meets needs	The church embodies the reality of the new creation
How Does the Church Change?	Change occurs incrementally	Change reflects culture Management principles "Church growth"	Change reflects the nature of the church's mission Spirit-driven change

9

Pastors
From Power to Servanthood

From the very beginning of Christianity, the question of leadership has been an issue in the local church. In Acts 2, church elders appointed deacons to serve the Hellenists who felt neglected; in Acts 7, bishops, elders, and deacons came together to discuss and solve the problem of what was expected of gentile converts; in the letters to the Corinthian church, many gifts and callings within the church are described; and in the pastoral epistles, Paul delineates three functions of ministry—oversight, teaching, and service. By the end of the first century, church leadership was situated in bishops, presbyters, and deacons; by the medieval period, there was a pope, cardinals, archbishops, bishops, priests, and deacons; in the sixteenth century, the Reformers placed leadership in a council of presbyters; by the seventeenth century, a more democratic form of government, congregationalism, emerged; and by the latter part of the twentieth century, leadership in many evangelical churches was modeled on business and the power of the CEO. Clearly the business model of the church is out of step with two thousand years of history.

The historic churches and the Reformation churches regard leadership in the church to be a matter of doctrine, but the megachurch sees the organization of leadership within the church as a pragmatic matter: whatever works, do it. Behind all these configurations is the nagging question, What about the laity? Do they have a calling to ministry, or are they primarily the sheep led by clerics? These issues have produced thousands of discussions, hundreds of books, and scores of models. This is not the place to review or attempt to shed any real light on all these questions. Instead, we turn to the current difference between the modern form of CEO leadership and the emergence of the servant model of leadership.

The Call to Servanthood

E. Glenn Wagner, pastor of Calvary Church in Charlotte, North Carolina, is deeply concerned about the effect of the CEO model of the church. In *Escape from Church, Inc.*, he writes of a concern for the "growing number of 'drop out Christians' who have been hurt and abused in churches that seem to see people as objects" and expresses concern for the "numbers of pastors being dismissed because they don't fit the corporate model now in vogue." Why is it, he asks, that the only continent in the world where the church is not growing is North America? His answer: "because we have bought into gimmicks and programs, the razzle dazzle Las Vegas syndrome of Christianity, all flesh and lights and gaudiness. But we have forgotten what it means to be the church and do ministry."[1]

Ministry, Wagner argues, is not task but relationship. He speaks of attending numerous seminars on how to grow a church or manage a church and reading hundreds of books on leadership development but never getting past his frustration. He eventually found that the answer was not in sociological, psychological, or managerial expertise but in the simple act of being a shepherd to God's people.

Robert and Julia Banks call attention to the unique nature of the smaller church or of the larger church built around small groups. In relational churches and small groups, the biblical injunction to love one another (1 Peter 1:22) or care for one another (1 Cor. 12:25) or bear one another's burdens (Gal. 6:2) can be fulfilled. In this setting Christians are better able to commit to long-term relationships with a specific group of people. Deeper relationships can be fleshed out as believers seek to incarnate God's words and to embody them within a particular group of people."[2]

Pastor Brian McLaren personally faced the issue of leadership burnout and had to rethink his role in church structures. Through his own struggles and through the breakthroughs he and others have made, he writes of seven characteristics of the new leader, the seventh being "Leadership must *once again* become a matter of love and spirituality, a place for spiritual sages, *not just organizational technicians*" (italics mine).[3]

This recovery of servant leadership in the church is not just incidental. It is missional in nature. The church is not just a "saving station," it is a place for spiritual formation, for healing, for the formation of a countercultural community, a locality in this world where people live under the reign of God and thus witness by their corporate relationships and lives that this world and its ways of being are not all there is. When relationships are structured on mutual servant-hood and not power, the world sees a glimpse of heavenly reality where the powers have been put away and God's *shalom* rests over the entire created order. In this way, the very structure of the church is a witness to what it means to be brought under the reign of Jesus Christ, to bow the knee and confess that Jesus is Lord. He is Lord, not only of personal salvation, but also of all relationships and structures. His lordship of structures calls us to live and work with each other by the servant leadership which Jesus modeled. He was not the CEO of his disciples; he was their servant.

The Shift toward Servant Leadership

This call to servant leadership is being heard by the younger evangelicals. For example, Dawn Haglund, a younger evangelical, puts the difference be-tween the younger evangelicals and the boomers rather succinctly: "We have been given structures, but we don't really like what they've produced. We want to be about making disciples."[4] Frank Nihart thinks "rubber stamp minis-try has had a strangle hold on evangelicalism for too long. Local churches need to customize their ministries to their communities and the people in their par-ticular congregation."[5] Another younger evangelical struggles with a boomer pastor who is concerned about "church growth, platform personality and pro-gram development."[6]

When it comes to church leadership, what is the thinking of the younger evangelicals? Their viewpoint is still developing, but there are discernible trends.

It is clear that the younger evangelical wants to turn away from business models of leadership and return to biblical principles. Ken Blanchard, the au-thor of *The One Minute Manager*, recently told the registrants of a leadership con-ference that "the popular model of pastor as CEO is brain dead. . . . This philos-ophy will only hurt the church in the long run."[7] Leroy Armstrong, pastor of a church in Kentucky, responded that the megachurch movement of the last twenty years has been led by "superstar" pastors who are now "dying out or burned out" without having mobilized lay people for ministry. As a result, the church, which should be an army, "still looks like an audience."[8]

In an email questionnaire I asked, "What is the leadership style of your pas-tor?" The most frequent response was a negative view of boomer leadership. One younger evangelical wrote, "The senior pastor at my church acts out of a *top-down mentality*. For the most part if there is a decision to be made or a minis-try to be started, he is the one to start it (or at least get the credit for it). He seems to be more interested in power and looking important than in being a servant. He is the head coach and everyone else (including the other pastors) are only players."[9] Another younger evangelical expressing the same concern wrote, "My pastor likes the role of CEO. He has told the ministerial staff that we should 'be ranchers and not shepherds.' He characterizes himself as a 'soft perfectionist.' Mix all of this with his Ph.D. in biblical studies and you have an indecisive theologue who likes to reach out and sporadically micromanage areas of ministry. He is very program oriented and church-growth motivated. I would change his style by letting him know that he is not omniscient and that he does not have to 'run the show.' I wish he had enough faith in the Holy Spirit to help him understand Philippians 2, but he doesn't know how to humble himself and be a servant. He would be a great person and a great pastor if he would simply relax and be authentic with everyone."[10]

Other boomers, however, have not bought into the CEO model. Nathan Coleson, coleader of Breaking Bread, a street ministry to the homeless in Chicago, writes, "The primary objective of my pastor is to make disciples of Christ. He is very relational and down-to-earth in his approach and rightly acknowledges that he is only a shepherd and teacher and that in order for the Body of Christ to be what it's supposed to be, each and every person in the congregation must do their part and exercise their gifts. I can think of nothing offhand that would make him more effective and am grateful that New Life Church is all about the work of the kingdom and not a cult of personality with the senior pastor heading the show."[11]

Implicit within these criticisms of boomer leadership, the younger evangelical expresses a concern for a more biblical kind of leadership.

Priesthood of All Believers

In an article called "The Next Reformation," Len Hjalimarson claims that the priesthood of all God's people, first introduced by Luther, was lost as the church quickly returned to hierarchical structures of leadership. The challenge we face in restoring the priesthood of all God's people is (1) current leaders are accustomed to control; (2) leaders fear disorder if they are not in control; (3) a sense of "professional" leadership has crept into the church, which means pastors often rely on their natural talent, instead of the Spirit, and insist on looking and sounding respectable; (4) modern individualism has impacted our thinking causing us to lose the biblical perspective of the Spirit; and finally (5) we use the wrong dominant model in the church. Most of our churches have the larger body and smaller groups. The mistake of most churches is to import the large group into the smaller group rather than allowing the small groups to impact the larger group. This wrongly directed model eventually kills the small group rather than promoting "every member ministry." Leaders, Hjalimarson argues, must work to create a congregational life of full participation.[12]

To accomplish this "every member ministry," the younger evangelical is calling for a return to servant leadership. Dann Pantoja in the "Paradox of Postmodern Leadership" sees Jesus as the ultimate model of a servant leader. Here is the paradox. Jesus has supreme authority in "heaven and earth" (Matt. 20–28), yet in the kingdom of God Jesus himself rejects power-based leadership. His dual position, Pantoja remarks, is symbolized "by the throne and the towel." Leadership in the church needs to emulate the servant leadership of Jesus Christ.[13]

In this image of the "throne and the towel," younger evangelicals are finding a theology for Christian leadership. Jesus said he came not to be served but to serve; this is the substance of Christian leadership. Christian leadership is the opposite of the exercise of power, the CEO model of the executive that everyone obeys. The true model of Christian leadership is the servant model. Like God who became incarnate, putting himself in our place as the second Adam to serve us and the world as redeemer and savior of all, so we are called to *kenosis* (the emptying of self) to be servants of each other. In congregations where this servant attitude is modeled by the pastor, the congregants soon see the spirituality of a life lived for others. Emulating the pastor, the whole church may become a vital community of servants to each other within the church and outside the church in its service to the world.

The Team Ministry Model of Leadership

The immediate translation of the servant model among younger evangelicals is found in their development of a "team ministry" leadership. In this model, writes younger evangelical Greg Warner, "the goal is to work with the teams to facilitate the ministry of others." The trend, he says, is "away from staff-led, committee-run hierarchies to team-based ministry, where decision making is dispersed to lay-led ministry teams." This "team trend promises to return ministry to the people, providing a corrective for staffers who want to hoard power and church members who expect hired staffers to do the work." Warner knows the traditional church will have a difficult time transitioning into a team-based church because it will require them to abandon "committees, democratic rule and other proven mechanisms."[14] Younger evangelicals in traditional church settings are becoming increasingly frustrated with church bureaucracy. This frustration has led many younger evangelicals to leave churches that are run like businesses to lead start-up churches where they don't have to deal with committee structures and controlling bureaucrats.

An example of a start-up church based on team ministry is Christ Community Church in Olathe, Kansas. The church, which David Pendleton started nine years ago, has more than four hundred people, most of them in their twenties. I interviewed Pastor David and asked how he came to a servant-based team leadership ministry while so many churches during the past nine years have embraced the CEO model.

"I don't find the CEO model in Scripture," he said. "We want a biblically based church, not a business model. We want to follow the leadership of Jesus. He spoke as one having authority. And when he spoke in the synagogue of his hometown, all eyes were fixed on him. He certainly must have been a charismatic leader. But, he says of himself, 'I came to serve, not to be served.' We get our clue from Jesus. If we want to be like him, we are to be servants and ministers of each other."

"Does that pertain primarily to the church staff?" I asked.

"No," said David, "we are all called to be ministers of each other and the world. At Christ Community Church everyone is a minister. Everyone is a minister of reconciliation, salt, light, a saint to be equipped for ministry, a member of the body of Christ with a gift to be exercised on behalf of the whole."

"How does that theory translate into action here at Christ church?"

"We have seven ministry action teams—leadership, worship, outreach, discipleship, compassion/missions, finance, and building/equipment. Each ministry team is made up of elected board members, lay ministers, and one staff member. These people meet regularly to decide what needs to be done, then they do it."

"Give me an example."

"Let's take preaching as an example. The team is made up of board members, the preaching staff, and lay ministers. We meet weekly. We begin by reading and reflecting on the text. Each person reflects on the text out of his or her own experience. We own the text and allow it to own us. We listen out loud to what the text says. So people begin to formulate their interaction and I hear where the congregation is, what they are thinking, what they are going through, what they need to hear from the Word of God. In this way the sermon is birthed within the community. My preaching is not so much what I think they should hear but more a reflection on what they are going through and how God meets us in the midst of our troubles and joys."

"What," I asked, "are the advantages of team ministry?"

"I've found that it has helped us move toward an authentic experience of community. We do the ministry of the church together. For example, a few years ago I took a full year away from the church to complete my doctorate. My role in the church was not replaced. Without me there, the team ministries carried on the full work of the church.

"The point we younger evangelicals are discovering is that we have to really die to self and to our agendas. The missional church and servant leadership is not 'me' or 'my' leadership, it's more about God's mission in the world and how we all do it together. So, while I have my place in the church, I'm only one of many. Everybody bears the weight and does the work of the church."[15]

In sum, the younger evangelicals are committed to a new form of leadership. Many younger evangelical leaders are frustrated with the leadership of both the traditional and the contemporary boomer church. In the start-up church movement, younger leaders are more free to express themselves in ways that they believe are consistent with biblical principles and the situation of the church living in a postmodern culture. The rejection of business models of the church and the embrace of an "every member ministry" working together in team ministry under a commitment to servant leadership is a new kind of leadership for the twenty-first century (see table 11).

Table 11
Approach to Leadership

	Traditional Evangelicals	Pragmatic Evangelicals	Younger Evangelicals
The Origin of Leadership	Ordination	Vision	Calling
Management of Ministry	Board of elders or deacons	One person with the gift of leadership	Team ministry Consensus
Power Base	Congregation or representation of congregation	Founder Leader	Rejection of power Affirmation of ecclesial servanthood
Model	Hierarchical Top down	Hierarchical Top down	A circle of equals
Driving Force	Denominational power base	High-energy leader	A community of committed relationships
The Place of Diversity	Diversity generally rejected	Leadership diffused among staff members	Leadership diffused among members
The Right to Lead	Denominational or congregational appointment	Inherent within the person or position	Recognition of God's calling

10

Youth Ministers
From Parties to Prayer

My wake-up call to the new shift in youth ministry came in 1998 at a Methodist conference on the future of ministry. Of all the presentations at the conference, the speech that struck me as most important was made by a youth worker in a local church.

In sum, his speech went like this: "I followed the traditional approach to youth work. It was party, party, party—of the Christian sort, of course. We did skating parties, pizza parties, sleepovers, trips, retreats, and all the usual 'entertainment' plus a devotion to reach the young. But all of this was to no avail. Hardly anyone came. It was like banging my head against a brick wall. The more 'entertainment' I offered, the less the kids seemed interested.

"As I began to think and pray about my frustration at being unable to reach these kids, it was as though God spoke into my despair and said, 'You're doing the wrong thing. These kids have more entertainment than they need. Television, MTV, school parties and the like. They don't want more of the same in church. What they want is me. Give them me and they will come.'

"In obedience to what I heard God saying to me but with skepticism, fear, and trembling, I put an end to all the entertainment stuff and announced that the main event of our youth group was to be a Friday night prayer meeting. To my shock but utter delight kids have come out of the woodwork everywhere.

They sit on the floor and sing, they lay hands on each other and pray. I literally don't have enough space for all the kids who want to come and participate in this event."

His testimony made a huge impact on me and forced me to ask some simple questions: What's going on here? Why is this happening? What might this mean for the next generation of the church?

Historical Background

Youth ministry needs to be put into historical perspective. The whole concept of "youth ministry" is a phenomenon of the last century and especially of the last fifty years. Interest in young people as a particular societal group can be traced back to the formation of the YMCA in 1844 and to the first public high school in 1875. Around the turn of the century G. Stanley Hall, the so-called "Father of Adolescence," first coined the word *adolescent*. His work called attention to the unique change of life that occurs during the teenage years. Then in the twentieth century the study of youth and their passage into adulthood became subject to various theories through the work of Piaget, Kohlberg, Erikson, and Fowler. Since the rise of the boomer generation a whole library of generational studies has appeared.

In the last fifty years the church has developed ministries for the various age groups. Larger churches have ministries directed to preschoolers, grade-schoolers, junior high, high school, college-age students, and single adults. These generational ministries seek to contextualize the faith along the lines of development studies.

The recent concern to focus on various generations of youth is connected to the rapidity of change experienced in society. For example, in the first part of the twentieth century, change was gradual and often imperceptible. Most people lived either in the rural setting of the agricultural society or in the urban setting of the industrial society. Even the concept of "suburbs" was generally unfamiliar. In this context generational studies were not needed nor even thought about. However, beginning with the revolution of the sixties, society began to show new changes in every generation. The changing nature of culture and the impact it made on youth became apparent as the boomers who were born in the late forties and fifties came to maturity in the seventies and eighties. Because culture has continued to change so rapidly, it appears that each new generation is shaped by a new set of cultural values.

As children, baby boomers were told that they were wonderful, brilliant, full of potential, and could accomplish anything they wanted to. This message translated into an attitude of "the bigger the better" and into CEO management skills and power. The contemporary Christian movement reflected these values. As corporate America became big, powerful, and strong with distinguished self-made leaders in business, medicine, education, and politics, so the boomer Christian used similar market techniques to grow bigger, better, and more efficient churches.

These boomers were called the "first" generation. They were the first generation of the media phenomenon; the first generation of rapid cultural change; the first hippie generation; the first generation to experience the all-pervasive rise of music; the first generation to throw away tradition and traditional values; the first generation to grow up in the civil rights revolution and the emergence of the minority rights movement; the first generation in a time of emerging globalization of the world; the first generation in an entertainment culture; the first generation of the narcissistic culture; the first generation in a society that became slick; the first generation in the "packing" culture; the first generation to live in a permissive sexual society; the first generation to go through a nearly 50-percent divorce rate; and the first generation to experience death through AIDS.

The contemporary Christian movement applied a radical contextual approach to reach this culture with the Christian message. They became what Steve Gerali, specialist in youth ministry and professor at Northern Seminary, calls "back-boomer value driven." They created the contemporary worship movement and the megachurch phenomenon. They emphasized reaching seekers through personal contact, seeker-driven services, and small groups designed for growth. Boomer Christianity also reflected corporate America by placing emphasis on "big churches," "spectacular worship events," and "casual dress and relationship." Schooled by the church growth movement, these churches grew to phenomenal sizes and influence in North America and spread around the world. Even though these churches are full, attracting worldwide attention and still growing, Gerali observes that "the Contemporary Church, having been built and enmeshed in the generational values of the baby boomer, is alienating a generation of adolescents."[1]

A distinguishing feature of the current generation is that they are anti-boomer. According to Gerali, "They do not want to be like the Boomer nor do they embrace Boomer values and culture."[2] The young generation grew up and came of age in the eighties and nineties and experienced the devastating effects of their parents' cultural revolution. They were influenced negatively by their parents' pursuit of success, which made them the most neglected teenage generation of the twentieth century; by their parents' materialism, which resulted in materialistic wealth but not relationships; by the consequences of permissive sex, which meant the rise of AIDS; and by the increase in violence, which translated into school shootings and terrorism.

According to George Barna, "We have a generation coming up that doesn't speak the same language, doesn't go to the same places, doesn't have the same needs and isn't looking to Christianity to answer their spiritual concerns. . . . We either change or we lose them."[3]

Today's twenty-somethings are less affluent than their parents; are products of either two-income or single-parent families; were raised to take care of themselves; are the MTV generation, who have never known a time when they were not surrounded by electronic gadgets like microwaves, electronic entertainment, and computers for everything; are an intimacy-starved generation; feel a lot of anger over their neglected childhood; feel a sense of cultural dislocation and alienation; and are characterized by a deep yearning to belong.

How do members of this generation see themselves? What is their self-image? Gerali writes that "they see themselves as an alternative nation with alternative music representative of alternative lifestyles. They have become content on living on less; desire more intimate relationships; are more embracing of diversity in race and gender; are more accommodating of social need; and their individual identity is not based on what they accomplish, but rather on who they are. Their definition of success is relational fulfillment as opposed to financial gain."[4]

Recent generational studies show that the different cultural circumstances of the boomer and twenty-something have resulted in a different set of values. For example, the boomer is attracted to trendy entertainment worship that is glitzy, fashionable, and costly. The twenty-somethings feel this approach to worship is slick and inauthentic, and prefer a more personal form of worship in smaller groups. Boomers are into large church buildings that look like a corporate headquarters—slick, plain, powerful. Twenty-somethings look on these buildings as symbols of corporate America. They want smaller, more intimate places of worship with lots of symbolism—the more the better. Success for the boomer is tangible and usually described in terms of numbers, big buildings, big budgets, and strong individual "hero" leaders. Younger evangelicals detest these symbols of power and prefer smaller to bigger and authentic to slick.

They want smaller groups, smaller space, and fewer people, but deeper relationships, lifelong personal friendships. Twenty-somethings value authentic relationships, a deep sense of community, and genuine love and commitment to each other. They are turned off by churches where they are greeted with pasty, phony smiles and condescending trite conversation. They want the church to be friendly but sincerely friendly with genuine commitment to a relationship based on self-giving. They are turned away by corporation Christianity, by small groups that exist for growth rather than for developing deep lifelong relationships, and by generationally oriented ministries. They are more multicultural and intergenerational than boomers. Also, they do not like to be set apart as Generation X because they don't like being labeled.

The millennial generation (born since 1982) is very similar in many ways to the twenty-somethings. Generally, they share a disdain for the boomer generation and the kind of Christianity modeled after corporate culture. Because culture has been changing so rapidly in the last twenty years, generational watchers suggest we need to be aware of the way this new generation is being shaped by cultural changes.

As we have seen, today's twenty-somethings were raised at a time when their boomer parents were "doing their thing," climbing the corporate ladder, and paying attention to their own needs. But the new generation is creating a child-focused society characterized by child-value movements in nearly every area of life including a focus on child legislation, concern for abuse against children, children's rights, safety for children, and new interest in and a commitment to better education for children.

Due to these changes, sociologist Francis Fukuyama claims society is under-going a renorming. In this changing society new changes will impact the millen-nial culture and have an effect on youth ministry. Consider the following nine changes that are taking place and will continue to take place in the culture of people currently in their early twenties and teenage years.

First, changes have occurred and will continue to occur within the family. Although future families are likely to be more stable, there are distinct ways in which the new family will differ from the traditional family of the fifties. For one, gender-role restrictions have started changing. In more cases mothers will be the primary wage earner and fathers will assume more of the nurturing of the children. In many homes family will be more important than career. Children will experience both quality and quantity time from their parents.

Second, there will be a shift away from big corporate business and a revival of small family-owned business in which the entire family may be involved. Work-ing and sharing together will reshape family life in many homes, creating a kind of alternative ideal to the money-oriented family of the boomer era.

Third, a general downsizing will take place whereby small is seen as better than big. The desire for smaller groups, more intimate and longer lasting rela-tionships at work, in the home, and in personal relationships will appear.

Fourth, societal changes will impact culture. For example, the changing sta-tus of women in society and places of leadership will become increasingly com-mon. Ethnic blending will result in less racism, more intermarriage between races, and a more homogeneous sense of society.

Fifth, the emergence of a world culture will be expressed in a more global consciousness and increasingly find its way into the entertainment industry and spirituality.

Sixth, new advances in technology such as the internet, cybernetics, and vir-tual technology have changed and will continue to change our forms of commu-nication. Access to chatroom relationships will continue to create a new form of virtual reality.

Seventh, the millennial generation is the first generation to be born into and to grow up with the postmodern philosophy of relativism. They know little of the old Newtonian mechanistic dualistic distinction between spirit and matter. This philosophical shift will have a multitude of cultural implications, such as the search for truth, a turn to community, a trust in image, and a sense of embodied reality.

Eighth, the spirituality of the New Age movement, which draws from Eastern philosophies and religions, has become an intricate part of our current culture. We as a society are literally preoccupied with the supernatural in movies, books, and life in general. The rise of astrology, witchcraft, and the occult as alternative and even respectable religions is now a fact of life that millennials deal with on a regular basis.

Ninth, living in the time of the war on terrorism has engendered a new patriotism but also a tentativeness about life and a vulnerability to the spiritual side of life. Life has become more restricted, less carefree. Younger people face a new world since September 11, 2001, a world whose changes will produce a person with a vastly different outlook than that of the sixties revolution or the eighties and nineties prosperity.

Examples of the Future of Youth Worker Ministry

How will the current cultural changes impact the way youth workers work with and reach out to the younger generation? First, youth ministry of the future will be more intergenerational and intercultural. Today's young people do not like to be segmented by either age or culture. They are "both-and" not "either-or." Andy Crouch, a leader of younger evangelical thought, writes, "The segmentation of the American church is dangerous to its health, because the church is not in the business of marketing a product. Segmentation, when not practiced with great care, self-consciousness, and humility, can be fatal, because the real danger of segmentation is that we will forget the gospel . . . The church, if it is to be the church, will undo what the marketers have done."[5]

But what will this church of an undone marketer's strategy look like? What kind of church and youth ministry will attract and hold the younger generation? Kevin Graham Ford, author of *Jesus for a New Generation*, suggests three characteristics for outreach to the younger generation.

First, the youth work of the future must be rooted in an embodied apologetic (see chap. 6). Ford rightly states that the question today is not "Can Christians prove what they believe?" but "Can Christians live what they believe?"[6]

Second, youth workers will reach youth through process evangelism (see chap. 15). Ford points to Jesus as the one who models process evangelism: "He committed himself to a process of evangelizing, not just an evangelistic event." This he accomplished by entering "into the world of the twelve disciples. He identified with their pain and their broken condition; he devoted great amounts of time building his life into their lives."[7]

Third, Ford argues that the young will be reached through narrative (see chap. 5). "As our culture increasingly moves away from logic and proposition-oriented thought forms and deeper into feelings-oriented and transrationally oriented thought forms, the only evangelism that speaks the language of the culture is a story-oriented evangelism."[8]

Wendy Murray Zoba has studied the twenty-somethings and millennial youth in particular. In her recent book, *Generation 2K*, she provides us with some examples of reaching youth with substance, not parties. One example of an embodied model of church is found in *Souled Out*, an innovative kids-ministering-to-kids ministry in Mount Prospect, Illinois. The main event is Thursday-night outreach worship. This service draws mostly unchurched kids whose lives are broken because of divorce, drugs, sex, and aimless living. After the service the Christian kids, most of them with their own history of brokenness, begin to minister to other kids. "Young people ministering to their peers put their arms around their hurting brothers and sisters and spend as much time as they need in prayers and ministry." One student leader, David, whose life was transformed at *Souled Out*, now ministers to his peers. "God is totally using me," he says. "I'm like, thank you, God."[9]

Process evangelism is found at Arbutus United Methodist Church in Baltimore, Maryland. Here the confirmation process drew from the Jewish bar mitzvah and the Christian catechesis process that goes all the way back to the third and fourth centuries. The process includes a "six-month period of preparation" during which each converting person is "assigned a lay adult mentor who [takes] the child under his or her wing for fellowship and spiritual inquiry." The process climaxes in a ritual ceremony on Pentecost Sunday where the young are engaged in a rite of passage that brings them into the full fellowship of the church.[10]

Another church, Shadow Mountain Community Church, in El Cajon, California, has pioneered small-group discipleship that is student led. In these meetings five things happen. First is a discussion time called *fresh bread* in which youth tell what God has been "baking" in their lives. Second, an *empty chair* is placed prominently in every group to remind them of the person that should be sitting there. Third, the *announcements* connect the more than forty groups that meet individually during the week and together on Sunday. Fourth is the *lesson*, where the student leader "gets into the Word," and fifth is a time called *prayer, care, share*, when recorded needs are presented to God and discussed week by week, as answers to prayer are forthcoming.[11]

I asked two youth workers from Christ Presbyterian Church in Edina, Minnesota, to reflect on how they do youth ministry, and here is how they responded:

Why are there so few young people at our Sunday services? Why don't our students experience God here at home like they do at camp? Has the culture and the world around us changed the way people experience God in worship?

With these questions at the forefront of our minds, last winter we set off on an experimental worship service called the Upper Room. Our goal was to create a worship service that would focus on restoring the sacred elements of Christianity through a uniquely experiential worship service. Although we knew the message and the values of our church needed to remain the same, the method of delivery was going to be radically different.

One way that the Upper Room is different is in the design of the service itself. Most worship services have a linear structure. . . . The Upper Room service, however, is designed organically. . . . The Upper Room focuses on the worship experience in a holistic way and uses every element of the service as potential points of worship.

In an Upper Room service, atmosphere is an integral tool in engaging people's senses in worship. Each service begins with the ringing of church bells, which calls people to worship. The lights are dimmed and candles are used to illuminate the Sanctuary, which brings people to a place of prayerful reflection. Lighting systems and video screens project stained glass windows and ancient Christian images that relate to the night's theme. The smell of burning incense calls people to lift their praises and petitions to God. By lowering a curtain from the balcony, the main floor of the Sanctuary is enclosed and a greater sense of community is created. Ultimately, our goal is to create an atmosphere that engages people's senses (sight, sound, touch, taste and smell) and to invite people to actively worship God.

Active participation in the worship service is another critical element of the Upper Room. The first way in which we encourage participation is through the use of ancient prayer corners. Placed in various locations throughout the Sanctuary, prayer corners invite people to come forward and kneel as they light candles and offer prayers to God. Another participatory element comes during the message. The speaker often interacts with the congregation, asking questions and soliciting responses that are then incorporated into the message. Finally, when celebrating Communion, the congregation is asked to come forward and kneel as they participate in the sacrament together as a community.

In addition to the service's structure, atmosphere and participatory elements, music is strongly emphasized in the Upper Room. Our desire is to weave together sacred hymns of the past with contemporary songs of today into a litany of music. As much as possible, we try to connect the music to the theme for the evening. Ancient images that relate to each song are used as backdrops for song lyrics and are projected onto video screens. By using a stage extension, the band is brought closer to the congregation, diminishing the performance-based feel of worship and bringing all participants closer together in worship.[12]

These examples demonstrate that youth work oriented around programs, parties, skits, entertainment, or market-driven techniques overlaid with a devotion are a style of the past. Youth work has become serious Bible study, prayer, and healing based on committed relationships and a nonjudgmental understanding of the brokenness of the lives of today's youth. It is driven by a missional understanding of the church and by a commitment to be an embodied presence of Jesus in and to the world (see table 12).

Table 12
Approach to Youth Work

	Traditional Evangelicals	Pragmatic Evangelicals	Younger Evangelicals
Outreach	Programs primarily for church families	Programs for outreach	Interactive worship, prayer, and Bible study
Context	Assume some Christian understanding	Secular world New Age spirituality	Postmodern pluralism and relativism
Focus	Provide alternative fun and games	Focus on individual needs	Create a community of open and real people
Approach	Parties with a devotion	Friendships that foster conversion opportunities	Immerse seeking persons into communities of faith
Message	Salvation of the soul Faith is birthed in a decision for Christ	Jesus can meet your need and give you meaning	Faith is birthed in a welcoming community where Jesus is embodied and lived out Discipleship is a lifelong process

11

Educators
From Information to Formation

Atlantic Monthly recently carried a four-part feature article entitled "The Opening of the Evangelical Mind." The introductory blurb stated, "'Of all America's religious traditions,' the author writes, 'evangelical Protestantism, at least in the twentieth-century conservative forms, has long ranked "dead last in intellectual stature." Now evangelical thinkers are trying to revitalize their tradition. Can they turn an intellectual backwater into an intellectual beacon?'"[1] The article dealt with evangelical colleges and seminaries noting that students at Wheaton College "are as outstanding as any students in America" and spoke equally as high of Fuller Theological Seminary and Calvin Theological Seminary.

We welcome the recognition of evangelical schools and the raising of the intellectual bar in local church education. But the younger evangelicals are raising some concerns about how one learns and processes information in a postmodern setting.

Twenty-eight-year-old David Clark puts his finger on the primary issue: "Information is important only if it leads to transformation. I teach theology for the purpose of developing character and wisdom. Information without transformation is pointless. Too much theology, seen as objective science, is taught from this point of view."[2] Younger evangelicals agree. They feel knowledge is often taught apart from its life connection, especially biblical and theological knowl-

163

edge. What younger evangelicals want is not mere information but a Christian way of thinking.

Paul Jones learned "how to think" at Regent College and claims, "Knowing how to think has enabled me to learn far more by enabling me to integrate thinking from different fields of study, and also by increasing my ability to grapple with real-life issues that have not necessarily even been dealt with in the classroom."[3] Paul Christenson agrees. "The classes I have taken," he writes, "where I had to memorize information to satisfy the teacher have had no lasting impact on me."[4] Dawn Haglund frequently comes across people in her ministry in the local church "who know a lot of information" but in whom there is no change of life. "For instance," she writes, "I have talked to people who communicate to me that they are having 'feelings' incongruent with their 'knowledge.' They will tell me that they feel hopeless or depressed or are having trouble with an addiction, but in the same breath they tell me all these things they 'know' about God being good and wanting to help with these things and being a powerful, healing compassionate God." Her concern is that there is a disconnect between knowledge and experience. She asks, "How do we get people to match their intellectual knowledge to their actions and hearts to bring about a change?"[5] Transformation is the issue for the younger evangelical leaders, an issue that will shape their teaching presence in the local church, in colleges, and in seminaries.

Conflict between Modern and Postmodern Approaches to Christian Education

My own college and graduate theological studies were all done in the context of a modern view of education. I completed my graduate studies in 1968 and was interviewed that year to teach in the theology department of Wheaton College. My entire interview was on the question of a Christian worldview. What is it? How do we develop it? How do we teach it? Wheaton College soon instituted a course for faculty members that dealt with these matters. This course and the writing of a paper on a Christian view of one's teaching discipline became and still is a requirement for tenure.

But today the younger evangelical questions the priority given to Christianity as worldview. Younger evangelical Charles Moore writes, "The idea of Christianity as a worldview is essentially Gnostic. It makes Christianity an idea, a philosophical viewpoint, a construct. Christianity is primarily a kingdom, an embodied reality and is more about a faithful discipleship than affirming an intellectual construct." Moore argues that making Christianity a worldview "abstracts reason from history and pits the existing, choosing subject against the object. It reduces Christianity to metaphysics."[6] This is the problem that so many young people in evangelical colleges and seminaries experience. Christianity, when presented as a worldview, is turned into a cognitive subject to be discussed, debated, and proven. What is lacking, as Dawn Haglund pointed out, is the personal dimension. "We have enough people," she writes, "who have all the 'right' information. We need to learn to be about the kind of disciples that God intends us to be."[7] Moore agrees. "Christ sought 'followers,' not 'believers.' He did not come to describe the world—he came to demonstrate and embody the coming reign of God."[8]

For Moore and Haglund, the evidence of the Christian faith is more than intellectual evidence. It is truth becoming truth. The evidence is not in the abstract—a thing "out there." No. The evidence of truth, as Moore states, "depends on the power of its beliefs to shape a community of truthfulness. . . . Christianity is more than a set of beliefs, because it is a form of life . . . a practice, an existence, a way of being in the world. . . . It is a pattern of acting and being."[9]

This emphasis on truth as a lived experience may cause modern evangelicals alarm. Moore does not mean to reject the metanarrative that sweeps from creation to the fall to the redemption and hope of the new heavens and the new earth. He addresses, rather, a problem that evangelical young people sense which is fostered, I believe, by a Christianity too thoroughly enmeshed with the modern outlook based on reason and science. In our schools and churches we have become ideological competitors who have bought into the "worldview" method of education to counter secularism and support the Christian worldview. But in doing so, says the younger evangelical, the side of education that has been neglected is embodied truth, the truth that lives in *me* and in *you*, the truth that we are called to live out, to be. This shift in emphasis, which derives from the general shift toward subjectivity and experience, is a much needed balance, a balance that needs to find expression in the education of the local church, in our seminaries, and in other places where people are trained for ministry.

The Younger Evangelical Speaks Out on Education

Education in the Local Church

How does this embodiment approach to education get translated into the local church? A good example is found in the work of Mark Driscoll, pastor of Mars Hill Fellowship in Seattle. First, Driscoll rejects the idea of Sunday school classes for different age groups. "Departmental churches," he writes, "are basically poor rip-offs of suburban malls where the entire family can walk in and consume products from a variety of stores waiting to serve them under one roof." Driscoll feels the boomer church has been too thoroughly shaped by a consumer mentality. We have been about creating the Wal-Mart church where "we have a 'store' for kids, moms, dads, divorcees, teens, singles, etc." What's wrong with what seems so successful in the megachurch? "Any sense of community," Driscoll writes, "is foreign." The mentality that presents spiritual consumer goods for each generation "has killed the ability for shepherding through difficult life transitions because you are expected to leap into a new ministry, with a new pastor and a new community, at the most difficult transition in your life (i.e., from junior high to high school to college, college to employment, employment to marriage, marriage to parenting, marriage to divorce, etc.)."[10]

Second, Driscoll thinks the generational approach to Sunday school "explains why most kids bail out after high school."[11] The younger evangelicals reject the concept of "generational targets." Their underlying passion is to participate in a community of people that embody the Christian community. It is difficult to emulate 1 Corinthians 12 about how the body works together so that "to each one the manifestation of the spirit is given for the common good" (v. 7) when members of the body are separated into different age groups. Today's twenty-somethings and the millennials want to be with their parents and grandparents; they want family, not isolation. They want the wisdom of their elders. When they do not receive an intergenerational perspective, the information they receive in their Sunday school often does not take root.

So, what do they do at Mars Hill? Driscoll writes, "We don't run Sunday school because one department can adequately build [faith and action] into a person. Instead we run classes and home Bible studies on a huge variety of topics, from missiology to prayer, according to what the teachers/leaders want to do. They have the pulse of our people and we trust them."[12]

When Bible courses are taught, the emphasis is not on memorizing Bible information but entering into the biblical story and becoming an extension of the narrative. "Narrative teaching" writes Driscoll, "is gaining popularity because it recognizes more fully the original context into which a revelation was given, and strongly interacts with what the original people and circumstances were, then moves to see the present, not as an application, but rather as an extension of the biblical story all connected to the gospel metanarrative."[13]

Leadership Training

The commitment of the younger evangelicals to an embodied Christian truth has compelled them to take new approaches to leadership training. In many places seminary education is in crisis, and training for ministry is shifting to alternative approaches. At least six factors are responsible for this shift.

First, most seminaries in North America are tied down to a curriculum that reflects modernity. For example, Brad Cecil, a younger evangelical who pastors Axxess at Pantego Bible Church in Arlington, Texas, dropped out of seminary for this reason. He says he has "no regrets." "Seminaries," he says, "ignore the shift in the way people think and process information."[14] Many other students who have dropped out of seminary and many who have stayed and graduated agree. "Seminary training," writes Pat Cole, "is too beholding to systematic and rationalistic thinking." Both are products of the Enlightenment. "Such dependence," he argues, "leaves little room for awe and mystery that ancient Christians valued and for which postmodern people yearn."[15]

Second, students feel strongly that those who are trained for ministry in the postmodern world need to listen to the text of culture, especially the culture of the poor and oppressed. John Wallis, an architect and lay leader in the church who studied at Northern Seminary, writes of his experience. As a young Christian he had been schooled in modernity and shaped by a separatistic and withdrawal approach to culture. He felt that he was living in a Christianized cultural cocoon—a white, middle-class existence of "separation and superiority" that "fit well with lessons my culture had taught me." His goal was "to return the church and the country to its Christian heritage." But at Northern, one of the most multicultural seminaries in the evangelical world, he began to be "awakened to God and *his* world."[16]

This world was the world of the poor, of the oppressed, a world that was multicultural. John and his wife enfleshed their faith. They adopted two biracial boys. John writes, "I sat one morning holding this baby, biracial and fresh to the world, in one hand and the book *God of the Oppressed* in the other. I felt as if I would explode. Then from nowhere it hit me, my context, my worldview, my faith had been shaped by a culture that wanted to dominate and control how I saw the world and God. . . . It was clear to me that my culture had formed my faith and when the construction was challenged, [the culturalized faith] collapsed. . . . I now see my call as one of helping others to see how their cultural view of the world and their faith needs to be expanded."[17]

Wallis's experience was that of being brought into "the real world." Much of the evangelical experience of culture seems to protect "white suburbia." Younger evangelicals reject the caricature of a white middle-class suburban evangelical faith and are turning to the urban culture to minister to the poor, the oppressed, and multicultural communities. They want seminary to equip them for the challenge, but most evangelical seminaries still educate students for the world of modernity and white suburbia, the old world of the twentieth century that no longer exists.

Third, the younger evangelical wants a training that approaches theology from a more traditional yet creative and applicable way. Jay Phelan Jr., president of North Park Theological Seminary, is aware of this need. He studied seminary, college, and Bible college catalogs from around the world to understand how evangelical schools treated theology. He found that evangelical schools declared the Bible to be the final authority. However, they bypassed the universal creeds of the early church and the great confessions of the Reformation to create their own statement of faith binding on all students and faculty. What he frequently found was "a detailed statement of faith that faculty was required to adhere to. This statement of faith was much more constricting than any creed I know, and not as carefully written as many confessions."[18]

Unfortunately the statements of faith in evangelical settings often reflect the assumptions of modernity. They stifle and suppress freedom of thought in the classroom. The younger evangelical is offended and put off by statements of faith that reflect modern culturalized interpretations of Christianity. On the other hand, the younger evangelical is committed to the authority of the Bible and to the value of ancient creeds and reformational confessions as important guidelines and signposts for the creative, thoughtful thinking of the church.

Phelan speaks for the younger evangelical when he writes, "Theological and biblical thought must be lively, controversial, relevant and alive. . . . We should not be afraid to question, to push, to challenge."[19] Theological education that is nothing more than information boxed in by a modern statement of faith will not attract, engage, or hold the minds and hearts of the new postmodern generation of evangelicals. The younger evangelicals believe theological education should allow students a good dose of freedom in their thinking. Such freedom is reflected in the thinking of Chad Allen, an editor for Baker Book House. In response to the culturalized notion of biblical inerrancy, he writes,

I still hold the Bible to be authoritative for my life, but I'm now aware that the Bible has to be interpreted. And because the Bible has "led" people to do all sorts of things, from embracing social outcasts (see Mother Teresa) to committing mass murder (see Adolf Hitler), whose interpretation you believe really matters. So, whose interpretation should we believe? I think a good place to start is the church because the church existed for quite a while before Scripture did and because the church gave us Scripture in the first place. When I read Scripture, more and more I find myself asking, How has the church interpreted this passage throughout history? Of course, often one has to discern between a number of interpretations that have existed within the church, and ecclesial interpretations still should be balanced with advances in archeology, new interpretive insights, one's own experience, and other biblically informed yet fresh thought, but in general they are a much better starting place than the thoughts of my own third-millennium head.

I'm moving away from the idea that Scripture is authoritative because so-and-so told me it's "God's infallible, inerrant Word" to the idea that Scripture is authoritative because God's faithful people have taken it to be authoritative throughout history. This is our book! For centuries we the church have chosen the Bible to be the book that calls our lives into question. When you read the Bible, you are stepping into a long line of saints—past, present, and future—who look to the Bible to learn about God, humanity, and the relationship between the two. I still believe Scripture is from God, but my understanding of this belief is more nuanced now. God didn't take a holy quill from on high and scrawl out a manuscript for us. He could have if he wanted to, of course, but God's more relational than that. He wanted to involve us in the process, loving God that he is, so he communicated his Word through his people. It is this people—this knock-kneed, bleary-eyed, sometimes very unlovable people, whom God loves anyway and through whom God chose to communicate himself—it is this people to whom I've chosen to belong. That is why the Bible is authoritative for me.

Fourth, the younger evangelical longs for training that will lead to wisdom and spiritual leadership. Seminaries that are still committed to an Enlightenment education tend to produce critical inquiry. Biblical studies have more to do with authorship and historical criticism than the message. A student may spend a semester on whether there were one or two Isaiahs or study Ephesians and wrestle with what portions came from Paul and what came from a later writer in the school of Paul. In the meantime the message of Isaiah or Paul is not adequately discussed or applied to pastoral ministry.

In more recent years some seminaries, highly influenced by the market approach to the church, have concentrated on training managers. David Wells points out that "many schools now train a pastor to be an institutional manager, a psychologist, a CEO, a denominational politician, an entrepreneur."[20] While the boomer megachurch may thrive on this misguided approach to ministerial education, many younger evangelicals will have none of it. For them it is not only *passé* but questionable. It lacks theological integrity.

This kind of pragmatism divides theology from praxis. For example, Ellen Charry speaks for the younger evangelical when she says, "The major doctrinal contributions of Athanasius, Basil of Caesarea, Augustine, Anselm, St. Thomas, Julian and John Calvin among others—all arose from a 'salutary principle' which read scripture in view of its 'aretegenic teleology'" (virtue producing aims). As these greats of the church labored in Christian doctrine, "moral, psychological, and social implications were uppermost in their minds. . . . They could not envision a notion of truth that is not salutary."[21]

The problem with modernity is that it has separated theology from practice. All the early church theologians were pastors. As time went on, theology and ministry became two disciplines that lost their relationship with each other. The goal of Christian education in our postmodern setting is to return these two disciplines to the unity they truly enjoy and to recover the salutary impact of good theology. The younger evangelical craves this unity between theology and practice knowing that in theology one finds wisdom for the practice of ministry and that all good practice is embodied in good theology.

Finally, recognizing that seminary education is in crisis, various seminaries are looking for ways to change the formation of ministers. Commenting on how difficult this assignment is for seminaries, R. Scott Rodin, former president of Eastern Baptist Theological Seminary, writes, "Consider the following: the marks of the postmodern worldview include a shift from knowledge to experience, from classroom learning to living-room learning, from belief in doctrine to belief in dialogue, from informational teaching to mentored learning, from right answers to right relationships, from the single leader to teams, and from church loyalty to distrust of institutional religion. In the face of all these new realities pastors must be skilled and prepared to be authentic, real, believable, relational leaders."[22] A student responding to a questionnaire sent out by Eastern Baptist Theological Seminary aptly stated the problem: "If you graduated from seminary before 1985, you were trained to lead a church that no longer exists."[23]

Consequently, Rodin reports, "The time has come to re-create seminary education in order to meet the needs of a church in a rapidly changing society." These changes include "relevance, agility, dynamism, transformational leadership, global and cross-cultural engagement, adult learning pedagogy, technology in the classroom, interdisciplinary team teaching, mentoring, reflection/praxis learning methods, core competencies, intensive internships, spiritual and character formation, assessments with teeth, agenda-setting courses, and contextualization."[24]

In the meantime the younger evangelical leadership is taking the issue into their own hands and creating postmodern ways of training leaders for the church. Andy Crouch and his colleagues have created Regeneration Forum. Rooted in historic Christianity, the mission of the forum is to "gather emerging Christian leaders across deep differences, advancing conversations and relationships that will impact the future of the church and the culture." The primary audience for the forum is "college educated Christians beginning careers for leadership in the academy, the arts, business and the professions, the home, media, politics and the church." The method is to bring Christians from Protestant, Catholic, and Orthodox backgrounds as well as multicultural situations together to focus on "conversations and relationships that cross disciplinary and professional lines, believing that interaction is essential to addressing the multi-faceted challenges of the postmodern flood." A concluding and, I think, very telling comment of the Regeneration mission statement is "we have a deep connection to historical Christianity that balances the general youthfulness of our audience."[25]

It is of equal interest to note the values of the Regeneration Forum, values that reflect younger evangelical leadership. They do not want conversation simply for the sake of conversation but to move toward five stated values: (1) the priority of community over privatized views of faith; (2) the comprehensive nature of the gospel extending it across every area of nature and culture; (3) the necessity of discernment in an attempt to cultivate clear thinking in the context of a sound-bite church; (4) to emphasize the primacy of culture engagement so to resist Christian marginalization and encourage Christian participation in the wider artistic culture; and (5) to stress the importance of realizing the unity of the church without abandoning deeply held convictions.[26]

Finally, the forum sponsors The Vine, a gathering of young Christians modeled after the Renaissance Weekends—when people gather together for open-ended discussion without a predetermined agenda. This conference does not bring in speakers. It is completely participant led. Each participant prepares a presentation to give to a small group gathered to discuss a topic of mutual interest. Then in plenary sessions a team of people engage all the participants in a discussion. The Vine has met with huge success around the country and in a few years has established chapters in many city centers. Kristin Fitzgerald, a professional staff member in the Education and Workforce Committee of the United States House of Representatives, wrote, "My husband and I love The Vine because of the relationships we have formed there. Coming from a Protestant-Catholic marriage, developing ecumenical community is of the utmost importance to both of us. The insight of others from different Christian walks builds and deepens our own faith."[27]

The impact of The Vine and of the Regeneration Forum on postmodern leadership in the church and the society is very important and holds the potential to be a key to training Christian leaders in a postmodern society. They have the right mission, values, and methods for our time. They probably will not replace seminary education, but they do offer seminary administrators and professors key insights into both the purposes and methods of leadership training for the twenty-first century.

I have attempted to show the crisis of Christian education in a postmodern world. While our educational institutions are rising in intellectual stature, they are decreasing in influence. The problem lies with the perpetuation of an Enlightenment agenda in a postmodern world. Administrators, clergy, and scholars need to recognize that education in the seminary and in the church should be more than the accumulation of information and knowledge. True education forms character, wisdom, spiritual sensitivity, and servanthood leadership. True education is not only knowledge but knowledge embodied and lived out individually and in community. The mission of the church in education is not to provide factual information that is memorized but wisdom that forms character and is embodied in a life (see table 13).

Table 13
Approach to Education

	Traditional Evangelicals	Pragmatic Evangelicals	Younger Evangelicals
Purpose	Knowledge	Answer felt needs	Spiritual formation
Style	Lecture	Lecture Discussion	Interactive All are learners and teachers
Context	Classroom setting	Small-group setting	Small groups Café setting Art centers Bookstores

(continued)

Table 13
Approach to Education

	Traditional Evangelicals	Pragmatic Evangelicals	Younger Evangelicals
Group Makeup	Generational	Generational	Intergenerational
Cultural Identity	Homogeneous	Homogeneous	Heterogeneous
Philosophy of Christianity	Christianity is a worldview	Christianity provides meaning	Christianity calls us to embody being truly human
Goal	Assurance of salvation	Therapeutic Christianity heals people	Discipleship Christianity challenges us to embody the new life in community

12

Spiritual Formation
From Legalism to Freedom

Those of us who grew up in the sixties and seventies remember the day when a secular humanist was behind every bush, the day when serious theologians declared that God had actually suffered a metaphysical death, and the time when any mention of the word spirituality was regarded as quaint and irrelevant.

But all that has changed. The introduction of New Age spirituality that espouses everything from "out of body" experiences to getting in touch with dead relatives, massaging a person's aura, reading astrology charts, conversations with your personal angel, and the spirituality of Oprah, has completely changed the meaning and use of the word *spirituality.*

For example, spirituality is a subject of study in secular universities. *The Chronicle of Higher Education* recently featured a syllabus from Emory University dealing with religion and ecology. "If you really want to become a tree," the syllabus proclaimed, "try to become it, sit beneath it. Match your breathing to the rustle of the wind ruffling its leaves. Soak up the sun beating on its roots. Listen to the birds in its branches." Ms. Patterson, the director of Emory's Theory, Practice and Learning Program, calls it "Forest Meditation" and claims it's one of the best ways to grasp "the connections between nature and what happens to us when we're in it."[1]

Spirituality is also happening in corporate America. Barbara Denman writes, "Corporate America, long portrayed as a den of thieves, focused on nothing but the bottom line, may be in the grip of a spiritual revival of sorts—a social sector in search of its soul."[2] A new book, *Jesus CEO* by Laurie Beth Jones, was on the *Business Week* best-seller list for eighteen months. Leaders are urged to follow the management principles introduced into the world by Jesus. His three primary principles were "self-mastery, action and relationship."

The author, who began her study of Jesus twenty years ago, was "struck by the fact that [Jesus] had only three years to train 12 people, none of whom were divine, to go out and change the world, and that he trained them so effectively that they went on to do the work after he left. I asked, What did he do with these people to turn them into such lean, clean marketing machines? What skills did he possess that we could duplicate or learn from?"[3]

Poor Jesus . . . the new corporate guru!

These examples show that the very concept or idea of spirituality or being a spiritual person has changed radically from the neglect of spirituality fifty years ago.

From Legalism to Freedom

I grew up in a home of rules, most of which would be considered quaint today. In my home it was forbidden to go to movies, play cards, drink alcohol, dance, smoke, neck, use words like *darn* or *gosh*, or do anything on Sunday other than go to church and rest. Even listening to a ball game or doing school work on Sunday was a no-no. I was taught that one who wanted to be spiritual was self-disciplined against all these worldly activities and that, if scorned in school, one wore the badge of suffering for Jesus. The other side of being a spiritual person resulted from a daily reading of Scripture, personal prayer, carrying a Bible to school, being a witness, and regular attendance at church—Sunday school, morning worship, young people's late afternoon fellowship time, evening service, and Wednesday night prayer meeting.

Spirituality was clearly defined. It was a discipline of do's and don'ts. The problem with this kind of spirituality is that it resulted in legalism and stood in the way of affirming the biblical concept of spirituality, which is to become free to be fully human.

My first real contact with the biblical concept of freedom came in 1964 through the reading of Daniel Stevick's *Beyond Fundamentalism*. Stevick, a graduate of Wheaton College, grew up with the same kind of rule-keeping emphasis that shaped my understanding of the spiritual life. I remember how struck I was with the following words from his text:

Fundamentalism has made over Christian life and obedience into a handy list of "do's" and "don'ts." Our world is faced by staggering problems affecting every person, family and community [here follows a list of the major problems facing the world in the early 1960s], yet in the face of the claim of a broken world—a world whose brokenness is ours—the fundamentalist ethic still concentrates on marking out the moral universe into black and white areas and avoiding contamination. It is principally concerned with its own purity.[4]

I began to discover that the legalism that had trapped me into the "handy list of do's and don'ts" prevented me from the full experience of grace and the freedom to become fully human. Stevick wrote these words that at first I could not comprehend:

Grace cannot move with pat formulas and ready-made answers. . . . Grace cannot be schematized. . . . Grace puts us in touch with ourselves—perhaps for the first time. It does not ask us to play a role or adopt a pose. If it is really grace, it opens the possibilities of individuality and spontaneity. . . . The Holy Spirit in every case, through all of the variety, means to take over weak, sinful human lives and re-create them in the image of Jesus Christ.[5]

It took years for the meaning of this biblical concept of God's grace and spirituality to gradually free me from legalism toward an affirmation of spirituality as authentic humanity. I finally came to see that my fallen sinful state is not normal but abnormal. When I choose to live by the sins of the flesh, I am choosing to bring my self under the bondage and condemnation of the law. But, because I am in Christ, I can choose to live by the Spirit. And when I do, I am choosing to become the person God created me to be, a human being made after the likeness of God. Jesus, by his death and resurrection, has made reconciliation with God possible. And, by his life, he has modeled for us all that it means to be truly human and in full union with God. This incarnate understanding of spirituality frees us from the constricting power of legalism into the glorious freedom of being authentic and real.

Examples of Legalism vs. Freedom

Perhaps a few examples given to me by twenty-somethings will help to clarify this tension between legalism and freedom. First, Julie Ann Vingers tells a story of her encounter with legalism in a seminary class. A case study is under discussion. Here is the case. A woman living with her boyfriend and involved in a local Bible study wants to become a Christian. She approaches the leader to lead her to Christ. But the leader says, "No, you can't become a Christian until you stop sleeping with your boyfriend." Here are Julie's comments:

Imagine my surprise and horror to discover that the majority of my classmates felt the leader had done the right thing! They were so hung up on the issue of sex, that they missed the fact this woman wanted a relationship with God! I asked them if a person was obese if they wouldn't allow them to know Christ until they lost weight since gluttony was also considered a sin . . . Don't we all enter into the relationship with God as sinners?[6]

Julie explains what this generation of younger evangelicals want. They want to be authentic, real and genuine. They are tired of the phony games people play, the pharisaical attitude that puts up a front and doesn't meet people where they are. She writes:

Evangelical Christians have an image in their minds of how a Christian is to look and act. I feel we look more like Pharisees than anything else! I mean, really, if Jesus had come to earth today, His disciples would have been drug dealers, crack addicts, gang leaders and hookers, and dare I say, women. I think He would stay as far away from evangelical churches as He could. And His ideas would be so radical and "blasphemous" that our churches would work as hard as they could to discredit Him in any way they could. I get scared sometimes that we wouldn't even recognize Him as anything but a "cult leader" if He came today.[7]

Julie speaks for the younger evangelical when she finds the answer to legalism in unconditional love:

When someone offers you true unconditional love, even in the face of hurt or failure on our part, the response is one of wanting to try harder, to do better, to please the one who loves you. I think humans are afraid that if you offer someone unconditional love you will get taken advantage of . . . but the opposite is true. When you try to extract punishment or revenge or demand a certain conformity of behavior, that is when rebellion takes place. People are drawn to love and repelled by someone dictating what they are to be or act like. Yet in churches we attempt to dictate a conformity of behavior that makes us feel comfortable. We don't offer unconditional love. Oh sure we say "love the sinner, hate the sin;" but let's be honest, we really hate the sinner too. I don't see us reaching out to the homosexual community. How many churches have AIDS support groups? How do we treat unwed mothers? How different would it look if we really truly reached out and loved these people? But then we would have to leave our safe walls and actually deal with issues, messy lives, complications and "shades of gray" rather than rest comfortably on our "black and white" principles. What would Jesus do, really!?[8]

A second example of the rejection of legalism and the affirmation of freedom comes from Timothy Roth, a member of my focus group (mentioned in the acknowledgments). Tim is a film critic. He tells a story of bumping into a young person who still functions in a legalistic framework:

As a staff writer for my college paper, my job is to write reviews of films and of the occasional new album. While my work is usually well received, my job sometimes gets me into trouble with well-meaning people who misunderstand what I do as a culture critic and my motivations for doing it.

This kind of trouble began when I first had in mind to try writing film reviews for the Wheaton College paper. As self-doubt is one of my weaknesses, I was very nervous about writing for the paper and how this kind of thing might be received at a conservative evangelical college. I went to the new recruits meeting to apply and talk with the editor of the arts and entertainment page. She hadn't had a film critic for quite some time and was enthusiastic about adding me to the staff.

Everything seemed to be going smoothly, except for one thing. Someone was hovering over me, eavesdropping on my conversation with my editor. This person followed me out of the door and onto the lawn on campus.

"Do I know you?" I asked.

The young, freshman girl opened her mouth, "So, I overheard you'll be writing movie reviews."

"That's right," I beamed. "I'm pretty excited about it."

"What kind of movies?"

This is an odd question, I thought. My stomach, turning faintly over, was sending me a signal that there was something wrong with this conversation.

"I'm not sure what you mean," I confessed. "Any kind of movies. Movie movies. You know, the kind you see in movie theaters."

"R-rated movies?"

Suddenly, I realized what this was. It was an inquisition. I stopped in my tracks. I didn't know what to say; knowing full well there was probably nothing I could say. But I had to answer. She was waiting.

"Well, yes," I stammered. "I suppose that since many of the films that appear in theaters are R-rated and that my new job is to see films that, yes, I will see a few R-rated movies."

"I would hate to see you compromise," she said without hesitation.

"I will pray for you," she said. I had nothing to say. I had been judged.

I went away from this encounter wounded, confused, and doubting myself more than ever. While I knew why this girl might misunderstand what I'm attempting to do as a film critic, I felt that it was unfair for her to judge me like she did on such a petty and legalistic basis. It is precisely because I do not compromise that I see and review "R-rated movies." Part of me wanted to defend my case to her, another part of me realized that defense would be the wrong approach. Even writing this essay, I have had doubts about how to present the heart and mind of this particular culture critic who happens to find himself, often, in a climate that is hostile or unappreciative towards the creative arts.

However, the truth is that, especially with the younger evangelicals, I see a revolution happening. More and more Christians are beginning to appreciate good music, film, and art and to see the value they have in exploring truth and spirituality in the current age. Perhaps the best apologetic, then, is not to defend but to simply open the door to my heart and mind; to explain why I think a thoughtful approach to popular films and music of all kinds is a valuable endeavor for Christians.

My goal as a culture critic is to encourage younger evangelicals to be discerning when they walk into a movie theater. My general rule of thumb here is provided by the apostle Paul, "All things are lawful, but not all things are profitable." This maxim from Paul works in two ways. First it guards our freedoms as children of God from legalistic and petty attitudes. Second, and most important, it challenges us to see our freedoms in the light of the bigger picture of the demands of love. Our rights are always subservient to love for God and our neighbor.

In my reviews I always have a desire to encourage younger evangelicals to go past two kinds of thoughtlessness that are addressed by this Pauline maxim. First is that shallow kind of legalism that insists that R-rated movies, no matter the context or content, are somehow "bad" or "un-Christian." Jesus rebuked the Pharisees for this kind of legalism that sees only the surface minutiae rather than the heart of a matter. He called it "straining out gnats but swallowing camels," or, as I like to say, missing the big themes of Good and Evil by getting hung up on the naughty and the nice. Second, I hope to encourage those who do see movies to do so with a sharp and discerning mind. Too many of us go to the theater to simply slump in the seat and turn off our minds.

The best way I know to respond to these two kinds of thoughtlessness is to present the big picture, to put music and film in their broader context. I believe that art in general is a kind of mirror held up to the culture it exists in. We can learn much about ourselves by looking into this mirror. Artists provide signposts that tell us where we are. Sometimes they give us reason to hope. Sometimes their work truthfully and honestly tells us how far east we have wandered from the Garden of Eden. In this sense the very best artists and their very best works are prophetic. Whether the message is pleasing or disturbing, it can help make us more aware of the cultural climate of our day. And as Christians, who are called to be salt and light in this world, this kind of cultural self-awareness is invaluable.

Finally, I'm a movie critic because I love movies. I love seeing a story play out for me visually. I love the aesthetic value and the beauty of a well-made film. I love to see good cinematography, good editing, good sound, good screenwriting, directing and acting. It is almost as though film is a kind of sacrament for me. My favorite movies have also been sources of some of my most profound and meaningful encounters with God. God speaks to me and moves me through good art.

It is to this end that Paul admonishes us, "Whatever is true, whatever is honorable, whatever is just, whatever is pure, whatever is pleasing, whatever is commendable, if there is any excellence and if there is anything worthy of praise, think about these things." Unfortunately, much of what the evangelical world has produced lacks excellence, integrity, and a proper sense of justice and is often so obvious or propagandist that it really requires little or no thought at all. I believe that I am part of a generation of Christians returning to a time where we are leaders in the art world once again rather than imitators who merely provide a safe, homogenized, and utterly irrelevant "Christian" alternative to "worldly" art. In order to do this we need to recover a sense of the intrinsic value of art as something that God has given us. H. R. Rookmaaker, the renowned Christian art historian, talks about this in his book *Art Needs No Justification*. He writes, "To fit into patterns of evangelism, artists have often compromised, and so prostituted their art. But Handel with his *Messiah*, Bach with his *St. Matthew's Passion*, Rembrandt with his *Denial of St. Peter* . . . worked to the glory of God. They did not compromise their art."

As Christians we need to recognize the value of art as a good in itself, created by God. When we succumb to sacred/secular thinking in the arts, we end up trivializing art. I have come to the conclusion that there is no such thing as "Christian art" just as there is no such thing as "Christian mathematics." There is only art. And as those who serve the God who gave us the capacity to make art, we should strive to pursue it to the best of our abilities.

I hope to encourage younger evangelicals not only to develop for themselves their own taste for excellent films and music but to also encourage them to make good work. Not good "Christian work" but good work made by Christians. I want to encourage younger evangelicals to recognize and make work that is truly without compromise: work that is not manipulative, work that is empathetic and gracious rather than sentimental, work that is redemptive rather than trite or cute, work that is true to life in its complexity and ambiguity rather than cheaply obvious. But as long as we refuse to be salt and light in the world by self-righteously refusing to "eat with sinners" in a cultural sense, we will find that we, as Christians, have already truly compromised.[9]

These illustrations point to the one word that I have heard over and over again from the twenty-somethings—authentic. They want to be real Christians in a real world—not phony Christians in a world of their own making. To achieve this goal, they know that they must break from the legalistic bondage of a spirituality defined by external rules and embrace the true meaning of freedom in Christ.

Current Sources of Younger Evangelical Spirituality

The primary source for younger evangelical spirituality, other than the Bible, is the past. Dawn Haglund writes, "We have introduced a number of things from past Christian history that have been left out of the contemporary church." She mentions "liturgy and creeds, *Lectio Divina*, icons and art during worship," and "saints and ancient writers for their questions, insights and depth."[10]

Haglund has put her finger on the fundamental theme I found recurring in the literature of the younger evangelical—the return to more ancient forms of spirituality, a trend that clearly fits their commitment to tradition, to resurrect the old and adapt it for use in a postmodern world.

For example, Maria Hoshaw has written an article for *Next-Wave* titled "Experience Ancient Spirituality." She says, "I desired to sit in a holy place, and feel God's awesome presence. I did what any normal person would do. I went on a personal retreat at a convent." Hoshaw says she is not alone in this "quest for an-

cient Christian spiritualities." She's been in contact with numerous young people who are interested in "Celtic spirituality, chant, and going to religious services with incense, candles and quiet music. . . . There's something going on
globally with the attraction to the spiritual."[11]

The numerous spirituality movements that have emerged in recent years may
be organized into two categories: the return to the sacramental and the restoration of premodern traditions.

The Return to the Sacramental

Traditionally evangelicals have stayed clear of the word *sacrament* because
they have associated it with the Catholics or high church people "who are into
religion but don't really care about being spiritual." This is unfortunate; it represents a misunderstanding of the word and of its use.

First, the fear of the word shouldn't be a Protestant fear at all. The word is
freely used in the writings of both Luther and Calvin and appears here and there
throughout Protestant history. If the founding fathers of the Protestant community were not put off by the word *sacrament*, neither should we.

The word's negative connotations come from the Catholic past, when at its
worst *sacrament* referred to a ritual that conferred God's saving grace without
need of corresponding faith. This was known as *ex opere operatum* (it works by
the work). Then came the Enlightenment, which replaced the mystery of sacramental action with an emphasis on the rational and understandable. Consequently, the free-church tradition (a tradition of churches that broke away from
the state and stood independent of state control) introduced the word *ordinance*.
Jesus *ordered* us to be baptized and receive the Lord's Supper. The term itself
suggests, "Do this because Jesus said to" or "It's what *you* do, not what God
does, that counts." Consequently, evangelicals are baptized "in obedience to
God's Word" and receive the Eucharist not because doing so is divine but as a
response to God's directive. Evangelicals substituted a premodern conviction
that the elements of Communion are God's symbols of sacred or divine action
with the reasoned conviction that they are personal symbols of faith.

One reason for the return of younger evangelicals to a sacramental consciousness is the recovery of the meaning of sacrament. The Latin word *sacramentum*
was used to translate the Greek word mystery *(mysterium)*. One could speak of
"the mystery of baptism," "the mystery of the Eucharist," or "the mystery of
marriage." The word sacrament comes from two Latin words: *sacra*, which
means "holy," and the suffix *mentum*, which means "to make holy." It also means
"to set aside." In Roman secular language the word was often used to "make an
oath." When a person was sworn into the Roman army, for example, an oath occurred between two parties, a covenant that "bound them together in a new relationship." The two sides of sacrament are reflected in this secular use: The Ro-

man government puts its imprint upon the soldier. The soldier receives the imprint and promises to wear it well. Likewise, in Christian thought "sacrament" refers to an action of God that is received, affirmed, treasured, and kept (see Eph. 3:3–6). "Sacrament" expresses the mystery of the union between God and man—effected by God, kept by man.

Early church writings taught there is only one sacrament, only one way to be holy, and that is through Jesus Christ. He alone presents us to the Father and represents us as holy before the throne of God. Today we make a distinction between the one sacrament (only Jesus makes us holy) and two dominical sacraments (Jesus instituted *baptism* and the *Eucharist* as sacred actions of his work on our behalf). We are to observe them as a reception of *his work for us* and *our faith response to him*. The five ecclesial sacraments (sacred actions affirmed by the church as special means of God's communication of himself to us) are: *confirmation*, the sealing of the Holy Spirit (Eph. 1:13); *confession*, the affirmation of the finality of our forgiveness and its continued effect in our lives (1 John 1:9); *marriage*, an affirmation of the presence of the love Jesus has for the church acted out in a relationship of mutual submission (Eph. 5:21–33, referred to as a "profound mystery" in v. 32); *ordination*, a special commissioning by God for the work of ministry and for the mentoring relationship of elder to younger (1 Tim. 1:2); and *healing*, an act of God communicated through the laying on of hands (James 5:13). Finally, all of life is considered to be sacramental. That is, in all relationships, prayer, the reading of Scripture, meditation, or in experiencing the beauty of creation, an actual, real, tangible, and authentic encounter with God can take place through the synergism of God's creational presence and the vulnerability and openness of the person who sees all things with an eye for God. Clearly, a large number of younger evangelicals are returning to baptism and the Eucharist as sacred actions, while some younger evangelicals are going even further, returning to a sacramental consciousness that encompasses all of the above sacraments.

Baptism is taking on a new importance as "God's stamp upon me" and as an embodiment of one's commitment to enter into the struggle of life that baptism symbolizes. Younger evangelicals, for example, are highly drawn to the way baptism is done in the indigenous church in Africa. Generally, new converts are baptized in the ocean. Here is what happens. After the words of the baptismal covenant have been exchanged, two deacons hold the person's hands and feet in a horizontal stretch, swing the convert back and forth, and then *throw* the convert into a wave "in the name of the Father." The convert is washed to shore. The deacons quickly pick up the convert and throw him or her again in the name of the Son. The convert is thrown a third time in the name of the Spirit. In this way the convert has been given a tactile baptismal experience that initiates the convert into the *struggle* of the faith. The younger evangelicals love this image because they are willing to make a sacrificial commitment to be real disciples of Jesus.

Younger evangelicals are also turning toward a more frequent celebration of the Eucharist. There is a fascination with ancient Orthodoxy and Eucharistic spirituality. For example, the writings of Father Alexander Schmemann have resurrected the ancient teaching that the Eucharist is an entrance into a momentary experience of the kingdom of God where the perfect love of God in the sacrifice of Jesus Christ is on full and permanent display. The younger evangelical longs for a sense of God's presence and finds it in the celebration of the Eucharist. Quiet meditative prayer songs, from ancient plainsong to Taizé worship music, often accompany this celebration. For many younger evangelicals, Eucharist is a high point of spiritual encounter and meaning.

This turn toward a more sacramental consciousness is found particularly in many new start-up churches led by the younger evangelicals. Many of these churches practice weekly Eucharist.

Restoration of Premodern Traditions

A second movement among the younger evangelicals is the restoration of certain premodern church traditions. These traditions are not sacraments as such, but they function on the level of the sacramental; they are means by which the power of the risen Christ is truly encountered and life is transformed.

For example, younger evangelicals are recovering the sacredness of time. Many of them recognize that time has been secularized so thoroughly that one has to fight hard to allow time to function in a sacramental way. They are recovering the Christian year, or the "church calendar," as it's sometimes called. This began in many churches in the evangelical culture through the reintroduction of the season of Advent. Now there's been a resurrection of Lent. Many younger evangelicals attend Catholic and Episcopal Ash Wednesday services and follow a Lenten fast or do Lenten spiritual readings. They often attend Holy Week services, including Tenebrae, Maundy Thursday, Good Friday Veneration of the Cross, and the midnight Paschal Vigil. Pentecost is taking on new meaning as well. Younger evangelicals are Spirit driven, and they want to celebrate in special ways the commemoration of the coming of the Holy Spirit and the birth of the church.

There is also a revived interest among younger evangelicals in the daily office, done either individually or communally. Maria Hoshaw writes of her experience of the daily office during her visit to the convent, mentioned earlier. She says, "I went through this cycle of events. . . . After about a full day, the cycle of the day prayerfully unfolded, and I found my breath slowing down. I found my thoughts slowing down . . . and felt more and more rested and at peace with each day. . . .

The day is regulated by the church bells and the call to prayer, and not by alarm clocks or a daily planner."[12]

Younger evangelicals also are recovering the spiritual pilgrimage. In many ways this phenomenon has continued throughout history and has taken on a commercial bent with trips to Israel, Rome, and places of the Reformation and the like. Mike Yaconelli, a pioneer in youth ministries, received a $600,000 grant from the Lilly Foundation to teach the ancient rituals to teenagers by taking them on pilgrimages to places like Taizé where they learn to pray and meditate. "What young people long for is not to be told about God," says Yaconelli, "not to be told about the spiritual life, but to get a chance to taste it for themselves." The ABC news article that presented Yaconelli's work reported that "last spring [1999] 70,000 Christian teenagers packed an arena in Michigan to sign their own Bill of Rights, condemning materialism and immorality and affirming 'their' commitment to live out spiritual values in their schools and communities." The report also stated that "on college campuses across the country, courses on religion have surged. In some places, there aren't even enough classes to fill the student demand." Young people are turning their backs on the material world and seeking meaning through spiritual retreats and pilgrimages.[13]

Two of my former students came by to tell me about their trip to Taizé in France. They had a pile of pictures to show me, but their most prized picture was of the Taizé cross. As I was looking at this wooden cross that lies on the ground, my former students said, "Look at the ends of the arms, the head and foot of the cross. Note how the wood is bare and worn down." Then, they said, "Want to know why the wood is so worn? . . . Because during worship, young people line up to come to the cross, to kneel before it and to place their foreheads against one of the tips of the cross as they pray." I was struck once again by the power of the pilgrimage and those acts of piety done in pilgrimage, like kneeling before the cross and letting all the weight of your body rest on the arm, foot or head of Jesus.

Another ancient tradition resurrected by the younger evangelical is the use of icons in worship or in private prayer. In Taizé services, for example, numerous icons are displayed in a center circle with scores of candles burning around them. Young people will sit on the floor, kneel, lie prostrate and meditate. Younger evangelical David Athey recently reviewed a book on praying with icons. He quotes the author, Jim Forest, as saying icons serve "both as an affirmation of the incarnation and of the significance of matter itself." Athey says, "We all need help to pray. And that is the primary gift of icons." Icons are "windows into heaven." Many younger evangelicals have purchased icons and place them on their walls, in dormitories and in their apartments.[14]

Another form of spirituality making a comeback is the labyrinth. A labyrinth is a "walk" that emerged in the medieval era to serve as a "kind of pilgrimage" for those who were unable to travel. It is a circular walk that also takes a person on an "inward" journey. In a *Faithworks* article, Robert Parham describes his experience this way: "Ever so slowly I gave up the cognitive struggle to discern where I was. I began to follow the path, letting it lead me. The need to understand the process and to rush through it disappeared." He describes this as the second stage of illumination when the pilgrim "prays for wisdom and listens for the spirit." By staying on the path and arriving at the center, he says, "I began to unwind into the third stage, called union." What, we may ask, is the value of this spiritual discipline? Parham answers, "In our high-tech, time-starved world, where speed is valued, life is compressed and only the output counts, surely this medieval exercise offers believers a countercultural way of reflection on mystery and gives renewal for the journey."[15]

An old approach to Scripture reading has been resurrected among many younger evangelicals and is being used in retreats and personal prayer. It's called *Lectio Divina* (Holy Reading). Developed by the Benedictine order of monks and used for centuries, it has been highly popularized through younger evangelical leaders. *Cutting Edge* magazine recently introduced this method of praying Scripture to its reading audience (a younger evangelical community). Here is how they presented it:

Preparation

Have the group members prepare themselves for prayer in whatever way is beneficial (e.g., silence, imagining Jesus, etc.).

First, let the group know you are about to read a verse or a short passage, and invite them to listen for a word or phrase that, as the Benedictines say, "shimmers"—something that "beckons you, addresses you . . . something that stirs, unnerves, disturbs, grabs, or touches you."

Read the Passage

Read it aloud twice in an unhurried way, the second time more slowly—perhaps by two different people.

Ask people to repeat the "beckoning" or "shimmering" word or phrase to themselves.

Invite each person in the group to speak that word or phrase one at a time. Allow this to be a slow movement, with spacious time between the speaking. Perhaps the group may agree simply to take turns around the circle, with each speaker indicating to the next person (by a gesture, a touch, a word) when he or she is finished.

The Passage Is Read Aloud Another Time (perhaps by a different person than above)

Have the group attend to the feeling or image in them which is connected to the word or phrase they have spoken.

Each person in the group briefly states his or her feeling/image. Use the same process as when the word/phrase was spoken.

The Passage Is Read a Final Time (perhaps by yet another person)

Have each person attend to the way this word or phrase, feeling or image, connects with the context and situation of their life right now. How does it relate to what they have heard and seen this day? How does it connect with what is happening at home, at work, in leisure time, in their community, in society, in the world, in nature?

Take an extended time of exploring this connection (in thought, in a journal, in art). How is God present to you in that connection? Is God calling you to anything in your present circumstance?

Briefly share with the group what you have discovered. Go around the group in the same process as above.

Invite the group to a time of silent contemplation, a time of simply resting with and receiving what God has offered them. Close with extended silence, resting in the presence of God. A spoken blessing or prayer may complete the silence.[16]

Another ancient practice resurrected by the younger evangelical is that of a spiritual director. Its purpose is to "help people discover—or stay in touch with—God's hints and nudges buried in the noise of everyday life." Melanie Arnold, a younger evangelical and former geologist, turned to a spiritual director to help her discern her future. She ended up quitting her work to give full-time attention to raising her two children.[17]

The foregoing examples illustrate that younger evangelicals communicate through symbols; they are a symbol-conscious generation. They want to "picture" words, "visualize" concepts, "symbolize" commitments. My generation and that of the boomers is primarily monolanguage (words), but the new generation is multilanguage. They are a visual, symbol-making generation attracted to the power and the mystery of many languages that go deeper than the cognitive, verbal, and print forms of communication.

In sum, younger evangelicals desire, as a young woman told me recently, a piety that has the force of tradition behind it, a piety that is communal and participated in by Christians always and everywhere, a piety characterized by structure and freedom. They are finding this kind of spirituality in the ancient, more enduring forms of piety discarded by the modern innovative boomer leaders. This piety, that of ancient and medieval Christianity, draws young people like a magnet. For many younger evangelicals, piety is not so much that of "keeping the rules" of evangelicalism but more that of keeping the rule of spirituality, especially the rule established in and passed down from the great ancient and medieval traditions of the spiritual life (see table 14).

Table 14
Approach to Spiritual Formation

	Traditional Evangelicals	Pragmatic Evangelicals	Younger Evangelicals
Prayer	Petition	Relationship with God	Union with God
Scripture	Read Bible in one year	Daily Bible reading	*Lectio Divina*

(continued)

Table 14
Approach to Spiritual Formation

	Traditional Evangelicals	Pragmatic Evangelicals	Younger Evangelicals
Church	Doing church	Innovative church	Being church
Witness	Four Spiritual Laws	Friendship witness	Communal witness
Goal	Sanctification	Getting one's life together Meaning	Discipleship
Setting for Spiritual Growth	Local church	Retreat centers	Monasteries' practice of the Christian year Labyrinth All of life
Rules	Do's and don'ts establish uniformity and abstinence	Freedom from cultural restrictions All things in moderation	Primary rule to become an authentic human being The freedom to be real
Sacramental Understanding of Life	Rejected	Rejected	Affirmed Seek to understand and live out through symbol and practice

13

Worship Leaders
From Program to Narrative

One of the most controversial revolutions in the church has been the recent changes in worship. Between 1900 and 1970 most churches had settled into the model of traditional worship handed down in their denomination or fellowship. There was little pressure to change until the music revolution of the fifties, the rise of the hippie movement in the sixties, and the emergence of the Jesus Movement in the seventies. The Jesus Movement, influenced by the music revolution and the hippie revolution, introduced music-driven casual worship, and the church has been in an uproar ever since. This genre of "praise and worship" has become the mark of the contemporary megachurch and the symbol of what attracts and holds the young. But will that genre be carried into the future by the younger evangelical?

I find that younger evangelicals feel somewhat "dizzy" over all the changes and the shouting matches going on between traditionalists on the one hand and those who demand a regular plate of contemporary worship on the other hand. David Di Sabatino, editor of *Worship Leader*, is so close to the issue that he says, "My head is swirling." There is, he says, "a sense in which I find myself in agreement with whatever I have heard last. . . . I find myself resonating with C. S. Lewis's quip that he didn't care much about the style of worship, save that you stopped changing it every five minutes so that he could get used to it. I am with him on that one."[1]

I find three trends in the worship of the younger evangelical. They are (1) a reaction to entertainment worship, (2) a longing for an experience of God's presence, and (3) a restoration of liturgical elements of worship.

Reaction to Entertainment Worship

Paul Christenson, a minister of music in the Church of God, says, "One way I differ from the boomer generation is that I am not as attracted to 'showy' worship and things that please my felt needs. . . . What I really desire is an experience with God."[2]

Christenson's sentiment seems to be borne out by a survey I conducted through the Institute for Worship Studies in 1999. The purpose of the survey, which was conducted with future evangelical leaders, was to determine whether or not the twenty-somethings would lead us beyond the current form of contemporary worship.

This question is a volatile one, so let's begin with a definition of contemporary worship. I am using the phrase "contemporary worship" to refer to a pattern of worship developed since the late 1960s that can be loosely characterized by the statement, "Let's put a band together, sing choruses for thirty minutes, and hear a sermon." This music-driven approach to worship spans the range from excellent musicians and worship leaders to extremely poor musicians and worship leaders. At its best it can be a moving experience of the Spirit. At its worst it's a show, a performance done for the people or to the people and seldom by the people. One form or another of this worship is found in the megachurches of evangelicalism, in boomer churches that want to reach the younger generation and in churches associated with Pentecostal or charismatic movements. Many of these churches are characterized by an energetic dynamism and are among the fastest-growing churches in America and even around the world. But, we must ask whether this style has a future or whether it will evolve into another form?

During the last two decades of the twentieth century, the church-growth experts have been saying, "Go contemporary or die," but recently I have been hearing an opposing voice. First of all, some pastors have confided in me that contemporary worship, which is all that they have ever known or done, now feels thin, even lifeless and rote. Second, in Christian colleges all over the country students are turning toward a much more quiet worship such as candlelight prayer vespers using Taizé music. Kirk Dearman, who wrote the song "We Bring the Sacrifice of Praise," has recently released a new CD, *Come to the Quiet*, a call to quiet meditative prayer characterized by a Celtic sound. These and other examples of a move away from contemporary worship rang in my ears for some time, so I decided to do a survey through the Institute for Worship Studies to find out whether younger evangelicals were going in a new direction with their worship.

The survey was administered to 176 twenty-somethings from Wheaton College and Wheaton Graduate School. Those surveyed represented thirty-eight states, forty-one denominations, and fourteen countries. The survey demonstrated some very interesting trends among the younger evangelicals. What they want is a God-centered worship that emphasizes the following nine features:

1. a genuine encounter with God
2. genuine community
3. depth and substance
4. more frequent and meaningful experience of Communion
5. challenging sermons and more use of Scripture in worship
6. participation
7. creative use of the senses; visual
8. quiet, characterized by the inclusion of contemplative music and times for quiet personal reflection and intimate relationship with God
9. a focus on the transcendence and otherness of God

A second set of answers demonstrated what the younger evangelicals do not want in worship. My interpretation of their answers suggests the following observations:

1. There seems to be a general reaction against the contemporary worship style. The highest negative response was given to entertainment and contemporary worship and to the music associated with this form of worship.
2. There also seems to be a general dislike of the style of worship we associate with the 1950s traditional worship of the boomers.[3]

What are we to make of this survey? Let me make several observations.

1. First, I called my friend, publisher of *Worship Leader*, Chuck Fromm, to share the results of this survey with him. He said, "Worship should always be contemporary. By contemporary, I don't mean 1960s contemporary but contemporary in the sense that it is always being incarnated into the current cultural situation. Our culture is changing, so it is no surprise that our worship tastes and style are changing as well." Chuck's response is the key to understanding the future and to getting ready for it.
2. The current change in worship taste and style is indeed a reflection of our shift into a postmodern world. The culture of post-2000 is very different than that of the sixties and seventies. It is a culture tired of noise, turned

off by phoniness, sick of glitz, and wary of the superficial. It is a culture searching for an authentic encounter with God, longing for depth and substance, craving quiet and spiritual contemplation and moved by visual, tactile forms of communication.

3. I don't interpret the negative responses to the music of contemporary worship as a rejection of the use of the band, keyboard, guitar, piano, and worship team, nor do I interpret the negative attitude toward the organ and choir as a rejection of the more traditional elements of worship. Rather, I think what is being said is this: We are tired of superficiality. What we want is an authentic experience of worship, an encounter with God that has life-changing results. What we don't want is phony, loud entertainment worship, or dead ritualistic worship.

4. All these styles of music and instruments will still have a place in worship so long as they serve the goal of achieving a genuine encounter with God characterized by depth and substance.

We are now in a new cultural situation. The demand for depth and substance speaks of a need to find biblical and transcultural principles of worship that have endured through two thousand years of history and to incarnate these principles into a new style that is relevant to the twenty-first century. If we can do that, the new generation will have taken us beyond the contemporary worship of yesterday to the contemporary worship of tomorrow.

For example, Dane Daker, the senior pastor at Coltin First Baptist Church in California, reports that they had split their congregation into two groups—the traditional and the contemporary—but, he writes, "we've found over time that the contemporary service left us wanting more, a deeper experience with God. My soul literally grieved that we had thrown out our heritage. I longed to hear our beautiful fourteen-rank pipe organ sound out a hymn with a full crowd of people singing. . . . I longed to recite the creeds again. . . . I wanted to do responsive readings. . . . I wanted more than seven songs which all sounded the same. So we started to experiment. We discovered that both the young and the old loved what we were doing. We decided to get rid of traditional and contemporary service designations and do worship together. It has been wonderful."[4]

Karen Daker, Dane's wife, wrote an article for Coltin First Baptist to help the members understand a richer and fuller way to worship. She titled the article "Beyond Contemporary Worship" and touched on what seems to me to be the major themes I see cropping up among younger evangelicals. Space does not permit an elaboration on her themes, but they speak for themselves. Here is my summary of Daker's points:

1. There is "a hunger for worship that not only helps us express our love for God, but also helps us grow in our understanding of who God is." This

point speaks to the shift among younger evangelicals away from the earlier forms of "me-ism" in worship to a focus on God.

2. There is "a growing recognition that all generations have a lot to gain if we can learn to worship together." This point illustrates the desire of the younger evangelical to do worship intergenerationally and interculturally.

3. There is a new concern for worship to challenge "the churched/unchurched paradigm." This speaks to the move of the younger evangelical to call into question the seeker-service model that focuses on the unchurched in a distinctly unchurched way.

4. Next there is "an increasing desire to use a variety of worship elements in our services, not just music alone." For the younger evangelical, worship is more than music.

5. And finally, "an intensified passion to experience the majesty and mystery of God." The younger evangelical is certainly characterized by "passion" and by a willingness to be humbled before the majesty of God who is mystery.[5]

The mood of the younger evangelical is to bring old and new together. For example, a recent letter from worship leader Candy Lynn Hanslik says to keep the great hymns of the past from the church "would be robbery." Yet she says, "I love meeting Jesus in new, contemporary worship." Worship through music, she says, "offers a time to physically express devotion to Jesus (i.e., clap hands, raise arms). The physical interaction is a tangible expression of surrender and submission to our mighty Creator." Like other younger evangelicals, she says we need both the old and the new because "both have reached multitudes and they will continue to do so."

The Longing for an Encounter with God's Presence

A boomer recently made this remark to me: "Face it, for the first fifteen hundred years of Christianity the presence of God was experienced in the Eucharist. The Reformers moved the presence of God from the Eucharist to the Word. Today, the new revolution in worship is locating the presence of God in music."

Perhaps this is why worship in many contemporary churches amounts to thirty minutes of music-driven activity. But is this sweeping statement true to biblical teaching and in continuity with the teaching and experience of the church throughout history? I think not, and the younger evangelical understands this.

In the twentieth century a great deal of scholarly work has been done on this question: How do we experience Christ's presence in worship? Recent liturgical scholarship affirms first of all that the presence of Christ is experienced in the gathering of people. God dwells in people, and as they come together to worship and exercise their gifts, they have been called by God to gather in God's presence and worship. For this reason many new churches are being built with relational seating. This makes the community more aware of the presence of Christ, the head of the church, who assembles with his people, the body of Christ.

Younger evangelicals are rediscovering that the God who is present in all creation becomes intensely present in our worship through sign and symbol. The primary symbol of God's presence is the assembled people. Within the assembled body the chief symbols of God's presence are expressed in the baptismal font, the pulpit, and the Eucharist table. The baptismal pool is there because it serves the community as a reminder that we have been baptized into the death and resurrection of Jesus. For this reason many new churches are actually putting the baptismal pool or font at the entrance to the sanctuary. In this way the worshiper is reminded of his or her baptism and the resulting indwelling of God.

The pulpit symbolizes God's presence in the Word. The Word was brought into being by the Holy Spirit who now brings the presence of God to us in the reading of Scripture and preaching. Younger evangelicals, unlike pragmatic evangelicals, are reintroducing Scripture readings in worship, and sermons have shifted away from the therapeutic to focus on the teaching of Scripture.

And then there is the Eucharist. At the table through bread and wine we enter into the Holy of Holies where the presence of God takes on a vital and personal intensity. In his presence we recall his victory over the powers of evil, and we are empowered by this presence to go forth and to live in his victory for us over the powers of evil. Younger evangelicals are rediscovering the healing presence of God at Communion. Numerous younger evangelicals see the Eucharist as a *necessary* element of full worship and want to restore weekly Communion.

While these symbols—the assembled people, the baptismal experience, the presence of God in the Word and Eucharist—are the primary symbols of God's presence, there are other symbols of God's presence in worship. We sing, we pray, we give our tithes and offerings, we confess our sins, we affirm our faith by singing or reciting creeds, we pass the peace of Christ to each other, and we offer testimony to God's grace in our lives. In all these ways and more, God is made present to the assembled people.

Younger evangelicals are also searching with some determination for God's presence in music and the arts. For example, younger evangelicals are reacting against the Christian contemporary music (CCM) industry because "of its lack of a foundation," says songwriter Wes King.[6] For this very reason, Delirious, a top Christian band in Britain, has swept the world with its authentic and biblically based music without the help of a Christian music category or distributor. Their mission, they say, is not "to a market of believers" but to the whole world because that is the mission of Jesus (see the "Description of Younger Evangelical Worship" by Brad Bessell, a pastor in south Australia, at the end of this chapter).[7]

The younger evangelicals are also turning from pop choruses; this is illustrated by the interest in a more contemplative form of music like that of Celtic, Iona, Gregorian, and Taizé genres. In a *Regeneration Quarterly* article, Amy Catherine Boucher wrote that she sees many younger evangelicals "seeking to express their faith through a shared, intentional life and stronger liturgical expressions of worship."[8] This may help explain the love younger evangelicals are finding for Taizé music and worship. It is a worship characterized by periods of silence and a contemplative hearing of Scripture. It is a liturgy of fewer words and quiet restfulness.

Michael Hawn, in a publication called *Worship Arts*, writes, "Leadership is indirect, that is, from within those assembled for prayer. No one ever leads the prayer from the front. Rather, the front of the prayer space is full of candles, greenery and Orthodox icons for meditation." Hawn takes students on trips to Taizé in France, where at the beginning of their experience of the built-in times of silence students remark on how long the silence seems, but by the end of the week they comment on how short the silence is. "None of the glitz, technology and popular culture" that dominates so much of contemporary worship is a part of the experience. Instead, people wait "for the still small voice of God that comes to us . . . when the clamor of popular culture fades away."[9] During the summer thousands of twenty-somethings and teenagers flock to Taizé from all over the world to pray, hear Scripture, camp out, eat simple meals, and work for free in the fields. Robert Parham observes, "Protestants seem more about filling the hour and sanctuary with sound than filling the soul with God's presence. Taizé is about listening to God, not a sermon."[10]

Younger evangelicals are also experiencing the presence of God through the arts. Ashley Olsen, a twenty-something and my assistant at Northern, is an artist. I asked her to write on art and worship from the perspective of a younger evangelical, and here is what she has to say about how the arts are a means through which an encounter with God may occur:

I believe the arts are being used to remind us of the invisible, those things that we sense, or imagine, that we dream with our inner eye. Instead of arts explaining our circumstances here on earth, I think there is a hunger for the arts to reveal the window into the heavenlies, the spiritual realm. We get glimpses of the beauty and glory of the eternal Kingdom. And in experiencing this, we also experience ourselves as new creation. We must constantly be reminded of God's Kingdom, and the arts that seek to behold God's beauty, mystery, awe, wonder and glory, help us to do this. When we are more and more exposed to these elements, our faculties and sensitivities that receive and respond are exercised. Through this exercising, we regain new eyes with which to perceive the world, our neighbor, and ourselves. Eyes and lives that respond with love and compassion, mercy and grace, forgiveness and reconciliation, peace and hope. The arts help strengthen our heart and mind's eye with which we see life.

But there is something troubling about the use of arts today. And it has to do with the way the arts are presented to the Christian community. I have experienced a dramatic upsurge in the push for arts in the church. Yet there has often been an attitude that more is better. There is a culture where people, young and old, are seeking to find a refuge of silence, simplicity, and a sense of otherness, something bigger than themselves. Worship is where we as individuals leave our other loves and come together to share our common first love. We leave things that we are doing, to honor him in his house with his children. It doesn't have to be complicated or cluttered. We have an hour to an hour and a half of focusing and praising God together, and yet I get a sense we are squeezing God out and sticking more of us in. We are having trouble emptying ourselves of our gifts and of what we do to come before the Lord and worship Him together. To just be. Can all of us, even artists, leave our vocations at the door and become children before God?

We can shed the things that make us different and be reminded of the things that unify us and draw us together as one. What unifies us is us acting out our worship together. Worship is like a banquet table already set plentifully with food. All that is asked of us is to come. Right now the table is ready for the feast. We need not bring anything to the table to validate why we are there. The more we come hungry and open handed, the more we can partake.

There is this disease called "self" that we bring into the church, clothed, masked, and disguised in so many ways. It is accepted, even celebrated the way the world celebrates self; the world esteems it, telling us that "self" should be our God. If we all responded to God in our own "self-expressive" way, it would be chaotic and not corporate worship. We have an hour and a half to "be" together, but instead we are practicing self-expression.

Through most of history, the people who made art never thought of themselves as making art. In fact, it's quite presumable that art was being made long before the rise of consciousness, long before the pronoun "I" was ever employed. The painters of caves, quite apart from not thinking of themselves as artists, probably never thought of themselves at all.

What this suggests, among other things, is that the current view, which equates art with "self-expression," reveals more of a contemporary bias in our thinking than an underlying trait of the medium. Even the separation of art from craft is largely a post-Renaissance development, and more recent still is the notion that art transcends what you do and represents what you are. In the past few centuries, Western art has moved from unsigned tableaus of Orthodox religious scenes to one-person displays of personal cosmologies. "Artist" has gradually become a form of identity which (as every artist knows) often carries with it as many drawbacks as benefits. Consider that if artist equals self, then when (inevitably) you make flawed art, you are a flawed person, and when (worse yet) you make no art, you are no person at all!

Doing art the way primitive peoples did is almost like coming before the Lord when I don't have to be a dancer anymore, or a painter, or a physician, electrician, mechanic, musician or whatever someone "does" or thinks that he or she "is." I can simply be, and that is sacred; it doesn't have to be complicated. The less of me I "need" to bring into worship, the more I am able to see of God, to be reminded and taught of His work in history and the world, to see Him in the faces of the people there worshiping with me. There are times that art enhances worship and can be used in an organic way. But when art is imposed on worship for the very purpose of it "having to be in there," . . . it will distract.

Honestly, I see my weekly corporate worship service as a performance art piece in itself. I see the procession as a dance, our body positions as choreography. When I watch people process forward to take Communion and lift their cupped hands for the bread and reach for the cup to drink, this is God's greatest piece of artwork happening, live. There is so much art happening in and around us, yet we are blind to see that, as Van Gogh has said, Christ was the greatest artist. We are His great work, His living and breathing sculptures, dancers, visual designs, and His most beautiful song. We have an hour and a half to just "be" together, to truly "see" one another. Once we do that, we are rejuvenated to go out and continue to create and live fully in the lives we are given. Art is not validated because it is done in the confines of the church walls. If all of life is sacred, then the times that we meet together to praise God can be climax times of not having to "be" or "bring" anything but just us.

As I come into the presence of the most high God, I can do little else except fall down, lift my hands, or just stand in awe. He is holy and mysterious and He is there, in the people, in word, song, prayer, bread and wine. And it is there I meet him in worship, an art form of the heavenlies, where I join with the heavenly throng to proclaim "Holy, Holy, Holy, the whole earth is full of His glory."[11]

A Restoration of Liturgical Elements of Worship

Many younger evangelicals, having reacted to worship as self-expression and to the me-ism of contemporary worship, are finding their way into liturgical churches. Others are incorporating more liturgical elements into their worship.

For example, Dale Dirksen, who works with college students, writes, "Younger people today seem to be more interested in worship that has silence, contemplation, historical elements (music, creeds, etc.)."[12] This observation is no guessing game for Dirksen. He teaches a course on worship at Briercrest College. In a recent assignment he divided his class into six groups and asked them to plan a worship service that drew from one of three models: *kerygma* (presentation oriented), *koinonia* (community/fellowship oriented) and *leitourgia* (God-focused liturgy). When he asked if students had a preference regarding the above models, 100 percent of the students wanted to do *leitourgia*. None of them were from liturgical backgrounds, but they were all intrigued with the idea and substance of liturgy.

Jay Greener, a worship director who sees a revival of liturgical forms of worship among the younger evangelicals, observes the impact of the media revolution. "Communication scholars," he writes, "have for some time been pointing to a shift away from the printed page to the visual, iconic method of receiving and interpreting information. Although it's a cliché to say it, this change is a major shift in paradigm. We have entered an era where propositional truth is not nearly so important as the experience of it . . . Walter Ong pointed out that as a society we are entering into a new 'orality,' away from the presentation of rational argument based on literary convention to an oral culture much like our distant past."[13]

Greener recognizes that the communications revolution takes us back in order to move us forward in this visual culture. He writes, "Our approach to worship should incorporate the means of communicating realities that were in place during the long phase of Christian worship where the people were non-literate, or at least, more non-rational. The visual arts, liturgical movement, the creeds, etc., all can have a newly discovered and important place for the church in the postmodern age."[14]

Younger evangelical Stephen Skaff, a graduate from Wheaton College, writes, "Four years ago I was first introduced to the liturgy—it was novel to me. When I began to understand the rich tradition and history of it I felt cheated and hurt by the churches I grew up in—they think they are better than two thousand years of tradition, or at least they think they are more exciting, relevant, accessible."[15]

Skaff's thoughts about emotion in worship run deep and are worth taking the time to read slowly:

As our youth groups taught us, we should be wary of MTV and Hollywood portrayals of love, for they portray infatuation, emotion, lust, and passion more than they portray love. Love, of course, is a verb. Love is something we do, and although love is often attended by deep feelings, it is not dependent on feelings.

I read a book written by a group of monks who described the honeymoon-like experience of joining a monastery (*In the Spirit of Happiness* by The Monks of New Skete). Just as a honeymoon is filled with passion and emotion, so are the first few months at a monastery for the newcomer. After the honeymoon the passion flickers, the emotions fade a little, reality hits, and the real work of love begins. Likewise, the head monk told the newcomer that he could really start becoming spiritual after his emotions had faded. Worship is work. "Liturgy" means literally "the work of the people." Worship is the action we do in community, not the passion I feel on my own; it is more about the whole body acting in unity than the individual "feeling" in privacy. Like love, it may be accompanied by good feelings, but it is not entered into in order to draw out these feelings. Emotion should be incidental in worship, not the goal of it. Worship should be the act or work of telling God how awesome he is. A line in the liturgy describes Communion as "our sacrifice of praise and thanksgiving." If worship is simply fun and good times, then we aren't sacrificing anything, only serving ourselves and catering to our need for emotional stimuli. I am not saying that worship should be dry and gloomy—it most certainly is not supposed to be boring. It is a joyful thing to remind ourselves what God has done for us. However, in order for worship to be a sacrifice, we can't take it too lightly. We don't want to haphazardly throw up generic praises to God all the time. Thus, being spontaneous isn't always a good thing. The resources of our spontaneity are relatively thin compared to what we can accomplish together when we plan, practice, and think deeply about what we are doing.

The liturgy is a rich resource, teacher, and vehicle of worship because it was carefully devised and has been carefully reworked, enriched, and added to through-out Christian history. Every little bit of the liturgy has been carefully considered and refined and every bit of it has been filled with symbolism on various levels. There is symbolism in the structure of the liturgy, the architecture of the church building, the vestments worn by the clergy, the ceremonial motions—all the sights, sounds, tastes, touches, and smells of liturgy.

With such depth of planning and intentionality we can better focus on what we are trying to say without fumbling for the right words with which to say it. And what we are saying throughout the liturgy is what is really important. It is not a new message, but it is always exciting, always cutting edge, always relevant: we are proclaiming the good news and acting it out every week. We are reminding our-selves constantly of what Almighty God, Father, Son, and Holy Spirit, has done for us, is doing for us, and will do for us. It is not an altar call or a "How to stay out of hell" message, but it is the fullness of the Christian narrative—past, present, fu-ture—every week. And I don't think that people necessarily need to hear the mes-sage of God in easier or more "modern" ways. God hasn't changed, the message hasn't changed, and although our surroundings and the particulars of our prob-lems have changed, people haven't changed either.[16]

Skaff represents a trend among younger evangelicals to return to liturgical churches—Catholic, Orthodox, and Episcopal. But the larger movement among younger evangelicals is to enrich their evangelical worship with liturgical re-sources.

For example, I recently received this email from Paul Blake, a worship leader in a contemporary church. He speaks of using the cross, light and shadow, quiet, and kneeling in a recent service.

For the past couple of weeks, I have done something a bit different in worship. Most of my "Charismaniac" friends would say what I've done is downright weird! I shut off all the lights in our sanctuary except for one! Which is a little white light that shines on this huge cross we have hanging at the front of our sanctuary! For music, we sing three or four "slow worshipful songs" that focus on intimacy with Jesus. Before I start, I teach for five minutes about worship and about what we are going to do in that service (I have started to do this also on Sunday morning with our adults!). I teach about what the cross means and how we are to worship with our whole bodies, so I invite the youth to something that they have never done, be it lifting their hands, clapping, bowing, or kneeling. I just have one rule: they can't sit and watch.

I usually ask them to spread out across the sanctuary as well, so they are not in-timidated from singing or doing something different! Last week I had finished playing and the church was silent. All of a sudden two of my youth got out of their pew and knelt in silent recognition of the cross! It was awesome! I believe that in my life (I am 20 years old!), I need something to focus my attention sometimes! I love worshiping in the dark with just that light on the cross because it reminds me that worship is all about Him and has nothing to do with me!! (By the way, I have even led worship from the front pew with me facing the cross. Now that was a unique experience!)[17]

Worship as an Art Form

What Blake discovered is that worship is an art form that reflects the meaning of human existence. Consider the following.

First, worship as an art form signifies that this world is not all that is. The very existence of the act of worship, personal and public, no matter where it is found or in what manner it is done, arises out of the fundamental conviction within the human psyche that there is something other than what is. Materialists proclaim there is no other. But worship uses the material to proclaim that the invisible God who is wholly other is the very ground and meaning of material existence. Worship says creation is good and, when released to express its rela-tion to transcendence, embodies the transcendence of God. Paradoxically per-haps, the transcendent God is immanent within the created order. This very material act—worship—evokes an encounter with the fundamental transcen-dent meaning of material existence. For this very reason we must be thoughtful about the way we do worship. Worship is not primarily for the worshiper, for his or her self-focused benefit. Its primary purpose is not the communication of knowledge, the stimulation of emotions, or the evoking of feelings. Worship is first an art form that signifies the reality of the wholly other upon whom we are dependent for our every breath.

Second, Christian worship signifies the truth about human history and God's involvement in the stuff of life. For this reason Christian worship must corre-spond to Christian truth. Worship is an art form that tells and enacts the story of the creating God, the rebellion of God's creatures, the personal and intentional involvement of God's active presence within the unfolding of historical events culminating in God's actual incarnate presence in which God became human flesh and took to himself our human condition (without sin), and made himself subject to time, space, history. He bore the consequence of our sin which is death, died, and was resurrected to conquer death and begin a new act of re-cre-ation in the church, the community called to bespeak the destiny of history.

Worship signifies the salvation of all who call on the name of Jesus and of the redemption of the whole material order in the heavens and the new earth. Wor-ship that proclaims any other message cannot qualify as Christian worship. The current self-help, self-esteem psychologizing of Christian worship has nearly ceased to be Christian. It is an art form (and usually a poor one at that) that too often celebrates human experience, not the experience of God who was in Christ reconciling the world to himself. The most crucial form of worship which clearly lifts us up into the true celebration of God's rescue mission to the world in Jesus Christ is the celebration of Eucharist in its classical content. I say "classical content" because, unlike the practice of the Lord's Supper in many evangelical churches, the practice of the Eucharist in renewal churches (churches renewed by the classical tradition of worship) gets Jesus off the cross and into the celebration of the resurrection and thus presents God's saving work in history more fully.

Third, worship as an art form signifies the mystery, the *Mysterium Tremendum*, of the wholly other. Modernity rejected mystery. We live, it was argued, in a rational world. For this reason, worship followed the curvature of culture and became secularized. The sermon became the essence of worship, it became the true art form. Our seminaries became centers of knowledge and homiletic skill and little else. Worship was seldom mentioned. When it was, it was "here is an order to follow, here is how to baptize or dedicate, here is how to marry, or bury." The revolution of the seventies rejected the overemphasis on the rational sermon and sought for the mystery of God's presence in music. Surely God dwells in the praises of his people, but the reduction of the mystery of God's presence to praise alone fails to grasp the presence of God unleashed through rituals.

Worship as an art form signifies the reality of otherness, the purpose and meaning of human history, and God's saving involvement within history. It evokes mystery and brings us into wonder and awe. Young evangelicals are tired of entertainment, self-focused, chorus-driven worship. They want more. They want mystery, awe, wonder, transcendence. The rediscovery of worship as an art form that signifies the Christian reality of the relation between God, creation, history, incarnation, and the ultimate re-creation of all that exists is where our new worship leadership can begin.

Younger Evangelicals' Approach to Worship

These changes are affecting the approach of the younger evangelical to the practice of Sunday worship. The younger evangelical seems to understand that worship celebrates the story of God's work in history through the proclamation of the Word and the enactment of the Eucharist. The content of worship is clear. It is the story of God creating and becoming involved in the created order through his presence in Israel, in Jesus, and now in the church to bring history to its completion in the *eschaton*. Worship is the *Missio Dei*, presented, celebrated, and thankfully praised. It has to do with God and the praise given to God for the salvation of the world. For this reason, worship is not presentational. It is not outreach but upreach. It is, as liturgist Marva Dawn says, "a royal waste of time." We gather together to remember the story, to let this story tell us who we are, and to allow the story to form us into the people of God. This content shapes the order of worship, the experience of the Eucharist, the use of symbol, and the recovery of the Christian year.

First, the younger evangelical understands the order of worship is not a presentational program. Many older evangelicals understood worship to be primarily an opportunity to present the gospel to seekers, so they formed believers' worship around this priority. The ultimate effect was a worship service that consisted of a sequence of programmed acts of worship with a musical piece or drama inserted here or there. In contrast, the story-formed view of worship, popular among the younger evangelicals, interprets worship to be an unfolding of the narrative of God's story. The narrative is expressed in four movements. First, the people gather. This is a theological act in which the church is actualized and brought into being. Second, the church hears the story of God in Scripture readings, the Psalms, and the sermon. Third, the church responds with praise and thanksgiving at the table, enacting God's redeeming story with bread and wine. Finally, the community of God goes forth, empowered by the Spirit to be a living member of God's story in the world.

Second, the younger evangelical is shaped by the experience of the Eucharist. The modern attitude toward the Eucharist stripped it of divine presence and action and turned it into an expression of divine absence. In modernity the Lord's Supper, as it has been called, is individually oriented. It's something I do to show God that *I* remember him. The ancient view is that in Communion God gives himself to the church. We "feed on him" in praise and thanksgiving for his work of saving the entire cosmos through his purposes in history revealed in Christ and interpreted in the Scripture. This understanding of the Eucharist has led to the inclusion of healing rites in the Eucharistic portion of worship. Worship, which celebrates God's healing of the world, communicates God's healing and results in the healing of mind, spirit, and body.

It is this understanding of the content of worship that accounts for the recovery of symbol and the arts in worship. The content of faith proclaims that this created order will be released from its enslavement to the powers of evil that have brought it into the "bondage to decay." In worship the arts put wood, stone, and textile into a new and released form of praise. The arts are not mere decorations that enhance worship, nor are they illustrations of truth. Instead the arts participate in their eschatological meaning. They are creation put to praise.

The Christian content also gave rise to the Christian way to celebrate redeemed time—the practice of the Christian year. So many Christians are not aware that Advent, Christmas, Epiphany, Lent, Holy Week, and Pentecost are the salvation markers. They do, of course, practice Christmas as the event of

God's incarnation and Easter as the event of Christ's resurrection, though many are unaware of the cosmic meaning and depth of these seasons. But the rest of the Christian year is often relegated to "dead ritual." When the younger evangelicals discover the true meaning of the Christian year—that following the Christian year is a corporate spiritual discipline—they are immediately drawn to it and embrace it.

In brief, worship is changing significantly among the younger evangelicals. They are discovering that worship that concentrates on presentational outreach has no upreach. By restoring and adapting the ancient triune theology of worship as well as historic aspects of worship, especially the Eucharist, the younger evangelicals are finding that upreach worship naturally reaches out. For them, worship is not entertainment that presents Christianity as a secular-like, appealing, you-can-be-just-like-the-world-come-and-be-happy movement but an engaging, challenging, authentic rehearsal of the *Missio Dei*, which demands a committed embodiment of the truth that all of life should be an offering of worship to God (see table 15).

Table 15
Approach to Worship

	Traditional Evangelicals	Pragmatic Evangelicals	Younger Evangelicals
Style	Traditional program	Contemporary presentation	Liturgical Ancient/Future Contemporary
Content	Thematic	Topical	Triune
Structure	Threefold: sing, preach, invite	Twofold: music set and preaching	Fourfold: narrative of gathering, hearing the Word, Communion, dismissal
Participation	Primarily congregational singing	Singing of choruses	Highly interactive
Arts	Banners	Art as illustration Drama	Art as embodiment Environmental arts
Seating	Rows	Theatre seats	Relational configuration
Space	Traditional turn-of-the-century buildings	Theatres or theatre-type spaces	Homes Warehouses Churches Modified cathedrals
Christian Year	Seldom followed	Almost never followed	Frequently followed

(continued)

Table 15
Approach to Worship

	Traditional Evangelicals	Pragmatic Evangelicals	Younger Evangelicals
Symbols	Stained glass Pulpit and table Baptist font or pool	No symbols	Strong use of symbols Icons in many churches
Eucharist	Quarterly or monthly	Quarterly, monthly, or sporadic	Weekly in many churches
Technology	Overhead projector in some churches	Widespread use of PowerPoint, video, etc.	Restore authentic symbols PowerPoint generally used for icon projection
Instruments	Organ and brass	Bands	Eclectic use of instruments
Music	Traditional hymns	Contemporary choruses	Eclectic use including ancient forms of singing
Preaching	Didactic	Therapeutic	Narrative with an emphasis on obedience and Christian living Interactive
Scripture Readings	At least one Scripture reading	Very little Scripture reading, often none	One to three Scripture readings
Intercessory Prayer	Weekly	Seldom	Weekly and usually engaging the people in participatory prayer
Choir	Traditional choirs Presentational	No choir Worship leader teams	Singing serves the text Strong emphasis on congregational leadership

Description of Younger Evangelical Worship
by Brad Bessell

The setting for worship is very primitive. We meet under a tin shed in my backyard. It is rectangular in shape. In the Center is a table covered with cloth of the liturgical year.

In the center of the table is a Celtic cross, made of stone. On one side of the cross is a beautiful ceramic plate with fresh bread and on the other is a large wine glass. (We can't afford a chalice yet.)

In a circle around the Eucharistic elements are various items from creation, mostly from the beach (we're not far from the beach): small stones, driftwood, and sometimes flowers. We don't use candles at present because we are semi-outdoors, and the wind blows them out.

Around the Communion table are regular chairs and some lounge chairs that are in a semicircle. The service starts at 6 P.M. (We don't do a morning service as most people that come are in the music industry and don't get out of bed until the afternoon.) We have coffee and fellowship. From the other end of the "shed," our worship leader will begin with some up-beat "gathering" songs.

Then I lead them in the prayer of humble access or something similar. The tone of the worship changes then from your typical Vineyard songs that have an "intimate feel." Then there is usually a song or two that helps us prepare for confession.

There is usually some time given for silence, then I lead them in a time of confession. My favorite one is from *Celtic Worship through the Year* by Ray Simpson (Hodder and Stoughton, 1997).

Reader: As we draw near to the place of at-one-ment:
Give us tears to see the wonder of your presence;
Give us tears to see the wasting of your people;
Give us tears to see the wounding of your Son.

All: We are the race that helped make the wood on
Which you were crucified, and still we misuse your creation;

We are the race that helped make the nails that pierced your body,
yet still we use work for gain at others' expense;

We are the race that did nothing to stop your betrayers, yet still we
are ruled by comfort or cowardice.

Reader: Mercy Lord; mercy Lord, have mercy Lord.

All: Mercy Lord, mercy Lord, have mercy Lord.

There is time allowed for silence. During this, anyone, or designated persons, may speak out hurts, pains, or sorrows with which they or the world around is oppressed. After this the Leader pronounces an absolution and says:

O Soul be joyful,
The saving God stretches out His hand to you,
To announce a loving reconciliation,
Washed and made whole, let us open our heart
To God in prayer.

We then have the Scripture readings. I use the revised common lectionary most of the time. I usually do a ten- to fifteen-minute reflective/expository homily. Sometimes we have some questions after or we silently reflect on what was said.

From there we move to the Eucharist and we use the "Thanks Giving" and include the part that asks the Holy Spirit to come upon the elements. Once the Eucharist is over, we have some ministry/healing time during which more reflective worship songs are sung.

After the ministry I give the blessing and encourage everyone to continue to meet with Christ as we eat a meal together. We then have more coffee and sometimes we even have wine or beer.

That is an average Sunday night.

14

Artists

From Constraint to Expression

My upbringing in the evangelical world was artistically deprived. It isn't that my family or church experience was hostile to the arts; it was more a matter of neglect, a sense of indifference. The arts didn't matter. Beauty was not considered to be important to the Christian faith. It wasn't until I heard Francis Schaeffer lecture on the arts that I had any sense of the way art communicates—for good or ill.

More recently, the megachurch movement added a new wrinkle to the evangelical view of the arts. They rejected any kind of "churchy" art—places of worship should not look like churches, so their wisdom went, and there should be no Christian symbolism on the inside. Yet they brought lounge music and life-oriented skits into the church. This kind of art—boomer art—is art as illustration.

Younger evangelical David Taylor is concerned about illustrative art. He says, "There is a desperate need for evangelicals to think theologically about the arts, lest we marry ourselves to the spirit of the age." He suggests we steer clear of a mere utilitarian function for the arts. Otherwise, "Christians will never be fully free to create works that are 'nonreligious,' 'nonevangelistic,' to simply be *good* artists who honor God in their works, regardless of their subject matter." Taylor has a vision for the arts. He wants to see "evangelicals released into the fullness of the life of the artist and of art-making, that they be freed to paint or photograph the naked body, to sculpt in the abstract, to dance in the forms of bhuto or classical ballet, to write about the little things of life, about old men on the sea, retarded boys caught in the grip of grace, war and peace and suicide—that they construct church buildings with architectural beauty, that they perform in movies like *Magnolia* and *Cookie's Fortune*, that they sing on a *Lilith Fair* tour or play with the Boston Symphony, that they create works that are excellent in content and form, that they are life-giving and prophetic, that reflect both the ordinary and the extraordinary of the world, created by God."[1]

Taylor gives us insight into the direction of the younger evangelical in the arts. They will go in directions very different from what we have seen in evangelical history over the last one hundred years. They want to create true art that reflects good theology, not "sentimental, narrow-minded, functionalist and trite" art. Taylor's goal in the church he serves is to teach art, "so that together we can grow as a body that understands why God created us with imaginations and the ability to make art, that understands what art has to do with the church, with the kingdom of God, and with this world that Christ is continually redeeming. I want us to see our work as artists in a complementary role to the Isaianic New Creation."[2]

Dealing with Resistance

Taylor's goal and that of other younger evangelicals involves an uphill battle. Not only are they dealing with the neglect and indifference of the evangelical church toward the arts, they are also up against hostility and resistance. Dale Dirksen, a young professor at Briercrest College in Saskatchewan, Canada, says, "The best way to value artists in our church is by valuing art." Unfortunately, the inhospitality toward the arts is often expressed in a cold indifference and sometimes outrage at the artist as a person. Dirksen suggests we start by "accepting the uniqueness" of the artist. If artists are expected to wear traditional clothing and wear their hair in an "accepted" style, artists, he feels, will "generally feel alienated. Churched people need to realize that for an artist, 'my body and clothing is a living piece of art.'"[3]

Taylor's greatest frustration is dealing with evangelical "resistance to the use of the imagination." He refers to the "propensity and deeply engrained" attitude toward "literalism and rationalism" as the view that says the only legitimate form of communication is a verbal form of preaching and teaching. This view, he thinks, is the source of evangelical resistance to artistic imagination. This fear of the imagination comes from the reality that art is "less controllable than the rational-factual." The imagination draws on forms of communication that are considerably less controlled—in fact, the imagination celebrates "ambiguity, paradox, mystery, and irony"—all of which is deeply mistrusted by the modern evangelical mindset, which is shaped by science and reason.[4]

But not all older evangelicals are resistant to the arts. Cathy Townley, a boomer, is a case in point. She heads up Wellsprings, an organization that seeks to train and provide resources to churches to develop "worship that is indigenous, expressive and creative." She understands the younger evangelicals' fear of illustrative art. "Art," she writes, is not canned. It is "not a program or the latest rage to bring people into the church. Don't use it like that." Instead, she asks us to remember "the artist is in all of us" and that the artist that is within us is "sacred space." God, she says, "lives there, in the midst of the struggles of life." Consequently, the very process of art is "creating a way of spiritual maturity." The artist is "like a midwife, unearthing the shards of their own and another's past, and providing a space where God and humans can meet." She calls upon evangelicals to "encourage the art and the artist, and watch Jesus transform a broken heart."[5] Good advice.

Poet Scott Cairns, another boomer, says alienation is "a rite of passage through which every adolescent (and certainly every nascent artist) must pass. But the issue is just that: the artist really must pass *through* it." But where do they go? What is the outcome of getting past the resistance and the feeling of alienation? It is this: "Art *isn't* the means by which the artist communicates already realized matter; on the contrary, it is the means by which the artist comes to apprehend elusive matter, and if she's lucky, a glimpse of mystery, the making of art is, first, a way of knowing; if it ever does serve as a way of distributing knowledge, that is something that happens after the fact and is exceedingly independent of the artist's intentions." The artist's primary concern is not to communicate but "to find out what she doesn't know—in part, what she doesn't know about the world, or about God, or about human relationships, but mostly what she doesn't know about herself."

Furthermore, an artist doesn't work alone. An artist works with tradition. Cairns advises all artists to "establish a relationship with his or her tradition." Tradition is "an enabling presence quite distinct from the ossified and repressive burden that most artist-wannabes presume." The past, Cairns believes, like T. S. Eliot taught, is "powerfully present." Eliot's version of the power of the past is this: "What happens when a new work of art is created is something that happens simultaneously to all the works of art which preceded it . . . whoever has approved this idea of order . . . will not find it preposterous that the past should be altered by the present as much as the present is directed by the past."[6]

Cairns offers advice to young artists who experience alienation from the mainstream and indifference and inhospitality from the church:

> So, you're feeling a little lonely as you go about your solitary task, you worry that the world doesn't understand you. You worry that you have this enormous drive to make things, but so little encouragement or appreciation from those around

you. Well, the world, our nation, your hometown, and your own family are largely comprised of folk who need to make—works of art. And the few "works of art" they appreciate are works that serve practical purposes—ceramic lamps, wooden spoons, macramé. When it comes to painting, they prefer Wal-Mart oil colors. When it comes to pottery, they prefer, well . . . Wal-Mart pottery. When it comes to photography, they prefer their own. And when it comes to poetry, they prefer poems that work like instructions for assembling a bicycle, poems that say clearly and directly one thing. I wouldn't waste a lot of time and energy in blaming them for that or seeking to convert them to your way of thinking; they are surely called to other vocations, which they'd do well to pursue with passion.

But you? You are potentially in contact with some of the most interesting people who have ever lived. What's more—as you develop as an artist, you're actually learning their language.

As for alienation? My guess is that, if you do go to the trouble of finding yourself a likely circle of dead artists to spend time with, you won't feel quite so alone.[7]

Good advice. Artists will take it. Let's hope the older evangelicals will heed it and make more room for the true artist and his or her art.

A Theology of the Arts

In order for evangelicals to become more attuned to good art, they will have to come to a good theology of art making. William Dyrness, a professor at Fuller Seminary, believes that "the Christian's involvement and impact on the arts will reflect his/her convictions about the nature of Christianity, the character of the world and the meaning of art."[8]

In a handout given to his students, Dyrness distinguishes between three approaches to the arts taken by various evangelicals: withdrawal, substitution, and infiltration. Those who withdraw from the arts (this group probably comprises the largest group of fundamentalist evangelicals) are those whose theology is based on the conviction that the "world is controlled by forces hostile to God." Such people believe that in history we are experiencing "a progressive development of anti-Christian forces." For them, salvation is a "total severance" from the world. Art is a profession "under a death sentence" because it is part of the world that is passing away; the material world will be destroyed. This Gnostic view of creation allows that art may be used to illustrate the gospel, to assist in evangelism, and express Christian sentiment. Art is generally approved for Sunday school illustration and tracts but questioned as a serious Christian subject for painters.[9]

The attitude of the second group, the substitutionists, is less Gnostic. It affirms the original goodness of creation but now sees the world as hopelessly fallen. They view creation as tainted so thoroughly by sin that it is not redeemable. For this group, salvation is found in creation of an alternative culture in which God is glorified. In this new culture art can express Christian values, but it does require a separate structure, a sanctified context, so to speak. The function of art is therefore to express the reality of the gospel and to glorify God directly. Consequently, it is possible to create a genre of art such as Christian music, painting, drama, poetry, and the like.[10]

The third view, infiltration, views creation as intrinsically good. While it acknowledges that the fall has had a drastic effect on creation, it affirms the lordship of Christ over all creation by virtue of *Christus Victor* and the present reign of Christ over the whole world witnessed to by the church. Salvation is the ultimate redemption of God over all the evil forces now working against creation. But now, before the reign of God is a literal reality over all creation, Christians individually and the church corporately can, through the arts, redeem creation from the perversion of evil so that creation embodies the reality of redemption it represents. In this theology of creation, which is where the younger evangelical finds a home, art is a "valid expression of the 'image of God in people.'" And art "reflects our divine capacity to create symbols of our value." Art then gives a "true and valid expression of the human situation (faith or unbelief) and glorifies God the creator."[11]

This third view is the historic view of the arts found in the great works of art associated with the ancient Orthodox church, the medieval era, and the Christian artists of the Renaissance period. This is the theology that now animates the younger evangelical and releases the imagination of the younger evangelical artists. A brief summary of that theology as it pertains to the arts is in order.

For centuries the focus of Protestant thought about worship has been on worship as a cerebral act. What made worship was the sermon. People gathered in church to get an "Aha!"—a morsel of thought they could chew on during the week. In this context there has been little need or use for the arts. Where do we go for a theology that will restore the use of the arts in our worship? Let me suggest that we return to the ancient way of thinking about the Christian faith, which involved three dogmas: Creation, Incarnation, and Re-creation.

First, creation. The Apostles' Creed begins with the words "I believe in God, the Father almighty, creator of heaven and earth." There is reason for this particular wording of the creed, and it lays the groundwork for our theology of the arts. In the middle of the second century a heretical form of Christianity (Gnosticism) became quite influential. One of its central doctrines was the argument that creation was intrinsically evil. Gnostics argued for two gods: the spirit god who is good and the creator god who is evil. The creator god is Yahweh of the Old Testament. (The Gnostic doctrine of creation resulted in a full repudiation of the entire Old Testament, including, obviously, its approach to the arts.) On the other hand, the god of Jesus is the spirit god unencumbered by materiality. Thus the Christianity Gnosticism espoused was a superspiritual faith that rejected all use of form and materiality. Even Jesus was not a material being but an apparition. Obviously in this theology there is no place for the arts—no place for anything material.

Irenaeus and Tertullian, the two most influential theologians of the second century, became the primary apologists against the Gnostics. They argued in keeping with the Old Testament tradition that God was the creator and that God's creation was good.

This affirmation of the goodness of creation provides a basis for the arts in and of itself. Because God created a material world—a world of sight, sense, touch, movement, and matter—all of creation is a worthy vehicle through which the truth about the creator can be communicated. While this argument provides a solid theological basis for the arts, another theological doctrine goes even deeper—the incarnation.

The early church interpreted John 1:14, "The Word became flesh," not as a mythological idea or an allegorical image but as an actual, physical embodiment of God in creation. God did not merely step into history, God became his own creation. Irenaeus described it this way: "Born by his own created order which he himself bore." God didn't just wear the creation as a cloak but became the creation and participated in the reality of time, space, and history just as we do. In God's enfleshment, the divine and immaterial God was united to the human and material reality of human existence. Tertullian said it well: "Therefore [materiality] is a worthy vehicle for grace." We can translate his insight into these words: *Just as God was embodied in human flesh, so also divine reality can be communicated through material reality.* In other words, the arts are not mere enhancers or illustrations of the Gospels but actual expressions of redeemed creation. In art, the creation is fashioned into the praise of God.

Third, re-creation. We must ask, as they did in the early church, Why did God become incarnate? The Gnostic answer to this question is quite different than that of classical Christianity. Because for Gnostics the incarnation was an apparition, their answer was that the spiritual presence of God was in the apparition called Jesus. For Gnostics salvation came from what Jesus, the apparition of the Spirit of God, taught. He taught that the spirit of man, which was good and came from the Spirit of God, was imprisoned in the body which was evil. The spirit of man, they argued, could be freed of its imprisonment to the body simply by knowing it did not have to be the slave of materiality. This truth was enough to set the spirit free. Salvation was knowledge.

Both Irenaeus and Tertullian countered that the God who created became the creation in order to re-create the world. Their answer, of course, recognized that creation had been adversely affected by the fall. God's mission in Jesus Christ was to bear the burden of the fall and its impact on creation—death—and to release creation from its bondage to death in order to re-create and thus restore the creation. The release that death holds over creation happened in the death and resurrection of Jesus and will be consummated in the second coming.

Thus salvation is not mere knowledge but the actual salvation of creation. Therefore, the arts function in a redemptive way. In the arts we release time, space, touch, sight, smell, sound, and movement from its bondage to sin to be an example of redemption and a foretaste of the coming kingdom of God, when all creation will be released completely from the effect of sin and be free to enter eternal praise. In this sense, the artist's work is to anticipate God's glory in the *eschaton*.

In sum, because of creation, and even more because of incarnation and the promise of re-creation, nothing is profane for those who know how to see.

The incarnational understanding of the arts means that the arts are not mere enhancements or adornments, nor merely functional acts of communication. They embody the message of redemption.

The arts take the very stuff of creation (e.g., stone, wood, sound, and light); vessels made of creation (e.g., textile, glass, gold, and silver); elements of creation (e.g., water, bread, and wine); and the human body (e.g., movement and gesture), and make these tangible expressions of redeemed creation. The arts open the portals of heaven, where all creation is in continual praise. This is the objective side of the arts, a side we see in Revelation 4–5. In this beautiful description of worship, there is no hint of performance or an audience—only a transfiguration of creation imbued with the magnificence of God's splendor and eternal glory.

On the subjective side, the arts both embody the historical events of God's saving action in history and evoke the experience of transcendence, wonder, and awe. They transform the natural, the human, and the material into the disclosure of otherness. They lift the ordinary into the extraordinary and return the transformed reality into the experience of the ineffable. In this way the arts lift us up into the transcendent reality of the future, into a momentary existential experience of the kingdom that is to come.

The younger evangelicals understand this deep creational, incarnational, and re-creational sense of the arts. Perhaps they will move us toward a reform of the arts and to the restoration of the arts to their rightful place.

Admonitions from the Younger Evangelicals

What does this restoration of aesthetics among the younger evangelicals look like?

First, they are listening to the wisdom of the ages. For example, Pope John Paul II wrote a *Letter to Artists* that holds great appeal for the younger evangelicals. *Regeneration Quarterly*, a think-tank magazine for the younger evangelicals, carried lengthy excerpts. Consider the pope's comments on the text, "God saw all that He had made, and it was very good" (Gen. 1:31). The pope distinguishes between the "creator" and "craftsman" and speaks of God "who bestows being itself." The craftsman, however, "uses something that already exists, to which he gives form and meaning." Artists are craftsmen whose vocation is beauty. The artist's central image of beauty arises from God's incarnation of himself in creation. This incarnation is "the central point of reference for an understanding of the enigma of human existence, the created world and God Himself." The pope then gives an overview of art in history and concludes with admonitions on beauty. "In so far as it seeks the beautiful . . . art is by its nature a kind of appeal to the mystery. Even when they explore the darkest depths of the soul or the most unsettling aspects of evil, artists give voice in a way to the universal desire for redemption." Art, the pope continues, "has a unique capacity to take one or other facet of the message and translate it into colors, shapes, and sounds which nourish the intuition of those who look or listen. It does so without emptying the message itself of its transcendent value and its aura of mystery." Finally, the pope challenges artists: "Use your creative intuition to enter into the heart of the mystery of the Incarnate God and at the same time into the mystery of man."[12]

The pope's encouragement to artists reminds me of my favorite story of evangelism through beauty. A man named Vladimir, who was prince of Kiev, sent several of his followers in search of the true religion. First, they went to the Moslem Bulgars of the Volga, but they found "no joy," only a "mournfulness and a great smell." Then they went to Germany and Rome and found the worship more satisfactory but still lacking in beauty. Finally they came to Constantinople and attending the Church of the Holy Wisdom, they discovered what they were seeking. Consequently, they reported to Vladimir, "We knew not whether we were in heaven or on earth, for surely there is no such splendor or beauty anywhere upon earth. We cannot describe it to you: only this we know, that God dwells there among men, and that their service surpasses the worship of all other places. For we cannot forget that beauty."[13]

In this true story, the subjects of Vladimir put their finger on three importance aspects of the arts: the first is found in their statement, "We knew not whether we were in heaven or on earth"; the second in the words, "God dwells there among men"; and the third in the phrase, "for we cannot forget that beauty." All three of these statements point to the unity between form and spirit in the beauty of God's creation.

Younger evangelical Mark Driscoll reflects on the power of beauty: "God is beautiful and His creation reflects His beauty. God created man and woman in His image and likeness to also create works of beauty. For this reason Mars Hill [the church he pastors] values the arts, expression and creativity. To be made in the image and likeness of God is to yearn for the creation of beauty that reflects our creator." But to accomplish this goal, Driscoll claims, "The artist cannot merely reflect the fallen state of things" but must also "cause a thirst for the beauty yet to be revealed in paradise." This kind of work, Driscoll argues, in the tradition of Dyrness's "infiltration" and the pope's *Letter to Artists,* creates "works of redemption that mirror the ministry of Christ, to the glory of the Father." This kind of artistic work is what lies at the "heart and essence of being a co-creator" with God in the re-creation of the created order.[14]

Second, this theology of art and its expression in beauty has led the younger evangelical to a new interest in icons and iconography. For example, I recently taught a course at Regent College, an international graduate school of Christian Studies located in Vancouver, British Columbia, Canada. On a section of the second floor of their campus building stood a beautiful icon, the product of one of their students. Prominently displayed next to the icon were nine "rules for the icon painter." Here they are:

1. Before starting work make the sign of the cross and pray in silence and pardon enemies.
2. Work with care on every detail of your icon, as if you were from the Lord Himself.
3. During work, pray in order to strengthen yourself physically and spiritually; avoid all useless work, and keep silence.
4. Pray in particular to the Saint whose face you are painting. Keep your mind from distractions, and the Saint will be closer to you.
5. When you choose a colour, stretch out your hands interiorly to the Lord and ask His Counsel.
6. Do not be jealous of your neighbour's work; his success is your success too.
7. When your icon is finished, thank God that His Mercy granted you the grace to paint the Holy Images.
8. Have your icon blessed by putting it on the Holy Table (of your parish church). Be the first to pray before it, before giving it to others.
9. Never forget:

    · The joy of spreading icons throughout the world
    · The joy of the work of icon writing
    · The joy of giving the Saint the possibility to shine through his/her icon
    · The joy of being in union with the Saint whose face you are revealing

It is not uncommon to find icons displayed where younger evangelicals worship. For example, younger evangelicals may sit in a circle on the floor, having all around them numerous burning candles and in the center a display of icons surrounded by many candles. As they sit in silence, or pray with Celtic, Iona, and Taizé songs playing in the background, they look at these icons as windows to heaven and see and experience the heavenly reality of the transcendent and Holy God.

Third, the interest in beauty has also led the younger evangelical to a new interest in church architecture and the beauty of space. Daniel Lee is the architecture guru of the younger evangelicals. He, like others, is concerned about "the reductionistic nature" of the architecture of corporate America and especially of the churches that follow this model. "Christians," he said, "are no longer heard in the public square." They cannot be "distinguished from the rest of culture." He's greatly concerned by the materialism expressed in recent corporate architecture. He calls it the "architecture of mammon" and suggests Christians should resist this kind of architecture and call into being an architectural style that "transforms life, including culture." He rejects the "Wal-Mart church" and says "we should build spaces crafted specially for a human-divine encounter with God."[15]

Westwinds Community Church in Jackson, Michigan, has created space that evokes an encounter with the divine. The pastor, Ron Martoia, a younger evangelical, was recently interviewed by Leadership Network. The church is a breathtaking fusion of the ancient cathedral with space that is contemporary, transcendent, and immanent all at once. Dave Driscoll, a member of the congregation and an award-winning architect himself, literally moved into the office for six months and posed the question, "What would a twenty-first century cathedral look like?" The church board wanted to know, "How can we take our mission to lead everyone toward full life development in Christ and allow the journey of life development to be reflected in the building?"

The first visual sight as you enter the front doors is a "cathedralesque" axial corridor. It is 175 feet long, 28 feet tall and 18 feet wide. Its largeness makes you feel like you have stepped into another world and you instinctively feel a sense of awe, majesty, and transcendence. As you walk down this monastery-like hallway with its high gothic-like arches, you note that it is a pathway that leads you off into various "life development studios"—places to pray, study, relate with others, or a place to be alone to stand or sit in silence, listening for the still small voice. Pastor Ron says there was some skepticism by the people of the church as the plans were being set forth, but now people say, "Wow, this is a place where people can encounter God in ways that you just couldn't in a plain old building." We want, he says, "to mediate deeply moving experiences with God that foster health. . . . We want people to move toward wholeness. . . . The facility helps to define the experience. Whether we're using aromatherapy, oil, or candles; whether it's media this week, or a reflection time of journaling; whether it's a fifth-century healing service where people are washing feet in basins and then being anointed with oil and dried off with a white towel by an elder; or whatever it happens to be, the space really helps to define the experience. Our auditorium is the only place where dramatic painting and glazing is not used so that every time people walk into the auditorium it can be configured differently." They keep no permanent art in their worship space, so they can continually change the art to reflect their worship and the changing Christian seasons.

The entire building, every inch of the 22,000-square-foot building, inside and out, is a work of art. And what goes on inside that place of housed art is art. "Art," says Pastor Ron, "provides an ambiguity that verbal communication does not." What this church creates is what Ron calls "moment collections." These are moments "that somebody hears God's voice. It might be upon entrance. It might be upon exit. Regardless of when it is, we have to steward those moments." I am really thankful, says Pastor Martoia, that we built "something that's artistic, that will bespeak our model of ministry, and be in harmony and consonance with that."[16]

I hope this chapter demonstrates that the younger evangelical is significantly different from his or her evangelical predecessors when it comes to art. Younger evangelicals are adding to the more word-oriented culture of modern evangelicalism the new dimension of art. Younger evangelical Thomas Hohstadt rightly states that the new language arising out of the dust of modernity is "the language of metaphor." "Like all arts, rituals, and symbols, this new metaphor—this new interplay of the senses—will represent something 'not there' . . . something beyond itself . . . something unseen. And it will embody the power—through God's grace—to transform us . . . to re-create us . . . even to heal us"[17] (see table 16).

Table 16
Approach to the Arts

	Traditional Evangelicals	Pragmatic Evangelicals	Younger Evangelicals
Dance	Never	Never	Moderate
Processions	Seldom	Never	Moderate
Candles	Moderate	Never	Seldom
Icons	Never	Never	Frequently
Banners	Moderate	Never	Moderate, used in processions
Drama	Seldom	Frequently	Moderate, used in church-year services
Environmental Art	Moderate	Never	Frequently, especially for church-year services
Photography	Not used	Not used	Moderate use*
Painting	Not used	Not used	Moderate use*
Sculpture	Not used	Not used	Moderate use*
Pottery	Not used	Not used	Used in Communion vessels*

*Used to create an atmosphere for worship. Also, many younger evangelical communities do neighborhood "art shows" as opportunities to connect with people in the neighborhood.

15

Evangelists
From Rallies to Relationships

I grew up in a Baptist church where we called an evangelist to come and preach a revival every year. I believed that raising my hand, walking down the aisle, and confessing Jesus as Savior was the only way evangelism was done. I still affirm the place of mass evangelism and would never deny that many people have heard God's call through the words of traveling evangelists and, responding to that call, have experienced a transformed life. In the eighties, a new form of evangelism was introduced called seeker evangelism. This evangelism proved to be highly effective. Thousands have come to Christ in this ministry. Their broken lives have been restored, and new hope for the future has been born. However, as effective as these forms of evangelism have been, both are being questioned by younger evangelicals. They are looking for a third way to evangelize in a postmodern world.

The Younger Evangelical Dilemma

Some younger evangelicals, especially those who study evangelism in some of our evangelical seminaries, are in a quandary about evangelism. The models they are taught don't ring true for effective evangelism in a postmodern world. For example, Bernie Van De Walle, assistant professor of theology at Canadian Bible College, says, "Live by entertainment-based services, die by entertainment-based services. The next guy with the next hot show . . ."[1] David Di Sabatino, editor of *Worship Leader*, goes so far as to say, "Silence every radio and television preacher, stop every evangelical book or tract from being published, take down every evangelical website from the net and simply ask Christians to show one tangible expression of Jesus' love to another person every day. We would be far better off."[2]

Dawn Haglund had a bad experience learning about evangelism in seminary. She found her course very difficult—emotionally. "We had standard lectures, required readings, and memorization, plus ten required 'interactions' with people to tell them about Jesus. . . . I thought I was just rebellious or just being a 'bad Christian' because I found myself internally reacting against the required interactions." Her problem was that the "rules" had standardized the process of evangelism, even "canned" it. She made it through the course but remained troubled by its requirements and uneasy about her own negative response. She even wondered if something was wrong with her. Why was she so turned off by this predetermined form of evangelism? Some time later, Dawn reports, she was reading "an interaction between Brian McLaren, Dallas Willard, and a small group of young pastors who were discussing how postmodernism impacts our thinking and the new ways postmoderns are looking at ministry including evangelism." She reports, "I began to cry . . . I was so moved and freed by the realization that I believe different things at the core and that is why I had such a struggle with the course on evangelism in the seminary."[3]

So what is the answer? Where is the younger evangelical going with evangelism?

John Green, founder of a ministry to gay and lesbian street prostitutes in Chicago, doesn't think "evangelism is people telling about Jesus" as much as it is "people hearing about Jesus."[4] The decisive turn among the younger evangelicals is summed up by Dale Dirksen, a young college professor, who says, "The most effective way I have been used in evangelism is when I am available for relationships with people God brings into my life."[5] Bruce McEvoy agrees: "Behind every conversion story is a story of a relationship."[6]

The new, younger evangelical approach to evangelism is more like a walk, a process on a spectrum. "It happens," Haglund says, "through community . . . through accountability. . . . It happens when we intentionally order our lives in such a way to be like Jesus."[7] "It's a kind of evangelism," says David Di Sabatino, "that is more like that of St. Francis who advocated preaching the gospel at all times, and if necessary use words."[8]

A word often used by the younger evangelicals to characterize their breed of evangelism is "authentic." David Hopkins, a college student, wrote a very thoughtful article on the phony "hyper-reality" of our time. What he says is worth noting, because he points us to the opposite of hyper-reality—the authentic.

His article begins by pointing to the "x-treme" that has captivated so many young people today—"sky diving, bungee cord jumping, rock climbing, snow boarding, skiing, skateboarding and paragliding are just a few examples." "Why," he asks, "is this society so obsessed with sport experiences that go to the edge?"[9]

He draws on the insights of French philosopher Jean Baudrillard who claims "we live in a world saturated by simulations. Simulations are reasonable facsimiles, or authentic replicas, of the world produced by the media, advertising, television, motion pictures and other influencing factors."[10]

We all know these stimuli. As we drive down the highway, we listen to the radio, see billboard signs, see advertisements for McDonald's, 7-Eleven, and Wal-Mart. But, says Hopkins, "none of these things is real, in themselves, but symbols or signs for something else." These simulations, he says, following the insights of Baudrillard, "have invaded our consciousness so greatly we confuse the facsimile with the real." Consequently, "We panic. . . . We desperately attempt to escape this plastic world by embracing events, activities, and lifestyles which assure us of our reality." But following Baudrillard these events are "hyper-reality or more-real-than-real." We pursue the x-treme to validate our existence. "Body-piercing, tattooing, talk-shows, 'real-TV', giant video screens at sporting events or concerts, celebrity worship, surround-sound, virtual reality, self-help manuals, telephone psychics, and fad diets" are some of the ways we attempt to find self-validation. But they are "just another simulation . . . hyper-real, not *really* real."[11]

Hopkins represents the thinking of many younger evangelicals. He carries this bold analysis one more step: "The church," he charges, "has also fallen into the panic pursuit of validation. . . . We are willing to sell out to anything that looks trendy in order to boost our attendance." Instead of worshiping Jesus Christ, who is the suffering servant of God, "we rally around Jesus Christ super star." In this context Jesus is not Jesus but a symbol for the divine, a concept of the holy. Church services transform into entertainment spectacles. The pastor is an entertainer, a comedian, and a deliverer of the weekly "warm fuzzy." The church service is nothing more than a talent show.[12]

Hopkins continues with his prophetic message to the church of the slick, the church of glitz and entertainment. Representing the voice of an untold number of younger evangelicals, he cries out: "For the churches trying to *do* postmodernism, you are missing the point. Postmodernism is the context we work in, not the goal. This next generation wants what anyone else would desire, the possibility to connect with the holiness of God in a loving community of honest people with the same hopes. And this cannot be solved simply by pursuing a postmodern paradigm. You can follow all the tactics, methods, and models, but if it doesn't connect people with the reality of God, forget it. All you will have is community-in-a-can. *This generation can see a sell-job from a mile away. Ultimately, they don't want the x-treme. . . . They want the authentic*" (emphasis mine).[13]

Hopkins's advice? "Truly humble yourself. Even to the point if God calls you to be a failure for His glory, you will embrace it with joy. Even to the point if God gives you a ministry where you will never see its blessings in your lifetime, you will embrace it with joy. Remember this, if you seek man's approval, you will get it . . . one tiny tombstone (maybe), a short funeral service (maybe), and a one-column obituary among a world of 5.8 billion people (maybe). If you seek God's approval, you will receive the honor of serving Him for all eternity and being among those written in the book of life."[14]

In David Hopkins's voice we hear commitment, passion, and authenticity. For younger evangelicals this is where evangelism starts. It's not seeing a show but hearing a life and experiencing that life incarnated into community. One becomes an evangelist by being evangelized in the whole of his or her being. With authentic evangelism, it takes an authentic Christian to generate another authentic Christian. And it takes an authentic community to grow an authentic Christian. That's how it works. Authenticity generates authenticity.

What Is Evangelism in a Postmodern World?

The younger evangelical asks not only "What is evangelism?" but more specifically "What is evangelism *in a postmodern world?*" The *Next-Wave* web magazine, a communiqué representing the younger evangelical, asks this question in a serious way. "The church," they write, "must learn to live and breathe in the postmodern world, and find ways to be the agent of change that Christ called her to be." So, how is evangelism accomplished? The younger evangelical confesses "relatively little has happened thus far, because all of us are starting at this from ground zero. The new landscape is like nothing we have seen before, and it takes time to find your path." This is a time they say "of re-calibration, re-focusing, re-thinking, and usually of profound paradigm shifts. One could compare it to a slow-motion earthquake. The landscape is changing, the ground is trembling beneath our feet, and our certainty is disappearing fast." Their desire "is to see people enter a relationship with Jesus Christ. Receive his forgiveness, enter his community with the saints, worship in ways that are meaningful to them, and reach out to others in their world."[15]

A clue, I think, to how the younger evangelicals will do evangelism in a postmodern setting is seen in the statement above. It's an old and new, ancient-future evangelism. What's old is the "relationship with Jesus" and "receive his forgiveness" parts. What's new is the context of "worship" and "community" and the kind of training envisioned to "reach out to others."

In order to do the "old," there needs to be a faithfulness to the gospel message which I clearly find among the younger evangelicals. They are committed to the tradition that goes back to the very beginning of the faith—*personal regen-*

erative faith in Christ. In order to do the "new," that is to speak into the postmodern world, they are again returning to tradition—*the church visible*, with an emphasis on worship, community, and witness training.

For example, worship has become the window to the postmodern church. Church start-up guru Steve Nicholson advises leaders of start-up churches to "ask God for a worship leader as a confirmation of your call. If you aren't finding a worship leader, you better be very certain you are even on the right track before you go. I can think of a number of people who eventually did it (a start-up church without the right worship leader), but boy, it's hard." Nicholson advises the young pastor to do "worship centered on an expectation of meeting with God." There is no hint of entertainment or glitz in his words. For Nicholson, worship is "people coming into the presence of God . . . the church being God's temple, the place where God dwells. . . . You teach people to be looking for that interaction, that connection with God in worship. . . . Folks have to *see* it."[16]

The community aspect of the church is another important component for the younger evangelicals. It has to be a welcoming, accepting community—of all sorts of people. Some time ago, for example, a good friend of mine was appointed pastor of a small church with about six or ten people. The church was located in a growing area but for some reason or another, the church failed to attract people, and the few it attracted did not remain.

My friend was told, "Let's give it a year. If the church hasn't grown, we will have to close it down." About six months later, I heard the church had sixty people in attendance. Naturally I was curious. What could have caused such rapid growth?

Because I had a Sunday free, I decided to visit the morning service. What struck me were the words the pastor said before the passing of the peace. Holding his hands out toward the people in a gesture of openness and vulnerability, he said, "Our God is a welcoming God. The only way our guests will know that God is a welcoming God is if we are welcoming people. The peace of the Lord be with you," he said, to which the people responded, "And also with you." Everyone broke from their pews and took a good five minutes to express to each other in attendance the peace of God. It was a rich time of spiritual hilarity and joy. The passing of the peace expresses the character of a welcoming God and of a community that cares enough to incarnate God's welcome.

The younger evangelical knows that community has the power not only to lead people into conversion, it also has the power to disciple and train new converts to be witnesses.

James Houston, whom many have labeled the senior theologian of the spiritual life, says, "What is destroying Christianity is the marketeering of Christianity. . . . Disciple-making is not about replicable, transferable methods, but about the mystery of two walking together. Methods treat discipleship as a problem to be solved, but mentoring treats discipleship as a relationship to be lived." Thus,

Houston said, "Christian maturity is always a social, and never an individual reality. There is no such thing as *my* maturity. There is only *our* maturity."[17]

One Local Church Example of Evangelism and Discipleship

Westwinds Community Church in Jackson, Michigan, is an excellent example of a postmodern church that combines evangelism with discipleship. Ron Martoia, the pastor, wrote me that their mission statement, "leading everyone to full development in Christ," has "gotten into the DNA of the church," because, he wrote, "we have modeled, storied, preached, visualized with art, this mission. In short we have beat the drum very loudly."[18]

To lead the congregation into a deep experience of the church's mission, Ron has developed the "Cross-Training" model. "The whole model is built on the notion that we have certain interior things that need cultivation that are then expressed, fleshed out or developed on the exterior. The goal is to help new and old Christians 'to be a healthy, viable and contributing Christ follower' by being 'imprinted, bonded, and teamed.' Each of these three realities have a 'ground' and a 'manifestation' that are rooted in biblical principles of the transformed and transforming life. Here, for example, is my simple diagram for the process:"

Illustration 1
The Cross-Training Model of Mission

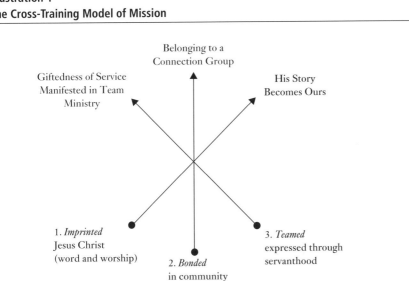

I should note that Ron works with a more complex and color-coded circle of relationship that can't be replicated here. Ron writes, "What we are essentially saying is, 'If you want to be healthy and more deeply maturing, wherever you are on the growth continuum, you need to be imprinted, through Word and worship; bonded, through being in a connection group; and teamed, where your personal mission and gifts can be expressed in serving with others of like passion and vision.' . . . If we beat this three-part drum often and creatively enough . . . we will move the church deeper. . . . We are convinced that both the brand new believer as well as the twenty-five-years-in-Christ veteran can benefit equally from this cross-training model. By design, it is tiered, flexible, and antilegalistic." The final comment in Ron's email to me was this: "The goal is not attracting a crowd but transforming a core."[19]

Process Evangelism

Westwinds Community Church, like other churches of the younger evangelical sort, is turning to process evangelism. This was the form of evangelism used in the pagan world of the third century and has been adapted to the present postmodern secular situation and set forth in my book, *Journey to Jesus: The Worship, Evangelism and Nurture Mission of the Church*[20] (see table 17, p. 225).

Journey to Jesus is designed to meet the need for authentic spirituality. The process is designed not only to convert the unchurched but to disciple, spiritually equip, and incorporate new Christians into a community of people where faith is nurtured by worship from week to week and year to year. What follows is a brief explanation of the steps involved in the ancient practice of process evangelism as detailed in *Journey to Jesus*.

The Seeker

The first step is to evangelize the seeker. Effective evangelism begins with personal contact and an eventual invitation to come to worship. Worship is faith proclaimed and acted out. In worship we embody truth, proclaim it, sing it, pray it, teach it, enact it. The idea behind process evangelism is that you bring the seeker to church where she is surrounded by truth expressed in the church's hospitality and in lively, engaging worship.

To aid the unchurched person in a thoughtful engagement with the person of Jesus, I wrote the booklet *Follow Me!*, which was designed to study with a Christian mentor and friend.

When the seeker has accepted Jesus as her personal Savior, she now goes through the first passage rite, "The Rite of Conversion." This rite, done in worship, does what good rites do. It is a rite of transition in which new converts publicly reject Satan and his ways and turn to Jesus. In this rite of renunciation and affirmation, the disciple of Jesus is born.

The Hearer

The new convert now enters into a second stage of evangelism and spiritual formation. In the early church this stage was a three-year process of discipleship during which new converts were *formed* into committed Christians. They were welcomed into the church and into the practices of being a disciple.

I wrote a booklet called *Be My Disciple!*, which leads the new convert into a period of discipleship. First, it introduces the new Christian to what it means to be in the church. Second, it helps the new Christian to worship the triune God in a way that praises the Father, thankfully remembers the work of the Son, and invokes the Holy Spirit. Third, it teaches the new Christian how to pray the Scripture using a method of contemplative Scripture encounter.

This stage ends with "The Rite of Covenant." This passage rite emphasizes the two sides of conversion: God has chosen you; you choose God's provision in Jesus Christ. While this choice was initially made in the rite of conversion, it is publicly proclaimed once more as the new convert digs into a deeper level of faith commitment and now commits to move toward baptism and a full life of spirituality in the church.

The Kneeler

In the third stage of process evangelism, the new convert is transitioned into a period of learning about spiritual warfare. In the early church, new converts were known as *kneelers*. The term *kneeler* captures beautifully this period of humility and submission, as the new convert learns how to be subject to the Spirit.

A contemporary equivalent is a booklet I wrote, entitled *Walk in the Spirit!* This booklet presents the principle of spiritual warfare. What does it mean to put off the old man and put on the new man? How do you do it? Then, like the third-century practice which *Journey to Jesus* adapts for the twenty-first century, the new convert learns the meaning of prayer through a study of the Lord's Prayer. Next, the kneeler looks at the meaning and uses of faith through an exposure to the Apostles' Creed. Finally, as in the early church, the convert is taught that the battle with the enemy is fought through prayer and steadfast faith.

This period ends with the passage rite of baptism. In baptism the new convert renounces the devil and all his works once again and affirms faith in Christ as God's sign of baptism is administered in the name of the Father, the Son, and the Holy Spirit. This rite is completed with the seal of the Holy Spirit as the new Christian is anointed with oil and the laying on of hands.

But the journey isn't over. Now the new convert is assimilated into the full life of the church, becoming a participatory member.

The Faithful

The final stage of *Journey to Jesus* is a full incorporation into the life of the church. Now the convert is a member of the *faithful*. Arriving at this stage doesn't mean that the journey is over by any means; it's simply the final step in beginning a path of spiritual formation that continues throughout life.

The booklet for this seven-week period of spiritual discipline is *Find Your Gift!*, a study that parallels the early-church practice of forming the new Christian into full, active, and conscious participation into the life of the new community.

The new Christian is schooled in three aspects of the Christian life. First, a spiritual mentor helps the new Christian to discern her gifts and gives her a ministry in the church. She is asked to see how all of her work is an offering to God. Here the emphasis is on integrating faith and worship with life vocation—praising God, as *The Book of Common Prayer* states, "not only with their lips, but also with their lives." Finally, now that the new Christian is within the fold of the church, she is directed to be a witness, to bring others to the church and to Christ by mentoring them on the journey to Jesus.

This stage of spiritual formation does not have a passage rite that leads to another stage of depth. Rather, the rite that characterizes this lifelong path is the Eucharist, a continuous rite of spiritual nourishment. In the Eucharist, a two-sided action occurs again and again. On the divine side, the Eucharist is God's spiritual nourishment given to us. In this divine action, we are brought again and again to a face-to-face personal encounter with God's incarnation, the Word made flesh, crucified and risen for our salvation. We feed on the personal and powerful presence of God's saving energy. As we remember his work on our behalf, as we eat bread and drink wine, we ingest this salvation, we allow ourselves to be fed by his saving presence and are transformed by his life within us.

In the rite of the Eucharist the "Journey to Jesus" is both ended and begun. What we moved toward, we now live out of. The new life has become a reality. Our new calling is to endure to the end. Our goal is a long obedience in the same direction.

This form of process evangelism is currently being tested in various local churches. While its usefulness is not yet fully known, it is clear that it has considerable potential in a postmodern world where evangelism has taken on the new dimensions of process and spiritual formation.

I hope I have been able to convey how unique the younger evangelical is when approaching the question of evangelism. Like their evangelical predecessors, the younger evangelicals are passionate about introducing people to Jesus. But they are highly aware that conversion in not individualistic, and it is no panacea for life's problems. They differ from the pragmatic evangelicals in that they are much lower in profile, more understated, and more committed to lifelong transformational relationships in small groups. Groups are intended for long-haul relationships as opposed to the megachurch use of groups, which are usually intended for rapid division and multiplication. In a word, the younger evangelicals are committed to a missional evangelism in their immediate neighborhood, an evangelism that is committed to making disciples and embodies the authentic reality of Christ in all of life (see table 18).

Table 17
Journey to Jesus

Stages of growth	Seeker	Hearer	Kneeler	Faithful
Spiritual Goal	Conversion	Discipleship	Spiritual formation	Incorporation
Passage Rite	Rite of Conversion	Rite of Covenant	Rite of Baptism	Eucharist (continuing rite)
Resource	*Follow Me!*	*Be My Disciple!*	*Walk in the Spirit!*	*Find Your Gift!*

Table 18
Approach to Evangelism

	Traditional Evangelicals	Pragmatic Evangelicals	Younger Evangelicals
Style	Mass evangelism	Seeker evangelism	Process evangelism
Emphasis	Decisionism by raising hand, walking aisle	Personal commitment generally made through one-on-one relationship	Personal commitment made in community with mentor and passage rites
Helps	Tracts Four Spiritual Laws	Seeker Services Christianity 101	Church as caring community receives people who eventually come to faith Spiritual Mentors
Time Expectations	Instant conversion	Gradual conversion	Conversion is a process
The Process	The sinner's prayer	Long time of guided inquiry followed by sinner's prayer	A converting person goes through stages of growth and turning points accompanied by passage rites that express the renunciation of evil and a commitment to Jesus Christ

(continued)

Table 18
Approach to Evangelism

	Traditional Evangelicals	Pragmatic Evangelicals	Younger Evangelicals
Baptism	Generally comes after decision	Generally comes after decision	A part of the process and major passage rite
Follow-up	Informational classes	Small-group involvement	Mentors and small groups

16

Activists

From Theory to Action

The nineteenth-century heritage of John Wesley and of the pietists before him was one that centered very much on the inner city, the plight of humanity, and a concern for the poor and downtrodden. During the first half of the twentieth century, fundamentalism and then the new evangelicalism focused more on doctrinal issues as historic Christianity came under attack. More attention was paid to the poor during the later half of the twentieth century. But attention to social issues was diverted by the megachurch movement and its emphasis on the seeker, a movement that reached many people but by all accounts the suburban yuppie more so than the inner-city poor. Bernie Van De Walle, bemoaning inattention to the poor, says, "Our heritage is found in reaching to the downtrodden and disenfranchised; we have sold this inheritance for a mess of pottage."[1]

Bernie raises the question now on the lips of younger evangelicals: What does it mean to say that the younger evangelicals have moved from theory to action?

To begin, let's look at the perspective of an anonymous author from the second century, a century much like the twenty-first in many ways:

Christians cannot be distinguished from the rest of the human race by country or language or customs. They do not live in cities of their own; they do not use a peculiar form of speech; they do not follow an eccentric form of life. . . . They live in

227

their own countries, but only as aliens. They have a share in everything as citizens, and endure everything as citizens, and endure everything as foreigners. . . . They busy themselves on earth, but their citizenship is in heaven. . . . They marry like everyone else. . . . They share their board with each other, but not their marriage bed. . . . What the soul is to the body, so Christians are to the world.[2]

This excerpt says three things about Christians: (1) they affirm the world and live in its political, economic, institutional, and family structures like anybody else; (2) they do not live by the ideologies of the world; and (3) in a sense, they hold the world together. They have a redemptive, transformative place in the world. These three tensions expressed in the literature of the early church are once again affirmed by the younger evangelical.

Younger Evangelicals Live *in* the World

Younger evangelicals are not separatists. They are not, like the Amish, withdrawing from life to create a distinct life and work culture within the world. They do not build their own cities. They have not developed a language of their own. They have not created their own political party. They work in every sphere of economic activity; they belong to both Republican and Democratic parties (in the United States); they are found in every educational institution; and they live in every city, town, and village. They drive cars, buy clothing and groceries, and go to sports events. They marry, have children, live in houses, go to block parties, and assimilate with their neighbors. This is their world, their culture, their place, and their time. In all this they are the same as all other citizens of the world.

Younger Evangelicals Are Not *of* the World

Just as Christians of the early church rejected the way of the world, so younger evangelicals are separating themselves from the ideologies of the world. This separation is occurring on both an individual level and in convictions about the corporate role of the church.

Personal Separation from the Ideologies of the World

For example, the moral context in which the younger evangelicals grew up was that of *values clarification*. This process taught young people that "desires represent valid moral and ethical values." This subjective emphasis has put our youth culture into a quandary and in need of an objective standard for right and wrong. They are fully aware that relativism in morality has produced disastrous results.

According to author Paula Rinehart, "This generation seems willing to be taught the biblical truth that might have been labeled 'sexist' only a few years ago." Chuck Milian is the singles pastor for Crossroads Fellowship in Raleigh, North Carolina. Milian offers a six-hour dating seminar and regularly has a packed house. He said, "Young people are ready to hear a biblical perspective on relationships when they are sufficiently sick of the pain of being loved and left, and when they can see something better in God's way." These are the kids that have spawned the chastity movement that has spread through the churches and beyond to teens who have discovered "it is better to wait."[3]

Regarding homosexuality, the younger evangelicals have grown up with discussions about gay rights, gay families, and gay lifestyles. What is their take on this controversial social issue? Generally, the younger evangelical seems to support two options.

First, Nelson González argues in a *Regeneration Quarterly* article for the nonsexual option for homosexuals, and he does so out of a resignation to the belief that homosexuals are incurable. Citing the biblical insight that people are made for relationship, he suggests choosing chastity in a community of people committed to the common life (e.g., a monastery, an evangelical fellowship of Christians who live communally, or a committed same-sex relationship without "genital relationship").[4]

On the other hand, Jeffrey Satinover is more hopeful that a homosexual can actually change, especially through healing prayer. In an article he cites the work of Leanne Payne and her Pastoral Care Ministry, which "incorporates the best of the secular, psychological approaches into vital, spiritual, orthodox Christian healing."[5] Younger evangelicals are more understanding and sympathetic to homosexuals than their boomer parents. However, like their parents, they teach that homosexual genital relationships are wrong.

Marriage continues to be a topic of interest and reflection among the younger evangelicals. Approximately 40 percent of "twenty-somethings" are children of divorced parents, so it is a matter of urgency to think seriously about marriage and family. Evangelicals have been bombarded by the romantic notion of marriage through the media and "marriage enrichment" seminars that promise couples all sorts of results such as "falling in love again" or finding ways to "stay in love forever." According to Jeffrey Greenman, "the dominant language of enrichment, intimacy, fulfillment and self-esteem suggests a deep and powerful trend toward a dangerous psychologization and privatization of the Christian faith." What is missing in evangelical circles, he says, is "serious reflection on the positive spiritual purpose of marriage: sharing together in a public 'life-partnership' dedicated to glorifying God."[6]

Rodney Clapp, younger evangelical commentator on love, marriage, and family, says we need to get over the myth of romantic love and base marriage on better footing. Romantic love, he claims, "is based on inconstancy, on feelings unanchored in reality." He thinks marriage should be an outgrowth of *koinonia* or churchly community. In this context married people *"become* people who love each other," he argues.[7]

The Church Is Separate from the Ideologies of the World

The younger evangelicals keenly aware that they live in a post-Constantinian world, a world where the church and state are separate. This knowledge has led them to reject the religious political solutions to our culture wars offered by both the right and left. The efforts of both the right and the left to lobby moral legislation was and continues to be a colossal failure. The Christian Coalition spent nearly $8 million on lobby efforts in 1997, but even Paul Weyrich, who influenced Jerry Falwell to start the Moral Majority, concedes they lost the war: "politics has failed because of the collapse of culture . . . the culture is an ever-wider sewer. We are caught up in a cultural collapse of historic portions, a collapse so great that it simply overwhelms politics. . . ."[8] Weyrich goes so far as to suggest that we need to drop out of the culture and assume a separatist stance.

The capstone of the turn away from religious political pressure on government came with the publication of *Blinded by Might* (1999) by two former employees of the Religious Right, Cal Thomas and Ed Dobson. They write, "We think it is time to admit that because we are using the wrong weapons, we are losing the battle."[9] Andy Crouch, editor-in-chief of *Regeneration Quarterly*, sees the younger evangelicals "embracing something that few players in the United States' fractious public square are willing to embrace: the complexity and ambiguity of moral choices—others and their own."[10]

Younger Evangelicals Believe Christians Are the Soul of the World

The goal of being the soul of the world is to be "salt" and "light"—a transforming presence. How is that accomplished? The common answer among the younger evangelicals is to return to a theology of the church as the "embodied presence" of Jesus Christ.

Dawn Haglund writes, "Programs are important . . . [but] I'm a strong advocate of an embodied presence of Jesus." But what, we may ask, does this mean? "I think," writes Haglund, "that Jesus' presence is communicated in many other ways besides our words—such as compassion, encouragement, love, grace, kindness, service, etc. . . . with no agenda to necessarily be telling them about Jesus. I believe He will be evident in the way we care for people."[11]

How exactly will the younger evangelicals integrate their commitment to be the embodied presence of Christ into our postmodern world? Nathan Coleson writes of his homeless ministry,

> The homeless outreach I colead is an example of embodied presence. Rather than set up a food kitchen and expect people to come to us, meet us on our terms, we take home-cooked meals and fellowship out to the streets. And we keep going back. Initially, it was simply about meeting people exactly where they're at and loving them the way we've been called to love. Over the months relationships have developed and we've learned a great deal about the men and women we minister to. I don't think we would've learned nearly as much or made as much of a difference in others' lives had we not been willing to put our fears and misconceptions aside and step into the "homes" of the homeless.[12]

A second example of an embodied and transforming presence is found in the work of John Green, founder of a Chicago-based ministry to reach sexually exploited males. John writes,

> These men are put out of sight and out of mind by society and the church. . . . In 1970 in America, 20 percent of prostitution arrests were male. By 1998 the percentage had risen to 40.2 percent. These are men sought after by the John Wayne Gacys and Jeffrey Dahmers of our world. . . . They are modern-day lepers left to wander streets, parks, and seedy bars waiting for the next trick. Sexual issues are explosive and divisive in our world today. This has made the church timid to meet the needs of people struggling sexually, largely because difficult social problems take an immense amount of energy to make a difference in. They fly in the face of our McWorld where fast food, fast happiness, and fast answers are the rule of thumb. Prostitution, homelessness, addiction, and mental illness: all of these resist and frustrate our efforts at providing fast solutions. . . . In truth they are solved through pain, sacrifice, relentless tenderness and long-suffering.

Tory Baucum served a church where both rich and poor worked together to embody a community that demonstrated the church as a visible society not divided by class. He writes,

> My last parish was socio-economically diverse. At the same altar rail I gave Communion to a man who had grease under his fingernails from pulling crank shafts all week and another whose nails were manicured, who owned his own company and sat on the board of an Ivy League University. I always felt we were counter-cultural at the Lord's Table.[13]

Dan Curran points to servanthood within the community, not power, as the goal of the church. He suggests the church will make its greatest impact only when it seeks "to engage in the holistic role of serving—building communities on the grass roots level rather than lobbying petitions or voting in special interest elections."[14]

These examples could be multiplied and drawn from every major city in the United States. These younger evangelicals are aware that the reign of God through Jesus Christ is demonstrated, not by power politics, but by a presence of humble servanthood within the structures of our social, political, economic, institutional, and relational existence.

Todd Hunter, former national director for the Association of Vineyard Churches, says, "God has always raised up an effective apologetic for His sovereign plan to save the world through Jesus. . . . I feel a great sense of expectancy to see what God will do. . . . God has a plan for the church in the transitional period we live in." This plan, according to Hunter, is found in the missional church that can influence "from the margins." The picture he sees is "a group of people who are highly intentional about truly obeying Jesus' commands so as to increasingly be like him. The *individuals* pursuing this life-goal are in *community*. . . . A key attitude is that this Christ-initiating community does not 'have a mission.' A mission 'has them!' . . . This is a life that marries conformity to Christ's clear teachings (discipleship) to Christ's mission (evangelism)." It is not, he writes, a "consumer Christianity," nor is it a "bumper sticker faith." It is an obedience to the commands of Jesus. "Look out world," he proclaims. "The world thrived best when it was least inclined to accommodate culture. . . . I have confidence that the young leaders I know will rediscover a pre-Constantine form of Christian life."[15]

One well-known pre-Constantinian type of ministry is Lawndale Community Church in Chicago, started by Wayne Gordon when he was a student at Wheaton College. By all accounts Lawndale is the most burned-out area of Chicago, not only figuratively but literally. After the murder of Martin Luther King in 1968, protestors literally burned the entire Lawndale area. Almost immediately every commercial enterprise, "factories, grocery stores, auto dealerships, clothing stores, drugstores—everything," moved out. People fled as well. Then the drug lords moved in, and soon crime and poverty became the dominant enterprise of an area sensible people avoided. But Wayne Gordon saw a mission field. He took a job teaching and coaching at the local high school and started a Bible study with his football players. Several became Christians and tried to fit into church, but because it was a bad fit, Gordon started a church. Gordon, who was already ensconced in the neighborhood with his wife, saw a vision for what could happen through the embodied presence of the church. Soon this ministry expanded into a thriving multigenerational and multicultural community that included a gymnasium for young people; a health clinic with doctors and dentists that serves seventy thousand people a year; a rehab program for housing; a halfway house for drug rehabilitation; tutoring classes; a clothing store; and even a thriving restaurant. Donna and Robert Holt find fulfillment here, they say, because this is a church that "cares about people and their well-being. . . . [People at church] exemplify that there's more to life than making money."[16]

The Younger Evangelical and the War on Terrorism

How does this threefold tension—(1) living *in* the world, (2) not being of the world's ideologies, and (3) being the soul of the world, an embodied and transforming presence—relate to the war on terrorism? Younger evangelicals, like all of us, are caught in the tension of being citizens of this country yet members of the church—an alternative worldwide community whose ultimate priority is found in the words of the Lord's Prayer: "Thy kingdom come, thy will be done, on earth as it is in heaven." My email correspondence with the younger evangelicals reflects this tension.

College professor Dale Dirksen thinks younger evangelicals will ask questions like, "Why does this hatred of America exist? . . . Is it possible to right any wrongs that have been committed by the West?"[17] David Taylor thinks, "It will confuse our sense of patriotism even more."[18] Dawn Haglund believes that "many of our generation have tended toward nonviolence and that certainly will be tested."[19]

My sense is that the war will call younger evangelicals to clarify four questions:

1. What is the church?
2. What is the nation?
3. What is the church in the nation?
4. How do we live as citizens of this world and the next?

What Is the Church?

Throughout American history the church has struggled with the continual temptation to confuse the church with the nation. The confusion between America and the church is a consequence of the reality that this country was founded on many values that correspond with Christian commitments. For example, America has honored the dignity of the human person, respected human rights, and calls on its citizens to serve their neighbors.

In recent history, the moral majority confused national and ecclesial spheres by trying to put the church into the service of the Republican party and its conservative policies, especially its support of life, and its concern to curb violence, pornography, and the breakup of the family. While these are all good values and are supported by the church, the church does not exist to support the political agendas of the government, no matter how righteous.

The church is not the nation, *it is the body of Christ*, and the younger evangelicals seem to understand this. As the body of Christ, it is a unique community of people among the nations. Its identity is not with this or that nation but with the kingdom of God. The church transcends all national and cultural boundaries and draws from every tribe and nation. It is not about the politics of the world but the politics of Jesus, the living out of kingdom principles.

What Is the Nation?

The first point to be made about the nation is that it is not the church. In the Old Testament, God called a particular people, the Jews, to be a nation of people under God to witness to the world of God's existence, of God's love and compassion, and of God's goal for humanity. But since the coming of Christ, God's witness in the world is no longer identified with a particular nation of people but with a people from every nation. No nation today, including America, is to be identified as God's unique and particular people.

What, then, is the work of the nation? Its work is to rule the people, to govern the well-being of the people, to restrain evil, to promote the good and the welfare of its people. A nation may choose to assert the state as an end in itself, subject only to its own arbitrary rules. Or a government may choose to affirm universal absolutes, as the American government did, and put itself "under God." Because of America's choice, Christians are comfortable living in this country but persecuted in Muslim and communist countries, where the government rules under other commitments.

What Is the Church in the Nation?

The brief remarks above should show that the church has a different *identity* than the nation. The identity of the nation is all of its citizens. In the case of America, the melting pot of the world, we are all immigrants from one country or another. We may be Polish American, African American, Indian American, Arab American, and so on. Together we make up the citizenry of the United States. But the identity of the church is not America, or Europe, or Africa, or any other geographical area. We are alien residents of every nation and tribe. Our true citizenship is the family of God that transcends all earthly boundaries.

The church also has a different *function* than that of the nation. The nation is called to care for its people, to protect them from danger, and to look out for their welfare. But the church's function is that of a witness. Paul's letter to the Ephesians reminds us that the church's battle is not against flesh and blood but against the principalities and the powers of spiritual evil (6:12). The church, collectively around the world, is called to witness to the work of Christ through which the powers of evil have been overcome (Eph. 3:10), and to live as a community of the kingdom now in this world.

What Should We Do?

How should we function as Christians, the body of Christ, in this new post–September 11 era? Essentially, *we live in two worlds simultaneously,* and our job is to be good citizens of our nation while we are first and foremost citizens of the kingdom that is to come. This means we have responsibilities to the state: we have a responsibility to obey its rules when they do not conflict with our heavenly citizenship, to pay our taxes, and to love our neighbors. We have responsibilities to the church: here we worship, study Scripture, grow spiritually, and anticipate God's ultimate rule over the world when every knee shall bow and every tongue confess that Jesus is Lord. Even though we live in two worlds, as Christians we live "under God" in every area of life, serving him in the church and in our vocation, knowing that the higher authority is the rule of the Spirit in the church. The kingdoms of this world will fall and fail. They have no eternal endurance. But the kingdom of God will endure throughout eternity.

The church, then, is a counterculture that has a different vision of the world than that of people who are not in the church. This vision is where our feet are planted—the place from which our hope springs. Yet, as citizens of a country, we can be patriotic and proud of our country, support it in prayer and participation, always knowing that our ultimate commitment is to the church, God's people everywhere and forever.

In sum, the younger evangelicals' presence in the world is clearly a threefold tension. They live in this world and want to be good responsible citizens, yet they are not of the world. They are moving away from the moral relativism of their postmodern world, seeking to offer a sharp alternative to the dominant culture. In personal and family and church life, they hope to be an embodied presence, an alternative culture that acts as salt and light, transforming society toward the kingdom ideal (see table 19).

Table 19
Approach to Social Action

	Traditional Evangelicals	Pragmatic Evangelicals	Younger Evangelicals
Sources	Chicago Declaration Moral Majority Christian Coalition Political activism	Megachurch	The local church
Focus	*National issues:* Abortion Family Pornography Conservative vote Violence	*Neighborhood issues:* Drugs and alcohol Rehabilitation Single mothers Divorce groups	*City issues:* The poor The homeless The abused

(continued)

Table 19
Approach to Social Action

	Traditional Evangelicals	Pragmatic Evangelicals	Younger Evangelicals
Goals	Cleaning up America World relief	Helping people meet needs in time of cultural breakdown	Rebuilding the cities and city communities Creating alternative communities

Conclusion

17

A New Kind of Leadership
for the Twenty-First Century

Like all other authors I spend a great deal of time thinking about the titles of what I write. My goal is for a title to fall into the category of what publishers call "truth-titles"—that is, to come up with a title that quickly reveals the content of a book. From the beginning I felt the title *The Younger Evangelicals* to be a truth title; this is a book about evangelical faith, and the title tells you it is mainly about the next generation of evangelicals.

Finding the right title for the last chapter has not been as simple. I have had three chapter titles in mind, each of which says something true about the younger evangelical.

One chapter title I considered was "A New Kind of Conservative for the Twenty-First Century." The truth is that younger evangelicals are conservative in that they believe the road to the future runs through the past. They definitely are not returning to a fifties past. Instead, they are returning to the Wesleyan past, to the Reformers of the sixteenth century, and to the ancient past of the first three centuries of the church, for inspiration and wisdom. This new movement is not a perpetuation of twentieth-century traditional evangelicalism but a much older faith and practice, more tested by time, more rooted in the tradition of the ancient church.

For this reason, a second title that came to mind was "An Ancient-Future Church for the Twenty-First Century." This chapter title captures the current sense of bringing the past into the future, of drawing on the wisdom of the ages for the current work of the kingdom.

In spite of my attraction to these titles, I've settled for "A New Kind of Leadership for the Twenty-First Century." The title includes the conservative nature of the younger leaders and speaks to their direction of an ancient-future ministry.

But what kind of leadership will the younger evangelical offer to the church? Where will they take us? One way to answer this question is to acknowledge their leadership will be very different than that of the evangelical traditionalists and pragmatists. Traditional evangelical leadership of the twentieth century is driven by the concerns formed out of the fundamentalist/modernist controversy. This traditional movement, its churches, publishing houses, mission boards, seminary and college education, have been and are now shaped by an apologetic Christianity that is fueled by the desire to be right. On the other hand, pragmatic evangelical leadership is driven by the market. It drinks from the hydrant of the church growth movement, the megachurch, the self-help books, and the program emphasis of the church that is fueled by religious consumerism. What do people want? How can we market to every need? How can we get the numbers?

The leadership of the younger evangelical is not shaped by being right, nor is it driven by meeting needs. Instead, it arises out of (1) a missiological understanding of the church, (2) theological reflection, (3) spiritual formation, and (4) cultural awareness. For this reason the most appropriate title of this chapter is "A New Kind of Leadership for the Twenty-First Century."

These four areas represent a *circle* of leadership, so there is not a correct point of entrance, nor a linear sequence of understandings through which a person must travel. Enter at any point and the entire arena explodes with connections and interrelationships that continue to expand in numerous directions, none of which come to closure. Consequently, leadership from the younger evangelicals will be dynamic, organic, and continuously changing paths as it constantly responds to cultural changes and to the hope for the eschatological reign of God over all of creation (see illustration 2 on p. 241).

I have decided to end this book with a brief presentation of the scope of each area of future leadership. This will help us gain a perspective on the kind of leadership the younger evangelical will offer.

First, younger evangelicals are increasingly affected by the missiological understanding of the church. The *Missio Dei* identifies God's purpose in the world to rescue the world, save it, redeem it, restore it. To this end God sent Jesus Christ. By his sacrificial death and resurrection he has conquered the powers of evil. He has sent his Holy Spirit to apply his saving work to the entire created

Illustration 2
The Younger Evangelical Leadership Circle

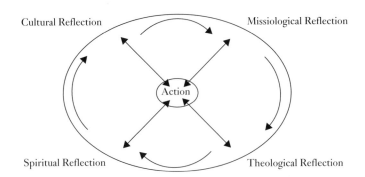

One may enter the leadership circle at any point. There is no linear sequence. Rather, all aspects of leadership are immediately connected and interrelated to each other all at once. The new leadership is a dynamic, unfolding interplay of "action—reflection—action" that touches every aspect of Christian life, thought, and ministry.

order, so that at the end of history God will reign over his restored creation and every knee shall bow and every tongue confess that Jesus is Lord. This is the *gospel*. It is the good news of God that we are to share with the world, calling people to repent from their sin and by God's grace through faith come under the present reign of God in their personal lives and in the church. We are to be individually and corporately the people of God's present rule in the world. The ramifications of the *Missio Dei* are manifold. We do not define God's mission. It defines us. It tells us who we are, what our mission is, how we are to do ministry, worship, spirituality, evangelism. There is no aspect of the Christian life, thought, and ministry that is not connected with God's mission to the world.

For this reason *theological reflection* is inextricably linked with the *Missio Dei*. It is not an abstract objective discipline that is subject to reason, logic, or science. It is instead a communal reflection on God's mission that arises out of God's people as they seek to discern God's work in history and his present action in the life of the community. As Jesus sends the Holy Spirit, so the Spirit fills the church, sends it forth, and remains within it always serving Christ, the chief minister of the church. Theological reflection is guided by the Spirit and clarifies for the church the nature of God's person and work in history. The practice of ministry is already theology—theology in action. The church, reflecting on this action, does theological thinking. This process has resulted in a universally embraced trinitarian and christologically based theological understanding. The mission of God in the world is the mission of the triune God manifested in Jesus, who is both fully human and fully divine. Every aspect of Christian life, thought, and action is inextricably linked with this universally affirmed understanding of God. God's union with Jesus, the empowerment of the Holy Spirit in the church, and the work of reconciliation in the world arise from the church's theology of God, Christ, and the Spirit, which is expressed in the ecumenical creeds of the ancient church. When one enters the circle of leadership through theology, one is driven to missiological reflection, to spiritual formation, to cultural awareness.

One can also enter the circle through *spiritual formation*. Spirituality is no longer exclusively identified with spiritual habits of prayer, Scripture reading, and attendance at church, or with an ethical list of do's and don'ts such as prohibitions against drinking and dancing. Rather, spirituality is informed by the *Missio Dei* and the theological reflection of the church, emphasizing the holistic message of becoming truly human. God's mission is to rescue the world. Through Jesus, the perfected second Adam, we see what man is called to be. The community of Jesus, the church, is called to be a corporate witness to what reconciled humanity, living as the extension of Jesus in the world, can become and will ultimately be in the kingdom of the future. True spirituality is the process of becoming human individually and corporately. This kind of spirituality, grounded in God's mission to the world, moves within the circle to action. True spirituality compels Christians to put themselves in the position of the poor and oppressed. It illuminates for believers how the exercise of Christ's ministry in the church and to the world works to liberate humanity from the demeaning affects of poverty and injustice. It releases the human spirit to participate in God's current, continuing redemptive action in history, which is moving toward God's ultimate victory over all evil and an eternal reign over all creation. Spirituality is a link between mission, theology, and ministry. It is not so much a knowing but a being—a true embodiment of God's mission.

Finally, this circle of leadership being formed by the younger evangelicals is not complete without recognizing the deep concern they have for *cultural awareness*. Younger evangelicals point us to a new hermeneutic which is grounded in Scripture, shaped by the reflection of the church throughout its history, and expressed in the concrete situation of the church in its particular place in culture. We now live in a postmodern culture—a culture shaped by globalization; historical nostalgia; spiritual hunger; mystery; oral, visual and interactive forms of communication; the longing for community; and the fear of terrorism. God's mission through the church, our theological reflection within the church, and our search for spiritual meaning take place within this particular kind of culture.

I have attempted to show throughout this book that the leadership of the younger evangelical will be distinctly different than that of the twentieth-century evangelical. It will be biblically informed by the *Missio Dei* to rescue the entire created order; it will be theological, rooted in the trinitarian and christological consciousness of the ancient creeds; it will be spiritual, reflecting the purposes of God to restore the fullness of his image in us and to bring all creation to its redemption and reconciliation to God; and it will be conscious in its action in and to the world of the new cultural situation in which we live, taking into consideration the new realities of the twenty-first century.

Notes

Introduction

1. See Robert E. Webber, *Ancient-Future Faith: Rethinking Evangelicalism for a Postmodern World* (Grand Rapids: Baker, 1999).

Part 1: Introduction to the Younger Evangelicals

Chapter 1—A Century of Evangelicals

1. Robert Webber and Donald Bloesch, *The Orthodox Evangelicals* (Nashville: Thomas Nelson, 1978), 43–44.

2. See Adolf Harnack, *What Is Christianity?* (New York: Harper, 1957).

3. See George M. Marsden, *Fundamentalism and American Culture: The Sharing of Twentieth-Century Evangelicalism 1870–1925* (Oxford: Oxford University Press, 1980).

4. Ibid., 6.

5. Ibid., 7.

6. Walter Lippman, *Preface to Morals*, in Marsden, *Fundamentalism and American Culture* (New York: MacMillan, 1929), 3.

7. William Jennings Bryan, in Marsden, *Fundamentalism and American Culture*, 4.

8. Marsden, *Fundamentalism and American Culture*, 184.

9. George Dollar, *A History of Fundamentalism in America* (Greenville, S.C.: Bob Jones University Press, 1973).

10. Marsden, *Fundamentalism and American Culture*, 166.

11. Ibid.

12. George M. Marsden, *Reforming Fundamentalism: Fuller Seminary and the New Evangelicalism* (Grand Rapids: Eerdmans, 1987), 38.

13. Marsden, *Fundamentalism and American Culture*, 37.

14. Ibid., 85–93.

15. Gary Dorrien, *The Making of American Liberal Theology: Imagining Progressive Religion* (Louisville: Westminster John Knox, 2001), xix.

16. Timothy P. Weber, "Fundamentalism Twice Removed: The Emergence and Shape of Progressive Evangelism," 260, in Jay Dolan and James Wind, eds., *New Dimensions in American Religious History: Essays in Honor of Martin E. Marty* (Grand Rapids: Eerdmans, 1993).

17. See ibid., 267. See also the full development of this shift in Marsden, *Reforming Fundamentalism*, especially chap. 2, "The History before the History."

18. Carl F. H. Henry, *Remaking the Modern Mind* (Grand Rapids: Eerdmans, 1946), 9, 19, 26, in Marsden, *Reforming Fundamentalism*, 78.

19. Weber, "Fundamentalism Twice Removed," 267–68.

20. Carl F. H. Henry, *The Uneasy Conscience of Modern Fundamentalism* (Grand Rapids, Eerdmans, 1947), 14, in Marsden, *Reforming Fundamentalism*, 80.

21. Harold J. Ockenga, introduction to *Uneasy Conscience of Modern Fundamentalism* (Grand Rapids: Eerdmans, 1947), 13, in Marsden, *Reforming Fundamentalism*, 81.

22. Marsden, *Reforming Fundamentalism*, 82.

23. Francis A. Schaeffer, "Should the Christian Tolerate the World Council? Or Is Liberalism Dead?" *Christian Beacon*, 29 July 1948, 4–5, in Marsden, *Reforming Fundamentalism*, 111.

24. Bela Vassaday, in Marsden, *Reforming Fundamentalism*, 111, 114.

25. Francis Fukuyama, *The Great Disruption* (New York: Free Press, 1999), 4–6.

26. Donald W. Dayton, *Discovering an Evangelical Heritage* (San Francisco: Harper & Row, 1976), 135.

27. See Richard Quebedeaux, *The Young Evangelicals* (San Francisco: Harper, 1974).

28. Mark A. Noll, *Between Faith and Criticism: Evangelicals, Scholarship and the Bible in America* (San Francisco: Harper and Row, 1986), 156–157.

29. Weber, "Fundamentalism Twice Removed," 270.

30. Noll, *Between Faith and Criticism*, 158–160.

31. Weber, "Fundamentalism Twice Removed," 270.

32. Ibid., p. 271.

33. Harold Lindsell, *The Battle for the Bible* (Grand Rapids: Zondervan, 1977), 17.

34. Ibid., 19.

35. Ibid., 25.

36. "The Chicago Statement on Biblical Inerrancy" (Oakland, Calif.: 1978).

37. Weber, "Fundamentalism Twice Removed," 274.

38. Harold Lindsell, *The Bible in the Balance* (Grand Rapids: Zondervan, 1979), 319–20.

39. See Webber and Bloesch, *The Orthodox Evangelicals*.

40. Ibid.

41. See Robert Webber, *Evangelicals on the Canterbury Trail* (Waco: Word, 1985); Thomas Howard, *Evangelical Is Not Enough* (Nashville: Thomas Nelson, 1984); and Peter E. Gillquist, *Coming Home: Why Protestant Clergy Are Becoming Orthodox* (Ben Lomond, Calif.: Conciliar Press, 1992).

42. Weber, "Fundamentalism Twice Removed," 279. See G. A. Pritchard, *Willow Creek Seeker Services: Evaluating a New Way of Doing Church* (Grand Rapids: Baker, 1996).

43. See Marva J. Dawn, *Reaching Out without Dumbing Down* (Grand Rapids: Eerdmans, 1995) and Pritchard, *Willow Creek Seeker Services*.

44. See Clark H. Pinnock et al., *The Openness of God: A Biblical Challenge to the Traditional Understanding of God* (Downers Grove, Ill.: InterVarsity, 1994).

45. Gregory A. Boyd, *God at War: The Bible and Spiritual Conflict* (Downers Grove, Ill.: InterVarsity Press, 1997) and *God of the Possible* (Grand Rapids: Baker, 2000).

46. John Sanders, *The God Who Risks: A Theology of Providence* (Downers Grove, Ill.: InterVarsity Press, 1998).

47. David F. Wells, *No Place for Truth: Whatever Happened to Evangelical Theology?* (Grand Rapids: Eerdmans, 1993).

48. Stanley J. Grenz, *Revisioning Evangelical Theology: A Fresh Agenda for the 21st Century* (Downers Grove, Ill.: InterVarsity, 1993).

49. "The Gospel of Jesus Christ: An Evangelical Celebration," The Committee on Evangelical Unity in the Gospel (Glendale Heights, Ill.). See also John N. Akers, John H. Armstrong, and John D. Woodbridge, eds., *This We Believe* (Grand Rapids: Zondervan, 2000).

50. Ibid., 7.

51. Ibid., 16.

52. William A. Dyrness, *Learning about Theology from the Third World* (Grand Rapids: Zondervan, 1990); *Invitation to Cross-Cultural Theology* (Grand Rapids: Zondervan, 1992); *Emerging Voices in Global Christian Theology* (Grand Rapids: Zondervan, 1994).

53. See James S. Cutsinger, ed., *Reclaiming the Great Tradition: Evangelicals, Catholics and Orthodox in Dialogue* (Downers Grove, Ill.: InterVarsity, 1997).

54. Charles Colson and Richard John Neuhaus, eds., *Evangelicals and Catholics Together: Toward a Common Mission* (Dallas: Word, 1995).

55. Ibid., xv.

56. "Universities Question Orthodox Conversions," *Christianity Today* 42 (10 August 1998): 21. See also Demetrios J. Constantelos, "The Evangelical Character of the Orthodox Church," *Journal of Ecumenical Studies* 9 (summer 1972): 544–555; "Orthodox, Evangelical Dialogue in Europe," *Journal of Ecumenical Studies* 22 (winter 1985): 200; Michael J. Christensen, "Evangelical-Orthodox Dialogue in Russia on the Eve of the Tenth Anniversary of Chernobyl," *Journal of Ecumenical Studies* 33 (winter 1996): 79–86.

57. Harold Lindsell, *Free Enterprise: A Judeo-Christian Defense* (Wheaton: Tyndale, 1982).

58. Ronald J. Sider, *The Chicago Declaration* (Carol Stream: Creation House, 1974).

59. Ronald J. Sider, *Rich Christians in an Age of Hunger: A Biblical Study* (Downers Grove, Ill.: InterVarsity, 1977).

60. See Nancy Hardesty and Letha Scanzoni, *All We're Meant to Be* (Waco: Word, 1974).

61. See Weber, "Fundamentalism Twice Removed," 285.

62. See Perry Troy, *The Lord Is My Shepherd and He Knows I'm Gay* (Los Angeles: Nash Pub., 1972).

63. Jeffrey D. Pulis, *Jerry Falwell and the Moral Majority: A Case Study of the Relationship between Theology and Ideology* (Ph.D. diss., Emory University, 1986).

64. James Dobson, *Solid Answers: America's Foremost Family Counselor Responds to Tough Questions Facing Today's Families* (Wheaton: Tyndale, 1997).

65. Beverly LaHaye, *FYI Confidential: A Confidential Bulletin Brief for Your Information from Dr. Beverly LaHaye and Concerned Women of America* (Washington, D.C.: Concerned Women of America, 1997).

66. See Ralph Reed, *How Christians Are Changing the Soul of American Politics* (New York: Free Press, 1996).

Chapter 2—A New Kind of Evangelical

1. Francis Fukuyama, *The Great Disruption* (New York: Free Press, 1999).

2. Charles Fromm, *New Song: The Sound of Spiritual Awakening: A Study of Music in Revival*, a paper presented at the Oxford Reading and Research Conference, July 1983, Oxford, England.

3. Wade Clark Roof, *Spiritual Marketplace: Baby Boomers and the Remaking of American Religion* (Princeton: Princeton University Press, 1999).

4. Ibid., 83.

5. Conrad Cherry, quoted in John Leland, "Searching for a Holy Spirit," *Newsweek*, 8 May 2000, 62.

6. Ibid., 53.

7. Angie Cannon and Carolyn Kleiner, "Teens Get Real," *U.S. News and World Report*, 17 April 2000, 50.

8. John Leland, "Searching for a Holy Spirit," *Newsweek*, 8 May 2000, 63.

9. Lynette Clemetson, "Color My World," *Newsweek*, 8 May 2000, 70.

10. Ibid., 72.

11. Ibid., 74.

12. "The Naked Truth," *Newsweek*, 8 May 2000, 58.

13. Wendy Murray Zoba, *Generation 2K: What Parents and Others Need to Know about the Millennials* (Downers Grove, Ill.: InterVarsity Press, 1999), 42.

14. William Strauss and Neil Howe, *The Fourth Turning: An American Prophecy* (New York, Broadway Books), 247.

15. David Taylor, email correspondence, 14 September 2001.

16. Email correspondence, summer 2000.

17. Paul Keith, email correspondence, summer 2000.

18. Bernie Van De Walle, email correspondence, summer 2000.

19. Dale Dirksen, email correspondence, summer 2000.

20. David Clark, email correspondence, summer 2000.

21. Jonathan Nelms, email correspondence, summer 2000.

22. Kyle Roberts, email correspondence, summer 2000.

23. Dawn Haglund, email correspondence, summer 2000.

24. Tom Beaudoin, *Virtual Faith: The Irreverent Spiritual Quest of Generation X* (San Francisco: Jossey-Bass Publishers, 1998), 178.

25. Dale Dirksen, email correspondence, summer 2000.

26. David Taylor, email correspondence, summer 2000.

27. Andrew Black, "Don't Call Us Slackers," *Faithworks*, November/December 1998, 4–7.

28. Todd Hunter, "The Church of the Future," *Next-Wave*, 14 January 1999, <http://www.next-wave.org/jan99/misscomm.htm> (7 December 2000).

29. See Kathy Juline, "Today's Hope for Tomorrow's Teens," *Science of Mind*, May 2000, 38–47.

30. Matt Redman, Andy Park, and Kevin Prosch, "Our Creed," *Next-Wave*, <http://www.next-wave.org/credo.html> (6 December 2000).

31. Sarah Diffenderfer, "The X Force," *Faithworks*, May/June 1999, 5–7.

32. David Taylor, email correspondence, summer 2000.

33. Ibid.

34. Thomas Hohstadt, email correspondence, summer 2000.

35. David Taylor, email correspondence, summer 2000.

36. Bruce McEvoy, email correspondence, summer 2000.

37. Jim Belcher, email correspondence, summer 2000.

38. Bernie Van De Walle, email correspondence, summer 2000.

39. William Forey, "Color and Marriage Outside the Lines," *Faithworks*, Jan./Feb. 1999, 8.

40. Bill White, in "Color and Marriage," 8.

41. Dieter and Valerie Zander, "The Evolution of Gen X Ministry," *Regeneration Quarterly* 5, no. 3 (1999): 16–19.

42. Todd Flanders, "Pascal: Talkin' 'bout My Generation," *Regeneration Quarterly* 1, no. 2 (1995): 32–33.

43. Correspondence, winter 1999.

44. Cherie Harder, "In Defense of Opacity," *Regeneration Quarterly* 4, no. 1 (1998): 9–17.

45. Jason Archer, personal conversation.

Part 2: The Younger Evangelical Thinkers

1. "The Antimoderns," *Christianity Today*, 13 November 2000, 76.

2. Sherri King, quoted in "The Antimoderns," 76.

3. Paul Jones, response to questionnaire, 13 July 2000.

4. David Di Sabatino, response to questionnaire, 13 July 2000.

5. Joseph Clair, paper, winter 2001.

6. Todd Johnson, email correspondence, fall 2000.

Chapter 3—Communication: From Print to Cultural Transmission

1. Sydney Westrate, faxed correspondence, 30 July 2001.

2. Doron Mendels, *The Media Revolution of Early Christianity: An Essay on Eusebius's Ecclesiastical History* (Grand Rapids: Eerdmans, 1999), 1, 5.

3. J. Jungman, in Pierre Babin, *The New Era in Religious Communication* (Minneapolis: Fortress Press, 1991), 20–21.

4. Pierre Babin, *The New Era in Religious Communication* (Minneapolis: Fortress Press, 1991), 4.

5. Ibid., 5.

6. Ibid.

7. Ibid.

8. Ibid., 58.

9. Ibid., 111.

10. Adrian Riley, "Impact of Multi-Media on Belief," 14 November 2000.

11. David Hopkins, "Sacred Distraction: Concerning the Art of the Spoken Word," *Next-Wave*, <http://www.next-wave.org/oct00/spokenword.htm> (22 April 2002).

12. Thomas Hohstadt, email correspondence, summer, 2000. For an expansion of these ideas see Thomas Hohstadt, *Dying to Live: The 21st Century Church* (Odessa, Tex.; Damah Media, 1999).

13. David Bunker, correspondence, summer 2000.

14. Mark Filiatreau, "Make It Real: The Imagination's Role in Living Our Beliefs," *Regeneration Quarterly* 2, no. 2 (1996): 23.

Chapter 4—History: From Ahistorical to Tradition

1. David Ray Griffin, ed., *The Reenchantment of Science: Postmodern Proposals* (New York: State University of New York Press, 1988), ix.

2. Michael Horton, "Evangelicals and Rome Sweet Rome," *Regeneration Quarterly* 2, no. 2 (1996): 26.

3. See John Milbank, *Theology and Social Theory: Beyond Secular Reason* (Oxford: Blackwell, 1990) and *The Word Made Strange: Theology, Language and Culture* (Oxford: Blackwell, 1997).

4. See Catherine Pickstock, *After Writing: On the Liturgical Consumption of Philosophy* (Oxford: Blackwell, 1998).

5. See John Milbank, Catherine Pickstock, and Graham Ward, *Radical Orthodoxy* (New York: Routledge, 1999) and D. Stephen Long, *Divine Economy: Theology and the Market* (New York: Routledge, 2000).

6. Milbank, *Theology and Social Theology*, 6.

7. Milbank, *The Word Made Strange*, 1.

8. Ibid.

9. Pickstock, *After Writing*, xii.

10. Milbank, *Theology and Social Theory*, 381.

11. Ibid.

12. Ibid., 384.

13. Milbank, Pickstock, and Ward, *Radical Orthodoxy*, the inside flap.

14. Robert L. Wilken, *Remembering the Christian Past* (Grand Rapids: Eerdmans, 1995).

15. Ibid., viii–ix.

16. Ibid., 13.

17. Ibid.

18. Ibid., 15.

19. Ibid., 17.

20. Ibid., 21; see Flannery O'Connor, *Mystery and Manners* (New York: Noonday Press, 1957), 178.

21. Timothy R. Phillips and Dennis L. Okholm, *The Nature of Confession: Evangelicals and Liberals in Conversation* (Downers Grove, Ill.: InterVarsity, 1996).

22. Ibid., 12.

23. Ibid., 20.

24. Mike Brecht, personal conversation, spring 1999.

25. Thomas Oden, *After Modernity . . . What?* (Grand Rapids: Zondervan, 1990).

26. Ibid., 14.

27. Ibid., 21.

28. Ibid., 22.

29. Ibid., 34.

30. Randy L. Maddox, "John Wesley and Eastern Orthodoxy: Influences, Convergences and Differences," *Asbury Theological Journal* 45, no. 2 (1990): 29–53.

31. D. H. Williams, *Retrieving the Tradition and Renewing Evangelism* (Grand Rapids: Eerdmans, 1999).

32. Ibid., 1.

33. Ibid., 4.

34. Ibid., 4–5.

35. Ibid., 7–8.

36. Cutsinger, *Reclaiming the Tradition*, 8.

37. Ibid., 8.

38. Rodney Clapp, *Border Crossings* (Grand Rapids: Brazos, 2000). See also his *A Peculiar People* (Downers Grove, Ill.: InterVarsity, 1996).

39. See Stanley J. Grenz, *Revisioning Evangelical Theology* (Downers Grove, Ill.: InterVarsity, 1993); *Renewing the Center* (Grand Rapids: Baker Academic, 2000); Stanley J. Grenz and John R. Franke, *Beyond Foundationalism* (Louisville: Westminster John Knox, 2000). The themes developed in these books are summarized in "Conversing in Christian Style: Toward a Baptist Theological Method for the Postmodern Context," *Baptist History and Heritage* 35, no. 1 (winter 2000): 82–103.

40. Grenz, *Revisioning Evangelical Theology*, 57–59.

41. Grenz, "Conversing in Christian Style," 87.

42. Ibid., 91.

43. Ibid., 92.

44. See James William McClendon Jr., *Doctrine*, vol. 2 (Nashville: Abingdon, 1994).

45. Gordon Lewis and Bruce A. Demarest, *Integrative Theology*, 3 vols. (Grand Rapids: Zondervan, 1986).

46. Boyd, *God at War*.

47. Loren Wilkinson, "Saving Celtic Christianity," *Christianity Today*, 24 April 2000, 79–85.

48. Ibid., 84.

49. Ibid., 85.

50. Joseph Huffman, "Faith, Reason and the Text: The Return to the Middle Ages in Postmodern Scholarship," *Christian Scholars Review* 29, no. 2: 281–301.

51. Ibid., 281.

52. *Regeneration Quarterly* 1, no. 2 (1995): 4.

Chapter 5 — Theology: From Propositionalism to Narrative

1. Gregory of Nyssa, in Georges Florovsky, *Creation and Redemption*, vol. 3 of *Collected Works of Georges Florovsky* (Belmont, Mass.: Nordland Publishing, 1976), 43.

2. Georges Florovsky, *Creation and Redemption*, vol. 3 of *Collected Works of Georges Florovsky* (Belmont, Mass.: Nordland, 1976), 48.

3. Ibid., 49.

4. Ibid., 82.

5. Ibid., 83.

6. Ibid., 84.

7. Ibid., 85.

8. Ibid.

9. Ibid.

10. Ibid.

11. Ibid., 86.

12. Ibid., 95.

13. See "The Nicene Creed," *The Book of Common Prayer* (New York: The Church Hymnal Corporation, 1977), 326–27.

14. See "The Chalcedon Creed," *The Book of Common Prayer* (New York: Church Hymnal Corporation, 1977), 864.

15. The ancient theme of *Christus Victor* is set forth in Gustaf Aulen, *Christus Victor: A historical study of the three main types of the idea of the atonement* (New York: Collier Books, 1969). This theme is becoming more pronounced among younger evangelicals. See Boyd, *God at War*, and Clinton E. Arnold, *Powers of Darkness: Principalities and Power in Paul's Letters* (Downers Grove, Ill.: InterVarsity, 1992).

16. Florovsky, *Creation and Redemption*, 105.

17. Ibid., 108.

18. Ibid., 120.

19. Ibid., 133–34.

20. John C. Polkinghorne, *Science and Creation: The Search for Understanding* (Boston: Shambhla Publications, 1988).

21. Ibid., 66.

22. Ibid., 65.

23. Ibid., 63.

24. See Pinnock et al., *The Openness of God;* Sanders, *The God Who Risks;* and Boyd, *God of the Possible.*

25. Polkinghorne, *Science and Creation*, 63.

26. Ibid.

27. Ibid., 51.

28. See John C. Polkinghorne, *Science and Theology: An Introduction* (London: SPCK, 1998).

29. The matter of ecology and the care of God's earth is related to beauty and truth. See Thomas Dubay, *The Evidential Power of Beauty: Science and Theology Meet* (San Francisco: Ignatius, 1990).

30. See Harnack, *What Is Christianity?*

31. See Harold Lindsell, *The Battle for the Bible* (Grand Rapids: Zondervan, 1976).

32. See William C. Placher, *Narratives of a Vulnerable God: Christ, Theology and Scripture* (Louisville: Westminster John Knox), 194.

33. Mark Driscoll, *What We Believe*, "Essay on Meaning," <http://www.marshill.fm/believe/meaning.htm> (22 April 2002).

34. David Mills, "Imaginative Orthodoxy," *Touchstone* 12, no. 6 (Nov./Dec. 1999): 28.

35. David Taylor, response to questionnaire, summer 2000.

Chapter 6—Apologetics: From Rationalism to Embodiment

1. See Barry J. Colman, ed., *Readings in Church History* (Westminster, Md.: Newman, 1960), 57.

2. Michel Foucault, *Ethics: Subjectivity and Truth*, ed. Paul Rabinow, in Michel Foucault, *The Essential Works of Foucault, 1954–1984*, vol. 1, trans. Robert Hurley et al. (New York: New Press, 1994), 278–79.

3. Carl F. H. Henry, *God, Revelation and Authority*, vol. 2 (Waco: Word, 1976), 12–13.

4. See Douglas Groothius, *Truth Decay: Defending Christianity against the Challenges of Postmodernism* (Downers Grove, Ill.: InterVarsity, 2000).

5. David Tracy, "Defending the Public Character of Theology," *Christian Century*, 1 April 1981, 350–56.

6. See for example the writings of third-world contributors to Dyrness, *Emerging Voices*.

7. Millard Erickson, *Christian Theology*, vol. 1 (Grand Rapids: Baker, 1983), 40.

8. See J. Wentzel Van Huyssteen, *Essays in Postfoundationalist Theology* (Grand Rapids: Eerdmans, 1997). Van Huyssteen seeks to find a way between what he believes is the extreme of *fideism* on the one hand and rationalism on the other.

9. John Milbank, *Theology and Social Theory* (Cambridge, England: Blackwell, 1993), 3.

10. John Milbank, in Jeff Sharlet, "Theologians Seek to Reclaim the World with God and Postmodernism," *The Chronicle of Higher Education* 46, no. 42 (23 June 2000).

11. William C. Placher, *Unapologetic Theology: A Christian Voice in a Pluralistic Conversation* (Louisville: Westminster John Knox, 1995).

12. Ibid.

13. George Lindbeck, *The Nature of Doctrine: Religion and Theology in a Postliberal Age* (Philadelphia: Westminster Press, 1984), 114.

14. Clapp, *Border Crossings*, 25.

15. Kenneth Kantzer, in Clapp, *Border Crossings*, 25.

16. Stanley Hauerwas, in Clapp, *Border Crossings*, 25.

17. Clapp, *Border Crossings*, 30.

18. Ibid., 31.

19. Grenz and Franke, *Beyond Foundationalism*, 24.

20. Ibid.

21. Ibid., 26.

22. David Clark, response to questionnaire, summer 2000.

23. Paul Jones, response to questionnaire, summer 2000.

24. David Di Sabatino, response to questionnaire, summer 2000.

25. Kyle Roberts, response to questionnaire, 13 July 2000.

26. Dawn Haglund, response to questionnaire, 4 August 2000.

27. Charles Moore, "The Only True Apologetic," *Regeneration Quarterly* 5, no. 2 (1999): 28.

28. Pierre Hadot, *Philosophy As a Way of Life*, ed. Arnold Davidson, trans. Michael Chase (Oxford: Blackwell, 1995), 265.

29. Joseph Clair, correspondence, spring 2001.

30. Joel Handy, correspondence, spring 2001.

31. Joseph Clair, "Rediscovering Communal Epistemology: Towards a Postmodern Apologetic," paper for an independent study in theology, Wheaton College, Wheaton, Ill., summer 1999.

Chapter 7—Ecclesiology: From Invisible to Visible

1. Kevin Offner, "Two Ways of Understanding Church," *Regeneration Quarterly* 3, no. 4 (1997): 11–12.

2. Stanley Hauerwas and William Willimon, *Resident Aliens* (Nashville: Abingdon, 1989), 23.

3. Ibid., 4.

4. Colson and Neuhaus, *Evangelicals and Catholics Together*, x–xi.

5. Ibid., xxv–xxvii.

6. Timothy George, "Evangelicals and Catholics Together: A New Initiative," *Christianity Today*, 8 December 1997, 34–35.

7. Ibid.

8. R. C. Sproul, *Getting the Gospel Right* (Grand Rapids: Baker, 1999), 10.

9. "The Gospel of Jesus Christ: An Evangelical Celebration," printed in *Christianity Today*, 14 June 1999, 51–56.

10. Nicholas Cabasilas, in John Meyendorff, *Byzantine Theology: Historical Trends and Doctrinal Themes* (New York: Fordham University Press, 1974), 175.

11. Cyprian, *On the Unity of the Church* (Willits, Calif.: Eastern Orthodox Books), in Robert Ferm, *Readings in the History of Christian Thought* (New York: Holt, Rinehart, and Winston, 1964).

12. Rodney Clapp, *A Peculiar People: The Church as Culture in a Post-Christian Society* (Downers Grove, Ill.: InterVarsity, 1996), 77.

13. Ibid., 82.

14. Miroslav Volf, *After Our Likeness: The Church as the Image of the Trinity* (Grand Rapids: Eerdmans, 1998), xi.

15. Brian D. McLaren, *The Church on the Other Side: Doing Ministry in the Postmodern Matrix* (Grand Rapids: Zondervan, 1998).

16. Gary Goodell, "Being a 'Third Day' Church," *Next-Wave*, October 2000, <http://www.next-wave.org/oct00/thirdday.htm> (6 December 2000).

17. Brian McLaren, "They Say It's Just a Phase," *Next-Wave*, October 2000, <http://www.next-wave.org/Nove00/phase.htm> (12 December 2000).

18. Ibid.

19. Mark Driscoll, *Who We Are*, "Seasons of Grace: The Story of Mars Hill," <http://www.marshill.fm/who/our-history.htm> (24 April 2001).

20. Ibid.

21. Dan Lee, "The Millennial Church: Postmodern, Spiritual Seeking, Post Denominational Currents" (unpublished article).

22. Eric Stanford, "The New Wave of Gen X Churches: Get Your Glimpse of the Future Here," *Next-Wave*, <http://www.next-wave.org/dec99/newwaveof genxchurches.htm> (7 December 1999).

23. Jim Belcher, "It's the Gospel, Stupid: Generation X and Religion," *Regeneration Quarterly* 1, no. 2 (1995): 23–26.

24. John Green, response to questionnaire, summer 2000.

25. Ibid.

26. Steven C. Ibbotson, "Survivor: Postmodern Paradox," *Next-Wave*, <http://www.next-wave.org/sep00/survivor.htm> (6 December 2000).

27. Tory Baucum, response to questionnaire, summer 2000.

28. Mark Driscoll, "Missional Community and the Art of Gardening," <http://www.marshill.fm/community/community_essay.htm> (11 December 2000).

29. Dawn Haglund, response to questionnaire, summer 2000.

30. Andrew Black, "Don't Call Us Slackers!," *Faithworks*, November/December 1995, 5.

31. Dieter and Valerie Zander, "The Evolution of Gen X Ministry," *Regeneration Quarterly* 5, no. 2 (1999): 17.

32. Barbara Parsole, "Evangelical Leaders Prepare for U.S. Ethnic Millennium," article in a Wheaton College newsletter, n.d.

33. William Frey, in Sarah Griffith, "Color and Marriage," *Faithworks*, January/February 2000, 8–10.

34. Mark Driscoll, "Seasons of Grace," *Faithworks*, January/February 2000, 8–10.

35. *What We Believe*, "Mars Hill Membership Covenant," <http//www.marshill.fm/believe/membership.htm> (11 December 2000).

36. Chris Alford, email correspondence, summer 2001.

37. David Clark, response to questionnaire, summer 2000.

38. *About Mosaic*, "Fulfilling the Vision," <http://www.mosaic.org/about/> (2 December 2000).

Part 3: The Younger Evangelical Practitioners

1. Joel Handy, correspondence, summer 2001.

2. Peter L. Berger and Richard John Neuhaus, eds., *Against the World for the World* (New York: Seabury, 1976).

3. Marva Dawn, *A Royal "Waste" of Time: The Splendor of Worshiping God and Being Church for the World* (Grand Rapids: Eerdmans, 1999), 41.

4. Os Guinness, *The Gravedigger Files: Papers on the Subversion of the Modern Church* (Downers Grove, Ill.: InterVarsity, 1983), 48.

5. Dawn, *A Royal "Waste" of Time*, 41.

6. Os Guinness, *Dining with the Devil: The Megachurch Movement Flirts with Modernity* (Grand Rapids: Baker, 1993), 48.

7. Gene Edward Veith Jr., *Postmodern Times: A Christian Guide to Contemporary Thought and Culture* (Wheaton: Crossway, 1994), 227.

8. Richard John Neuhaus, "The Christian and the Church," in James M. Boice, ed., *Transforming Our World: A Call to Action* (Portland, Ore.: Multnomah, 1988), 120.

9. Lauren Winner, "Gen X Revisited: A Return to Tradition?" *Christian Century*, 8 November 2000, 1147.

10. C. S. Lewis, in Don E. Eberly, *Restoring the Good Society: A New Vision for Politics and Culture* (Grand Rapids: Baker, 1994), 80.

11. Henri Nouwen, in Guinness, *Dining with the Devil: The Megachurch Movement Flirts with Modernity* (Grand Rapids: Baker, 1993), 64.

12. Johnny Seel, "A Cultural Literacy Primer: Ten Resources Christians Need for Understanding Today's World," *Christianity Today*, 28 April 1997, 66.

13. W. Tullian Tchividjian's essay, "A Cry for Difference from the Culturally Weary," printed with permission, was transmitted by email, 29 August 2001.

Chapter 8—Being Church: From Market to Mission

1. B. Joseph Pine and James Gilmore, *The Experience Economy: Work Is Theatre and Every Business a Stage* (Boston: Harvard Business School Press, 1999).

2. George Barna, in Eddie Gibbs, *Church Next: Quantum Changes in How We Do Ministry* (Downers Grove, Ill.: InterVarsity, 2000), 37.

3. George R. Hunsberger, "The Newbigin Gauntlet: Developing a Domestic Missiology for North America," *Missiology: An International Review* 19, no. 4 (October 1991): 391. See the following books by Lesslie Newbigin: *The Other Side of 1984* (New York: Friendship Press, 1983) and *The Gospel in a Pluralistic Society* (Grand Rapids: Eerdmans, 1990).

4. Ibid., 395.

5. Ibid., 396.

6. Ibid., 397.

7. Ibid., 399.

8. Ibid., 403.

9. George R. Hunsberger and Craig Van Gelder, *The Church Between Gospel and Culture* (Grand Rapids: Eerdmans, 1996).

10. Ibid., xvii.

11. James Stump, response to questionnaire, 28 August 2000.

12. Ibid.

13. Dawn Haglund, response to questionnaire, summer 2000.

14. David Taylor, response to questionnaire, summer 2000.

15. Tim Erdell, response to questionnaire, 11 August 2000.

16. Dawn Haglund, response to questionnaire, summer 2000.

17. James Stump, response to questionnaire, 28 August 2000.

18. Jonathan Nelms, response to questionnaire, summer 2000.

19. James Stump, response to questionnaire, summer 2000.

20. R. Scott Gornto, "Journey Missional Community," <http://www.youngerleader.org/webzine/webzine.htm>.

21. John Graham, email correspondence, December 2000.

22. Dann Pantoja, "Please Don't Start Another Postmodern Ministry," *Next-Wave*, November 2000, <http://www.next-wave.org/nov 00/please.htm>.

23. Ibid.

24. Ibid.

25. Ibid.

26. Ibid.

27. Erwin McManus, *About Mosaic*, "Fulfilling the Vision," <http://www.mosaic.org/about/> (24 April 2002).

28. Ibid.

29. Ibid.

30. Ibid.

31. Ibid.

32. Ibid.

33. Ibid.

34. Email correspondence, 5 December 2000.

35. John Graham, correspondence, 31 March 2000.

36. Jeff Bailey, in J. Panner, "Incarnation Ministry," an email response sent to *Cutting Edge* 2, no. 2 (Spring/Summer 1998): 13.

37. Rob Bell, personal correspondence, August 2001.

Chapter 9—Pastors: From Power to Servanthood

1. E. Glenn Wagner, *Escape from Church, Inc.: The Return of the Pastor-Shepherd* (Grand Rapids: Zondervan, 1999), 10.

2. Robert and Julia Banks, *The Church Comes Home* (Peabody, Mass.: Hendrickson, 1998).

3. McLaren, *The Church on the Other Side*, 117.

4. Dawn Haglund, response to questionnaire, summer 2000.

5. Frank Nihart, response to questionnaire, summer 2000.

6. Response to questionnaire, summer 2000.

7. Ken Blanchard, in Greg Warner, "The Power of Teams," *Faithworks*, November/December 1999, 9.

8. Ibid.

9. Response to questionnaire, 30 June 2000.

10. Response to questionnaire, summer 2000.

11. Nathan Coleson, response to questionnaire, 12 September 2000.

12. Levi Hjalmarson, "The Next Reformation," *Next-Wave*, <http://www.next-wave.org/Oct99/nextreformation.htm> (October 1999).

13. Dann Pantoja, "The Paradox of Postmodern Leadership," *Next-Wave*, <http://www.next-wave.org/Dec99/paradox_of_postmodern_leadership.htm> (December 1999).

14. Greg Warner, "The Paradox of Postmodern Leadership," *Next-Wave*, <http://www.next-wave.org/Dec99/paradox_of_postmodern_leadership.htm> (December 1999).

15. Personal interview with David Pendleton, 6 October 2001.

Chapter 10—Youth Ministers: From Parties to Prayer

1. Steve Gerali, "Paradigms in the Contemporary Church that Reflect Generational Values," *The Church and Youth Ministry* (Oxford: Lynx Communications, 1995), ed. Pete Ward, 52.

2. Ibid., 54.

3. George Barna, in Gerali, "Paradigms in the Contemporary Church", 52.

4. Gerali, "Paradigms in the Contemporary Church," 54.

5. Andy Crouch, "Generation Complex," *Regeneration Quarterly* 5, no. 3 (1999): 3.

6. Kevin Graham Ford, *Jesus for a New Generation: Putting the Gospel in the Language of Xer's* (Downers Grove, Ill.: InterVarsity, 1995), 174.

7. Ibid., 191.

8. Ibid., 221.

9. Zoba, *Generation 2K*, 68.

10. Ibid., 69–70.

11. Ibid., 72–73.

12. Joe McDonald and Kurt Vickman, faxed correspondence, 3 October 2001.

Chapter 11—Educators: From Information to Formation

1. Alan Wolfe, "The Opening of the Evangelical Mind," *Atlantic Monthly*, <http://www.theatlantic.com/issues/2000/10/wolfe.htm> (24 April 2002).

2. David Clark, response to questionnaire, summer 2000.

3. Paul Jones, response to questionnaire, summer 2000.

4. Paul Christenson, response to questionnaire, summer 2000.

5. Dawn Haglund, response to questionnaire, summer 2000.

6. Charles Moore, "The Only True Apologetic," *Regeneration Quarterly* 5, no. 2 (1999): 29–31.

7. Dawn Haglund, response to questionnaire, summer 2000.

8. Moore, "The Only True Apologetic," 29–31.

9. Ibid.

10. Mark Driscoll, *What We Believe*, <http://www.marshill.fm/believe/index.html> (24 April 2002).

11. Ibid.

12. Ibid.

13. Ibid.

14. Brad Cecil, personal correspondence.

15. Pat Cole, "Learning to Lead," *Faithworks*, February 2000, 11.

16. John Wallis, "Seminary Experience Overwhelms Students' Faith," *Next-Wave*, November 2000, <http://www.next-wave.org/nov00/faith.htm> (24 April 2002).

17. Ibid.

18. John E. Phelan Jr., "Markings," *The Covenant Companion* (Chicago: North Park Theological Seminary), 6.

19. Ibid.

20. David F. Wells, "Educating for a Countercultural Spirituality," in *Theological Education in the Evangelical Tradition*, ed. D. G. Hart and R. Albert Mohler Jr. (Grand Rapids: Baker, 1996), 293.

21. Ellen T. Charry, *By the Renewing of Your Mind: The Pastoral Function of Christian Doctrine* (Oxford: Oxford University Press, 1997), 18–19.

22. R. Scott Rodin, "Vision Ministry," *Ministry*, autumn 1999, 3.

23. Ibid.

24. Ibid.

25. "The Regeneration Forum," <http://www.regenerator.com/aboutus.html> (24 April 2002).

26. Ibid.

27. Kristin Fitzgerald, comment on a brochure for "The Vine." For information about "The Vine" write to vine@regenerator.com or see <http://www.the-vine.org>.

Chapter 12—Spiritual Formation: From Legalism to Freedom

1. "Religion and Ecology at Emory U., Teaches Connections Between Nature and Spirituality," *The Chronicle of Higher Education*, 20 October 2000, <http://chronicle.com/weekly/v47/i08/08a01202.htm>.

2. Barbara Denman, "The Soul at Work," *Cross Culture*, March/April 1999, 5; Laurie Beth Jones, *Jesus CEO* (New York: Hyperion, 1996).

3. Ibid.

4. Daniel Stevick, *Beyond Fundamentalism* (Richmond: John Knox, 1964), 58–59.

5. Ibid., 73.

6. Julie Ann Vingers, correspondence, July 2001.

7. Ibid.

8. Ibid.

9. Timothy Roth, faxed correspondence, July 2001.

10. Dawn Haglund, response to questionnaire, summer 2000.

11. Maria Hoshaw, "Experience Ancient Spirituality," *Next-Wave*, March 2000, <http://www.next-wave.org/mar00/experience_ancient_spirituality.htm> (24 April 2002).

12. Ibid.

13. Peggy Wehmeyer, "Spiritual Youth Boom: More Teenagers Finding Answers Through Faith," ABCNews.com, <http://www.more.abcnews.go.com/onair/c..._cl_youthspirituality_feature_.html> (summer 2001).

14. David Athey, "Prayed Any Good Books Lately?" *Regeneration Quarterly* 4, no. 1 (1999), 35.

15. Robert Parham, "Labyrinth," *Faithworks*, May/June 1999, 22–23.

16. "Lectio Divina: A Way of Praying with Scripture," *Cutting Edge* 4, no. 2 (summer 2000): 18.

17. Melanie Arnold, "More People Turning to Spiritual Directors," *Faithworks*, January/February 1999, 27.

Chapter 13—Worship Leaders: From Program to Narrative

1. David Di Sabatino, response to questionnaire, 13 July 2000.

2. Paul Christenson, response to questionnaire, summer 2000.

3. Institute for Worship Studies, survey (Wheaton, Ill., 1999).

4. Dane Daker, correspondence, n.d.

5. Karen Daker, article presented to the congregation of Colton First Baptist Church, Colton, California, and sent to me by mail, n.d.

6. Wes King, in Candi Cushman, "Salt or Sugar," *World on the Web* 15, no. 19, 13 May 2000 <http://www.worldmag.com/world/issue/05-13-00/cover_1.asp> (summer 2001).

7. Candi Cushman, "Salt or Sugar," *World on the Web* 15, no. 19, 13 May 2000 <http://www.worldmag.com/world/issue/05-13-00/cover_1.asp> (summer 2001).

8. Amy Catherine Boucher, "The Poetry of Liturgy," *Regeneration Quarterly* 3, no. 3 (1997): 32.

9. Michael Hawn, "Taizé: That Little Spring Time!" *Worship Arts*, March/April 2000, 3.

10. Robert Parham, "Rediscovering the Power of Silence," *Faithworks*, September/October 1999, 29.

11. Ashley Olsen, correspondence, August 2001.

12. Dale Dirksen, response to questionnaire, summer 2000.

13. Jay Greener, correspondence, summer 2000.

14. Ibid.

15. Stephen Skaff, correspondence, n.d.

16. Ibid.

17. Paul Blake, email correspondence, 2000.

Chapter 14—Artists: From Constraint to Expression

1. David Taylor, response to questionnaire, summer 2000.

2. Ibid.

3. Dale Dirksen, response to questionnaire, summer 2000.

4. David Taylor, response to questionnaire, summer 2000.

5. Cathy Townley, "Musing on Art—and the Relationship to Worship in the 21st Century," *Next-Wave*, April 2000, <http://www.next-wave.org/apr00/musings_on_art.htm> (24 April 2002).

6. Scott Cairns, "It's Not Just You: Artists, Alienation, and Getting On with It," *Regeneration Quarterly* 5, no. 4, winter 1999/2000, 14–16.

7. Ibid.

8. William A. Dyrness, handout given in class, n.d. See also William A. Dyrness, *Visual Faith: Art, Theology, and Worship in Dialogue* (Grand Rapids: Baker Academic, 2001).

9. Dryness, handout.

10. Ibid.

11. Ibid.

12. Pope John Paul II, "A Letter to Artists," 4 April 1999, in *Regeneration Quarterly* 5, no. 4 (1999/2000): 9–12.

13. This story is cited in Timothy Ware, *The Orthodox Church* (Baltimore: Penguin, 1963), 269.

14. Mark Driscoll, *What We Believe*, "Essay on Beauty," <http://www.marshill.fm/believe/beauty.htm> (24 April 2002).

15. Daniel Lee, in Duncan G. Stroik, "Is There a Christian Architecture? An Interview with Daniel Lee," *Regeneration Quarterly* 4, no. 1 (1998): 18–22.

16. See <http://www.westwinds.org>.

17. Thomas Hohstadt, email correspondence, quoted from Thomas Hohstadt, *Spirituality and Emotions: Faith, Flesh, or Friend* (forthcoming). See also <http://www.capnok.net/damahmedia>.

Chapter 15—Evangelists: From Rallies to Relationships

1. Bernie Van De Walle, response to questionnaire, summer 2000.

2. David Di Sabatino, response to questionnaire, 13 July 2000.

3. Dawn Haglund, response to questionnaire, summer 2000.

4. John Green, response to questionnaire, 20 July 2000.

5. Dale Dirksen, response to questionnaire, summer 2000.

6. Bruce McEvoy, response to questionnaire, 31 July 2000.

7. Dawn Haglund, response to questionnaire, summer 2000.

8. David Di Sabatino, response to questionnaire, summer 2000.

9. David Hopkins, "The Deception of the X-treme Church," *Next-Wave*, October 1999, <http://www.next-wave.org/oct99/Deception.htm> (24 April 2002).

10. Ibid.

11. Ibid.

12. Ibid.

13. Ibid.

14. Ibid.

15. *Next-Wave*, "Concerning the Church and Culture," <http://www.next-wave.org/credo.html> (24 April 2002).

16. Steve Nicholson, in Jeff Bailey, "Everything You Ever Wanted to Know About Church Planting from Facing Fears to Launching Services: A Conversation with Steve Nicholson," *Cutting Edge* 4, no. 2 (July 2000), 2–10.

17. James Houston, in "Make Disciples, Not Just Converts: Evangelism without Discipleship Dispenses Cheap Grace," editorial, *Christianity Today*, 25 October 1999, 28.

18. Ron Martoia, email correspondence, summer 2000.

19. See "Introduction to Cross Training," <http://www.westwinds.org>.

20. See Robert E. Webber, *Journey to Jesus: The Worship Evangelism and Nurture Mission of the Church* (Nashville: Abingdon, 2001). The journey to Jesus process includes four books, one for each stage of spiritual development. These books are *Follow Me!*, *Be My Disciple!*, *Walk in the Spirit!*, and *Find Your Gift!*—all Wheaton IWS resources, 2001.

Chapter 16—Activists: From Theory to Action

1. Bernie Van De Walle, response to questionnaire, summer 2000.

2. See "The Epistle to Diognetus" in Cyril Richardson, *Early Christian Fathers* (Philadelphia: Westminster Press, 1953), 216–18.

3. See Paula Rinehart and Stacy P. Rinehart, *Choices: Finding God's Way in Dating, Sex, Marriage, and Singleness* (Colorado Springs: NavPress, 1996).

4. Nelson R. González, "Exploding Ex-Gay Myths," *Regeneration Quarterly* 1, no. 3 (1995): 17–22.

5. Jeffrey Burke Satinover, "Hope for Healing Homosexuality," *Regeneration Quarterly* 1, no. 4 (1995): 24–29.

6. Jeffrey P. Greenman, "The Good News about Marriage," *Regeneration Quarterly* 1, no. 3 (1995): 11–13.

7. Rodney Clapp, "Why Christians Have Lousy Sex Lives," *Regeneration Quarterly* 1, no. 3 (1995): 7–10.

8. Paul Weyrich, in "Is the Religious Right Finished? The Moral Minority," *Christianity Today*, 6 September 1999, 54.

9. Cal Thomas and Ed Dobson, in Bruce L. Shelley, "An On-Again, Off-Again Love Affair," *Christianity Today*, 6 September 1999, 54.

10. Andy Crouch, "Paradoxical Politics," *Regeneration Quarterly* 5, no. 1 (1999): 3.

11. Dawn Haglund, response to questionnaire, summer 2000.

12. Nathan Coleson, response to questionnaire, 10 September 2000.

13. John Green, response to questionnaire, summer 2000.

14. Dan Curran, response to questionnaire, summer 2000.

15. Todd Hunter, "The Church of the Future: Missional Communities," *Next-Wave*, January 1999, <http://www.next-wave.org/Jan99/misscomm.htm> (24 April 2002).

16. Norman Jameson, "Out of the Ashes," *Faithworks*, November/December 1999, 11–13.

17. Dale Dirksen, email correspondence, fall 2001.

18. David Taylor, email correspondence, fall 2001.

19. Dawn Haglund, email correspondence, fall 2001.

Bibliography

Part 1: Introduction to the Younger Evangelicals

Chapter 1—A Century of Evangelicals

Abraham, William J. *The Coming Great Revival: Recovering the Full Evangelical Tradition*. New York: Harper and Row, 1984.

Ammerman, Nancy Tatom. *Bible Believers: Fundamentalists in the Modern World*. New Brunswick: Rutgers University Press, 1987.

Askew, Thomas A., and Peter W. Spellman. *The Churches and the American Experience*. Grand Rapids: Baker, 1984.

Bloesch, Donald. *The Evangelical Renaissance*. Grand Rapids: Baker, 1973.

Carpenter, Joel A. *Revive Us Again: The Reawakening of American Fundamentalism*. Oxford: Oxford University Press, 1997.

Carter, Stephen L. *The Culture of Disbelief: How American Law and Politics Trivialize Religious Devotion*. New York: Doubleday, 1993.

Cole, Stewart Grant. *The History of Fundamentalism*. New York: R. R. Smith, 1931.

Dayton, Donald W. *Discovering an Evangelical Heritage*. San Francisco: Harper & Row, 1976.

Dayton, Donald W., and Robert K. Johnston. *The Variety of American Evangelicalism*. Knoxville: University of Tennessee Press, 1991.

Dollar, George. *A History of Fundamentalism*. Greenville, S.C.: Bob Jones University Press, 1973.

Erickson, Millard. *The Evangelical Mind and Heart*. Grand Rapids: Baker, 1993.

Gasper, Louis. *The Fundamentalist Movement*. The Hague: Mouton, 1963.

Gier, Nicholas F. *God, Reason, and the Evangelicals*. Lanham, Md.: University Press of America, 1987.

Henry, Carl F. H. *Remaking the Modern Mind*. Grand Rapids: Eerdmans, 1946.

———. *The Uneasy Conscience of Modern Fundamentalism*. Grand Rapids: Eerdmans, 1947.

Hoge, Dean R., Benton Johnson, and Donald A. Luidens. *Vanishing Boundaries: The Religion of Mainline Protestant Baby Boomers*. Louisville: Westminster John Knox, 1994.

Hollinger, Dennis. *Individualism and Social Ethics: A Syncretism*. Lanham, Md.: University Press of America, 1983.

Hunter, James Davison. *American Evangelicalism: Conservative Religion and the Quandary of Modernity*. New Brunswick, N.J.: Rutgers University Press, 1983.

———. *Evangelicalism: The Coming Generation*. Chicago: University of Chicago Press, 1987.

Kelley, Dean M. *Why Conservative Churches Are Growing*. New York: Harper and Row, 1972.

Lightner, Robert P. *Neoevangelicalism Today*. Schaumburg, Ill.: Regular Baptist, 1978.

Marsden, George M. *Evangelicalism and Modern America*. Grand Rapids: Eerdmans, 1984.

———. *Fundamentalism and American Culture: The Shaping of Twentieth-Century Evangelicalism, 1870–1925*. New York: Oxford University Press, 1980.

———. *Reforming Fundamentalism: Fuller Seminary and the New Evangelicalism*. Grand Rapids: Eerdmans, 1987.

McGrath, Alister. *Evangelicalism and the Future of Christianity*. Downers Grove, Ill.: InterVarsity, 1995.

Nash, Ronald H. *Evangelicals in America: Who They Are, What They Believe*. Nashville: Abingdon, 1987.

———. *Evangelical Renewal in the Mainline Churches*. Westchester, Ill.: Crossways, 1987.

Nelson, Rudolph. *The Making and Unmaking of an Evangelical Mind: The Case of Edward Carnell*. New York: Cambridge University Press, 1987.

Noll, Mark A. *The Scandal of the Evangelical Mind*. Grand Rapids: Eerdmans, 1994.

Noll, Mark A., and Ronald F. Thiemann, eds. *Where Shall My Wond'ring Soul Begin? The Landscape of Evangelical Piety and Thought*. Grand Rapids: Eerdmans, 2000.

Peshkin, Alan. *God's Choice: The Total World of a Fundamentalist Christian School*. Chicago: University of Chicago Press, 1986.

Quebedeaux, Richard. *The Young Evangelicals: The Story of the Emergence of a New Generation of Evangelicals*. San Francisco: Harper and Row, 1974.

Ramm, Bernard W. *The Evangelical Heritage: A Study in Historical Theology*. Waco: Word, 1973; Grand Rapids: Baker Academic, 1981, 2000.

Sandeen, Ernest Robert. *The Roots of Fundamentalism*. Chicago: University of Chicago Press, 1970.

Schaeffer, Francis. *The Great Evangelical Disaster*. Westchester, Ill.: Crossway, 1984.

Shibley, Mark A. *Resurgent Evangelicalism in the United States: Mapping Cultural Change Since 1970*. Columbia, S.C.: University of South Carolina Press, 1996.

Smith, Christian. *American Evangelicalism: Embattled and Thriving*. Chicago: University of Chicago Press, 1998.

Soper, J. Christopher. *Evangelical Christianity in the United States and Great Britain*. New York: New York University Press, 1994.

Sweet, Leonard I. *The Evangelical Tradition in America*. Macon, Ga.: Mercer University Press, 1984.

Tidball, Derek J. *Who Are the Evangelicals: Tracing the Roots of Today's Movement*. London: Marshall Pickering, 1994.

Webber, Robert. *Common Roots: A Call to Evangelical Maturity*. Grand Rapids: Zondervan, 1978.

Wells, David F. *No Place for Truth: Or Whatever Happened to Evangelical Theology?* Grand Rapids: Eerdmans, 1993.

Wells, David F., and John D. Woodbridge. *The Evangelicals: What They Believe, Who They Are, Where They Are Changing*. Nashville: Abingdon, 1975.

Woodbridge, John D., Mark A. Noll, and Nathan O. Hatch. *The Gospel in America: Themes in the Story of American Evangelicals*. Grand Rapids: Zondervan, 1979.

Wuthnow, Robert. *The Restructuring of American Religion*. Princeton, N.J.: Princeton University Press, 1998.

———. *The Struggle for America's Soul: Evangelicals, Liberals and Secularism*. Grand Rapids: Eerdmans, 1989.

———. *Rediscovering the Sacred: Perspectives on Religion in Contemporary Society*. Grand Rapids: Eerdmans, 1992.

Chapter 2—A New Kind of Evangelical

Beaudoin, Tom. *Virtual Faith: The Irreverent Spiritual Quest of Generation X*. San Francisco: Jossey-Bass, 1998.

Bernardi, Janet, and William Mahedy. *Generation Alone: Xer's Making a Place in the World*. Downers Grove, Ill.: InterVarsity, 1994.

Celek, Tim, and Dieter Zander with Patrick Kampert. *Inside the Soul of a New Generation*. Grand Rapids: Zondervan, 1996.

Ford, Kevin Graham. *Jesus for a New Generation: Putting the Gospel in the Language of the Xer's*. Downers Grove, Ill.: InterVarsity, 1995.

Hahn, Todd, and David Verhaagen. *GenXers after God: Helping a Generation Pursue Jesus*. Grand Rapids, Baker, 1998.

Hohstadt, Thomas. *I Felt God . . . I Think: Authentic Passion in the 21st Century*. Odessa, Tex.: Damah, 2001.

———. *Dying to Live: The 21st Century Church*. Odessa, Tex.: Damah, 1999.

Long, Jimmy. *Generating Hope: A Strategy for Reaching the Postmodern Generation*. Downers Grove, Ill.: InterVarsity, 1997.

Rabey, Steve. *In Search of Authentic Faith: How Emerging Generations Are Transforming the Church*. Colorado Springs: WaterBrook, 2001.

Riddell, Michael. *Threshold of the Future: Reforming the Church in the Post-Christian West*. London: S.P.C.K., 1998.

Riddell, Michael, Mark Pierson, and Cathy Kirkpatrick. *The Prodigal Project: Journey into the Emerging Church*. London: S.P.C.K., 2000.

Roxburgh, Alan J. *Reaching a New Generation: Strategies for Tomorrow's Church*. Vancouver: Regent College Publishing, 1993.

Schieber, Andrea Lee, and Ann Terman Olson, eds. *What Next? Connecting Your Ministry with the Generation X*. Minneapolis: Fortress, 1999.

Sweet, Leonard I. *Post-Modern Pilgrims: First Century Passion for the 21st Century World*. Nashville: Broadman and Holman, 2000.

Zoba, Wendy Murray. *Generation 2K: What Parents and Others Need to Know about the Millennials*. Downers Grove, Ill.: InterVarsity, 1999.

Part 2: The Younger Evangelical Thinkers

Chapter 3—Communication: From Print to Cultural Transmission

Brogyanyi, Bela, ed. *Prehistory, History and Historiography of Language, Speech and Linguistic Theory*. Amsterdam, 1992.

Burnett, Ron. *Cultures of Vision: Images, Media and the Imaginary*. Bloomington, Ind.: Indiana University Press, 1995.

Carey, James W. *Communication as Culture: Essays on Media and Society*. New York: Routledge, 1988.

Cassirer, Ernst. *Language and Myth*. Translated by Susanne K. Langer. New York: Dover, 1946.

Chappell, Warren. *A Short History of the Printed Word*. Boston: Nonpareil, 1980.

Czitrom, Daniel J. *Media and the American Mind: From Morse to McLuhan*. Chapel Hill, N.C.: University of North Carolina Press, 1982.

Febvre, Lucien, and Henri-Jean Martin. *The Coming of the Book: The Impact of Printing 1450–1800*. Translated by David Gerard. London: Verso, 1976.

Freedberg, David. *The Power of Images: Studies in the History and Theory of Response*. Chicago: University of Chicago Press, 1989.

Goodman, Nelson. *Languages of Art: An Approach to a Theory of Symbols*. Indianapolis: Hackett, 1968.

Henderson, David W. *Culture Shift: Communicating God's Truth to Our Changing World*. Grand Rapids: Baker, 1998.

Lyon, David. *The Information Society: Issues and Illusions*. Cambridge, England: Polity, 1988.

Manguel, Alberto. *A History of Reading*. New York: Penguin, 1996.

McLuhan, Marshall. *Understanding Media: The Extensions of Man*. New York: McGraw-Hill, 1974.

———. *The Gutenberg Galaxy*. Toronto: University of Toronto Press, 1965.

Mendels, Doron. *The Media Revolution of Early Christianity: An Essay on Eusebius's Ecclesiastical History*. Grand Rapids: Eerdmans, 1999.

Negroponte, Nicholas. *Being Digital*. New York: Vintage, 1995.

O'Donnell, James J. *Avatars of the Word: From Papyrus to Cyberspace*. Cambridge: Harvard University Press, 1998.

Ong, Walter J. *The Presence of the Word: Some Prolegomena for Cultural and Religious History*. New Haven: Yale University Press, 1967.

———. *Orality and Literacy*. London: Routledge, 1982.

Owens, Virginia Stem. *Media Development*. London: World Association of Christian Communication, 1984.

Postman, Neil. *Amusing Ourselves to Death*. New York: Penguin, 1986.

———. *Technopoly: The Surrender of Culture to Technology*. New York: Vintage, 1993.

Rossi, Philip J., and Paul A. Soukup, eds. *Mass Media and the Moral Imagination*. Kansas City: Sheed and Ward, 1994.

Slaughter, Michael. *Out on the Edge: A Wake-up Call for Church Leaders on the Edge of the Media Reformation*. Nashville: Abingdon, 1998.

Schramm, Wilbur, and Donald F. Roberts, eds. *The Process and Effects of Mass Communication*. Urbana, Ill.: University of Illinois Press, 1971.

Schultze, Quentin J. *Televangelism and American Culture: The Business of Popular Religion*. Grand Rapids: Baker, 1991.

———. *Winning Your Kids Back from Media*. Downers Grove, Ill.: InterVarsity, 1994.

———. *Communicating for Life: Christian Stewardship in Community and Media*. Grand Rapids: Baker Academic, 2000.

———. *Dancing in the Park: Youth, Popular Culture, and the Electronic Media*. Grand Rapids: Eerdmans, 1991.

Stephens, Mitchell. *The Rise of the Image of the Word*. Oxford: Oxford University Press, 1998.

Stock, Brian. *Listening for the Text: On the Uses of the Past*. Philadelphia: University of Pennsylvania Press, 1990.

Sweet, Leonard I., ed. *Communication and Change in American Religious History*. Grand Rapids: Eerdmans, 1993.

Traber, Michael. *The Myth of the Information Revolution: Social and Ethical Implications of Communications Technology*. London: Sage, 1986.

Williams, Raymond, ed. *Contact: Human Communication and Its History*. London: Thames and Hudson, 1981.

Wolterstorff, Nicholas. *Divine Discourse: Philosophical Reflections on the Claim That God Speaks*. Cambridge, England: Cambridge Press, 1995.

Chapter 4—History: From Ahistorical to Tradition

Cutsinger, James S. *Reclaiming the Great Tradition: Evangelicals, Catholics and Orthodox Dialogue*. Downers Grove, Ill.: InterVarsity, 1997.

Hall, Christopher A. *Reading Scripture with the Church Fathers*. Downers Grove, Ill.: InterVarsity, 1998.

Hall, Stuart G. *Doctrine and Practice in the Early Church*. Grand Rapids: Eerdmans, 1991.

Hemming, Laurence Paul. *Radical Orthodoxy? A Catholic Inquiry*. Burlington, Vt.: Ashgate, 2000.

Kelly, Gerard. *Retrofuture: Rediscovering Our Roots, Recharting Our Routes*. Downers Grove, Ill.: Inter-Varsity, 1999.

Milbank, John. *Theology and Social Theory: Beyond Secular Reason*. Oxford: Blackwell, 1990.

———. *The Word Made Strange: Theology, Language, Culture*. Oxford: Blackwell, 1998.

Milbank, John, Catherine Pickstock, and Graham Ward, eds. *Radical Orthodoxy*. London: Routledge, 1999.

Oden, Thomas. *After Modernity . . . What? Agenda for Theology*. Grand Rapids: Zondervan, 1990.

Webber, Robert E. *Ancient-Future Faith: Rethinking Evangelicalism for a Postmodern World*. Grand Rapids: Baker, 1999.

Wilken, Robert L. *Remembering the Christian Past*. Grand Rapids: Eerdmans, 1995.

Williams, D. H. *Retrieving the Tradition and Renewing Evangelicalism: A Primer for Suspicious Protestants*. Grand Rapids: Eerdmans, 1999.

Chapter 5—Theology: From Propositionalism to Narrative

Anderson, Bernhard W. *From Creation to New Creation: Old Testament Perspectives*. Minneapolis: Fortress, 1994.

Arnold, Clinton E. *Powers of Darkness: Principalities and Powers in Paul's Letters*. Downers Grove, Ill.: InterVarsity, 1992.

Aulén, Gustav. *Christus Victor: An Historical Study of the Three Main Types of the Idea of the Atonement*. New York: Collier, 1969.

Bevans, Stephen B. *Models of Contextual Theology*. Maryknoll, N.Y.: Orbis, 1992.

Boyd, Gregory A. *God of the Possible: A Biblical Introduction to the Open View of God*. Grand Rapids: Baker, 2000.

Braaten, Carl E., and Robert W. Jenson, eds. *Sin, Death and the Devil*. Grand Rapids: Eerdmans, 2000.

Carlson, Richard F., ed. *Science and Christianity: Four Views*. Downers Grove, Ill.: InterVarsity, 2000.

Clapp, Rodney. *Border Crossings: Christian Trespasses on Popular Culture and Public Affairs*. Grand Rapids: Brazos, 2000.

Colyer, Elmer M., ed. *Evangelical Theology in Transition: Theologians in Dialogue with Donald Bloesch*. Downers Grove, Ill.: InterVarsity, 1999.

Dembski, William A., and James M. Kushiner. *Signs of Intelligence: Understanding Intelligence Design*. Grand Rapids: Brazos, 2001.

———. *Intelligent Design: The Bridge between Science and Theology*. Downers Grove, Ill.: InterVarsity, 1999.

———. *Mere Creation: Science, Faith and Intelligent Design*. Downers Grove, Ill.: InterVarsity, 1998.

DuBay, Thomas. *The Evidential Power of Beauty: Science and Theology Meet*. San Francisco: Ignatius, 1999.

Fackre, Gabriel. *The Christian Story: A Narrative Interpretation of Basic Christian Doctrine*, third edition. Grand Rapids: Eerdmans, 1996.

Florovsky, Georges. *Creation and Redemption*. Volume 3 in *The Collected Works of Georges Florovsky*. Belmont, Mass.: Nordland, 1976.

Frei, Hans W. *The Eclipse of the Biblical Narrative: A Study in Eighteenth- and Nineteenth-Century Hermeneutics*. New Haven, Conn.: Yale University Press, 1974.

Goldberg, Michael. *Theology and Narrative: A Critical Introduction*. Philadelphia: Trinity, 1991.

Green, Joel B., and Mark D. Baker. *Recovering the Scandal of the Cross: Atonement in New Testament and Contemporary Contexts*. Downers Grove, Ill.: InterVarsity Press, 2000.

Grenz, Stanley J. *Revisioning Evangelical Theology: A Fresh Agenda for the 21st Century*. Downers Grove, Ill.: InterVarsity, 1993.

———. *Renewing the Center: Evangelical Theology in a Post-Theological Era*. Grand Rapids: Baker Academic, 2000.

Hauerwas, Stanley, and L. Gregory Jones, eds. *Why Narrative?: Readings in Narrative Theology.* Eugene, Ore.: Wipf and Stock, 1997.

Horton, Michael, ed. *A Confessing Theology for Postmodern Times.* Wheaton, Ill.: Crossway, 2000.

Kraft, Charles H. *Christianity in Culture: A Study in Dynamic Biblical Theologizing in Cross-Cultural Perspective.* Maryknoll, N.Y.: Orbis, 1979.

Lindbeck, George W. *The Nature of Doctrine: Religion and Theology in a Post Liberal Age.* Philadelphia: Westminster, 1984.

McKnight, Edgar V. *Postmodern Use of the Bible: The Emergence of Reader-Oriented Criticism.* Nashville: Abingdon, 1988.

Nicodemus of the Holy Mounted, ed. *Unseen Warfare.* Revised by Theophan the Recluse. Crestwood, N.Y.: St. Vladimir, 1995.

Pfitzner, Victor, and Hilary Regan, eds. *The Task of Theology Today: Doctrines and Dogmas.* Grand Rapids: Eerdmans, 1999.

Pickstock, Catherine. *After Writing: On the Liturgical Consummation of Philosophy.* Oxford: Blackwell, 1998.

Placher, William C. *Narratives of a Vulnerable God: Christ, Theology and Scripture.* Louisville: Westminster John Knox, 1994.

Polkinghorne, John C. *Science and Theology: An Introduction.* London: SPCK, 1998.

———. *Science and Creation: The Search for Understanding.* Boston: New Science Library, 1988.

———. *Science and Providence.* Boston: New Science Library, 1989.

———. *Belief in God in an Age of Science.* New Haven, Conn.: Yale University Press, 1998.

———. *Scientists As Theologians.* London: SPCK, 1996.

Scalise, Charles J. *From Scripture to Theology: A Canonical Journey into Hermeneutics.* Downers Grove, Ill.: InterVarsity, 1996.

Stackhouse, John G., Jr., ed. *Evangelical Futures: A Conversation on Theological Method.* Grand Rapids: Baker Academic, 2000.

Torrance, T. F. *Reality and Evangelical Theology: The Realism of Christian Revelation.* Downers Grove, Ill.: InterVarsity, 1999.

Volf, Miroslav, ed. *The Future of Theology: Essays in Honor of Jürgen Moltmann.* Grand Rapids: Eerdmans, 1996.

Von Balthasar, Hans Urs. *Truth Is Symphonic: Aspects of Christian Pluralism.* San Francisco: Ignatius, 1987.

Wheatley, Margaret J. *Leadership and the New Science: Discovering Order in a Chaotic World.* San Francisco: Berrett-Koehler, 1999.

Wink, Walter, *When the Powers Fall: Reconciliation in the Healing of Nations.* Minneapolis: Fortress, 1998.

Chapter 6—Apologetics: From Rationalism to Embodiment

Chang, Curtis. *Engaging Unbelief: A Captivating Strategy from Augustine to Aquinas.* Downers Grove, Ill.: InterVarsity, 2000.

Clapp, Rodney. *Border Crossings: Christian Trespasses on Popular Culture and Public Affairs.* Grand Rapids: Brazos, 2001.

Davis, John Jefferson. *Foundations of Evangelical Theology.* Grand Rapids: Baker, 1984.

Dembski, William A., and Jay Wesley Richards. *Unapologetic Apologetics: Meeting the Challenges of Theology Studies.* Downers Grove, Ill.: InterVarsity, 2001.

Grant, Robert M. *Greek Apologists of the Second Century.* Philadelphia: Westminster, 1988.

Grenz, Stanley J., and John R. Franke. *Beyond Foundationalism: Shaping Theology in a Postmodern Context.* Louisville: Westminster John Knox, 2001.

Groothuis, Douglas. *Truth Decay: Defending Christianity Against the Challenges of Postmodernism.* Downers Grove, Ill.: InterVarsity, 2000.

Hauerwas, Stanley, Nancey Murphy, and Mark Nations, eds. *Theology without Foundations: Religious Practice and the Future of Theological Truth*. Nashville: Abingdon, 1967.

Helm, David R., and Jon M. Dennis. *The Genesis Factor: Probing Life's Big Questions*. Wheaton, Ill.: Crossway, 2001.

Loscalzo, Craig A. *Apologetic Preaching: Proclaiming Christ to a Postmodern World*. Downers Grove, Ill.: InterVarsity, 2000.

Murphy, Nancey. *Anglo-American Post Modernity: Philosophical Perspectives on Science, Religion, and Ethics*. Boulder, Colo.: Westview, 1997.

———. *Beyond Liberalism and Fundamentalism: How Modern and Post Modern Philosophy Set the Theological Agenda*. Valley Forge: Trinity, 1996.

Phillips, Timothy R., and Dennis L. Okholm. *Christian Apologetics in the Postmodern World*. Downers Grove, Ill.: InterVarsity, 1995.

Placher, William C. *Unapologetic Apologetics: A Christian Voice in a Pluralistic Conversation*. Louisville: Westminster John Knox, 1989.

Plantinga, Alvin, and Nicholas Wolterstorff, eds. *Faith and Rationality: Reason and Belief in God*. Notre Dame, Ind.: University of Notre Dame Press, 1983.

Ramm, Bernard. *The Pattern of Religious Authority*. Grand Rapids: Eerdmans, 1959.

Shults, F. LeRon. *The Postfoundationalist Task of Theology: Wolfhart Pannenberg and The New Theological Rationality*. Grand Rapids: Eerdmans, 1999.

Thiel, John E. *Nonfoundationalism*. Minneapolis: Fortress Press, 1994.

Van Huyssteen, J. Wentzel. *Essays in Postfoundationalist Theology*. Grand Rapids: Eerdmans, 1997.

Wolterstorff, Nicholas. *Reason within the Bounds of Religion*. Grand Rapids: Eerdmans, 1976.

Wood, W. Jay. *Epistemology: Becoming Intellectually Virtuous*. Downers Grove, Ill.: InterVarsity, 1998.

Chapter 7—Ecclesiology: From Invisible to Visible

Ahlen, J. Timothy, and J. V. Thomas. *One Church, Many Congregations: The Key Church Strategy*. Edited by Lyle Schaller. Nashville: Abingdon, 1999.

Arnold, Eberhard. *Why We Live in Community with Two Interpretive Talks by Thomas Merton*. Farmington, Pa.: Plough, 1995.

Banks, Robert, and Julia Banks. *The Church Comes Home*. Peabody, Mass.: Hendrickson, 1998.

Braaten, Carl E., and Robert W. Jenson, eds. *Marks of the Body of Christ*. Grand Rapids: Eerdmans, 1999.

Clapp, Rodney. *A Peculiar People: The Church as Culture in a Post-Christian Society*. Downers Grove, Ill.: InterVarsity, 1996.

Coalter, Milton J., John M. Mulder, and Louis B. Weeks. *Vital Signs: The Promise of Mainstream Protestantism*, Grand Rapids: Eerdmans, 1996.

Gibbs, Eddie. *ChurchNext: Quantum Changes in How We Do Ministry*. Downers Grove, Ill.: InterVarsity, 2000.

Groff, Kent Ira, *The Soul of Tomorrow's Church: Weaving Spiritual Practices in Ministry Together*. Nashville: Upper Room, 2000.

Guder, Darrell L. *The Continuing Conversion of the Church*. Grand Rapids: Eerdmans, 2000.

Hauerwas, Stanley. *A Community of Character: Toward a Constructive Christian Social Ethic*. Notre Dame, Ind.: University of Notre Dame Press, 1981.

Hutcheson Jr., Richard G., and Peggy Shriver. *The Divided Church: Moving Liberals and Conservatives from Diatribe to Dialogue*. Downers Grove, Ill.: InterVarsity, 1999.

McLaren, Brian. *The Church on the Other Side: Doing Ministry in the Postmodern Matrix*. Grand Rapids: Zondervan, 1998.

Meyendorff, John. *Catholicity and the Church*. Crestwood, N.Y.: St. Vladimir's Seminary Press, 1983.

Mittelberg, Mark. *Building a Contagious Church: Revolutionizing the Way We View and Do Evangelism*. Grand Rapids: Zondervan, 2000.

Rausch, Thomas P. *Catholics and Evangelicals: Do They Share a Common Future?* Downers Grove, Ill.: InterVarsity, 2000.

Reeves, Thomas C. *The Empty Church: The Suicide of Liberal Christianity.* New York: Free Press, 1996.

Van Der Ven, Johannes A. *Ecclesiology in Context.* Grand Rapids: Eerdmans, 1993.

Van Gelder, Craig. *The Essence of the Church: A Community Created by the Spirit.* Grand Rapids: Baker, 2000.

Vanier, Jean. *Community and Growth.* Revised edition, New York: Paulist, 1989.

Wagner, E. Glenn. *Escape from Church, Inc.: The Return of the Pastor Shepherd.* Grand Rapids: Zondervan, 1999.

Part 3: The Younger Evangelical Practitioners

Chapter 8 — Being Church: From Market to Mission

Bosch, David J. *Transforming Mission: Paradigm Shifts in Theology of Mission.* Maryknoll, N.Y.: Orbis, 1994.

Guder, Darrell, ed. *Missional Church: A Vision for the Sending of the Church in North America.* Grand Rapids, Eerdmans, 1998.

Hunsberger, George R., and Craig Van Gelder. *The Church between Gospel and Culture: The Emerging Mission in North America.* Grand Rapids: Eerdmans, 1996.

Newbigin, Lesslie. *Foolishness to the Greeks: The Gospel and Western Culture.* Grand Rapids: Eerdmans, 1986.

Pritchard, G. A. *Willow Creek Seeker Services: Evaluating a New Way to Do Church.* Grand Rapids: Baker, 1996.

Ramachandra, Vinoth. *The Recovery of Mission: Beyond the Pluralistic Paradigms.* Grand Rapids: Eerdmans, 1996.

Sanneh, Lamin. *Translating the Message: The Missionary Impact on Culture.* Maryknoll, N.Y.: Orbis, 1999.

Chapter 9 — Pastors: From Power to Servanthood

Banks, Robert, and Julia Banks. *The Church Comes Home.* Peabody, Mass.: Hendrickson, 1998.

Cladis, George. *Leading the Team-Based Church.* San Francisco: Jossey-Bass, 1999.

Davis, Kortright. *Serving with Power: Reviving the Spirit of Christian Ministry.* New York: Paulist, 1999.

Easum, William M., and Thomas G. Bandy. *Growing Spiritual Redwoods.* Nashville: Abingdon, 1995.

——— . *Sacred Cows Make Gourmet Burgers.* Nashville: Abingdon, 1995.

——— . *Leadership on the Other Side.* Nashville: Abingdon, 2000.

Gibbs, Eddie. *ChurchNext: Quantum Changes in How We Do Ministry.* Downers Grove, Ill.: InterVarsity, 2000.

Hansen, David. *The Art of Pastoring.* Downers Grove, Ill.: InterVarsity, 1994.

McLaren, Brian D. *The Church on the Other Side: Doing Ministry in the Postmodern Matrix.* Grand Rapids: Zondervan, 1998.

Messer, Donald E. *Contemporary Images of Christian Ministry.* Nashville: Abingdon, 1989.

Sofield, Loughlan, and Carroll Juliano. *Collaboration: Uniting Our Gifts in Ministry.* Notre Dame, Ind.: Ave Maria, 2000.

Wagner, E. Glenn. *Escape from Church, Inc.: The Return of the Pastor-Shepherd.* Grand Rapids: Zondervan, 1999.

Woods, C. Jeff. *Better Than Success: 8 Principles of Faithful Leadership.* Valley Forge: Judson, 2001.

Chapter 10 — Youth Ministers: From Parties to Prayer

Borgman, Dean and Christine Cook. *Agenda for Youth Ministry: Cultural Themes in Faith and Church.* London: SPCK, 1998.

Ford, Kevin Graham. *Jesus for a New Generation: Putting the Gospel in the Language of the Xer's*. Downers Grove, Ill.: InterVarsity, 1995.

Hahn, Todd, and David Verhaagen. *Gen Xer's after God: Helping a Generation Pursue Jesus*. Grand Rapids: Baker, 1998.

Long, Jimmy. *Generating Hope: A Strategy for Reaching the Postmodern Generation*. Downers Grove, Ill.: InterVarsity, 1997.

Mahedy, William, and Janet Bernardi. *Generation Alone: Xer's Making a Place in the World*. Downers Grove, Ill.: InterVarsity, 1994.

Rabey, Steve. *In Search of Authentic Faith: How Emerging Generations Are Transforming the Church*. Colorado Springs: WaterBrook, 2001.

Roxburgh, Alan J. *Reaching a New Generation: Strategies for Tomorrow's Church*. Vancouver: Regent College Publishing, 1993.

Ward, Pete. *The Church and Youth Ministry*. Oxford: Lynx Communications, 1995.

Celek, Tim, and Dieter Zander with Patrick Kampert. *Inside the Soul of a New Generation: Insights and Strategies for Reaching Busters*. Grand Rapids: Zondervan, 1996.

Zoba, Wendy Murray. *Generation 2K: What Parents and Others Need to Know about the Millennials*. Downers Grove, Ill.: InterVarsity, 1999.

Chapter 11—Educators: From Information to Formation

Astley, Jeff, Leslie J. Francis, and Colin Crowder. *Theological Perspectives on Christian Formation*. Grand Rapids: Eerdmans, 1996.

Charry, Ellen T. *By the Renewing of Your Minds: The Pastoral Function of Christian Doctrine*. Oxford: Oxford University Press, 1997.

Groome, Thomas H. *Sharing Faith: A Comprehensive Approach to Religious Education and Pastoral Ministry*. San Francisco: Harper Collins, 1991.

———. *Christian Religious Education: Sharing Our Vision and Story*. San Francisco: Jossey-Bass, 1980.

Hart, D. G., and R. Albert Mohler Jr. *Theological Education in the Evangelical Tradition*. Grand Rapids: Baker, 1996.

Kelsey, David H. *To Understand God Truly: What's Theological about a Theological School*. Louisville: Westminster John Knox, 1992.

———. *Between Athens and Berlin: The Theological Education Debate*. Grand Rapids: Eerdmans, 1993.

Leith, John H. *Crisis in the Church: The Plight of Theological Education*. Louisville: Westminster John Knox, 1997.

Palmer, Parker J. *To Know as We Are Known: Education as a Spiritual Journey*. San Francisco: Harper, 1993.

Willimon, William H., and Thomas H. Naylor. *The Abandoned Generation: Rethinking Higher Education*. Grand Rapids: Eerdmans, 1995.

Zagzebski, Linda Trinkaus. *Virtues of the Mind: An Inquiry into the Ethical Foundations of Knowledge*. Cambridge, England: Cambridge University Press, 1996.

Chapter 12—Spiritual Formation: From Legalism to Freedom

Barry, William A., and William J. Connolly. *The Practice of Spiritual Direction*. San Francisco: Harper, n.d.

Bass, Dorothy C., ed. *Receiving the Day: Christian Practices for Opening the Gift of Time*. San Francisco: Jossey-Bass, 2000.

———. *Practicing Our Faith: A Way of Life for a Searching People*. San Francisco: Jossey-Bass, 1997.

Bushnell, Horace. *Christian Nurture*. Cleveland: Pilgrim, 1861; New York: Charles Scribner, 1994.

Byrne, Lavinia, ed. *Traditions of Spiritual Guidance: Collected from the Way*. Collegeville, Minn.: Liturgical, 1990.

Chambers, Oswald. *Christian Disciplines*. Grand Rapids: Discovery House, 1995.

Cloninger, Claire. *A Place Called Simplicity: The Quiet Beauty of Simple Living*. Eugene, Ore.: Harvest House, 1993.

Collins, Kenneth J., ed. *Exploring Christian Spirituality: An Ecumenical Reader*. Grand Rapids: Baker Academic, 2000.

De Waal, Esther. *Living with Contradiction: An Introduction to Benedictine Spirituality*. Harrisburg, Pa.: Morehouse, 1989.

Dykstra, Craig. *Growing in the Life of Faith: Education in the Christian Practices*. Louisville: Geneva, 1999.

Forest, Jim. *Praying with Icons*. Maryknoll, N.Y.: Orbis, 2000.

Foster, Richard J. *Celebration of Discipline*. Revised edition, San Francisco: Harper and Row, 1988.

French, R. M., trans. *The Way of a Pilgrim and the Pilgrim Continues His Way*. New York: Seabury, 1965.

Gill, David W. *Becoming Good: Building Moral Character*. Downers Grove, Ill.: InterVarsity, 2000.

Hauerwas, Stanley, and Charles Pinches. *Christians among the Virtues: Theological Conversations with Ancient and Modern Ethics*. Notre Dame, Ind.: University of Notre Dame Press, 1997.

Henrichsen, Walter A. *Disciples Are Made Not Born: Equipping Christians to Multiply Themselves Through Ministry to Others*. Colorado Springs: Cook, 1988.

Jones, W. Paul. *A Table in the Desert*. Brewster, Mass.: Paraclete, 2001.

Kenneson, Philip D. *Life on the Vine: Cultivating the Fruit of the Spirit in Christian Community*. Downers Grove, Ill.: InterVarsity, 1999.

Kreeft, Peter. *Prayer for Beginners*. San Francisco: Ignatius, 2000.

Macaulay, Ranald, and Jerram Barrs. *Being Human: The Nature of Spiritual Experience*. Downers Grove, Ill.: InterVarsity, 1978.

McBride, Alfred. *The Ten Commandments: Covenant of Love*. Cincinnati: St. Anthony Messenger, 2001.

McGrath, Alister E. *Christian Spirituality*. Oxford: Blackwell, 1999.

Merton, Thomas. *Spiritual Direction and Meditation*. Collegeville, Minn.: Liturgical, 1960.

Meyendorff, John. *St. Gregory Palamas and Orthodox Spirituality*, Crestwood, N.Y.: St. Vladimir, 1974.

Nemeck, Francis Kelly, and Marie Theresa Coombs. *The Way of Spiritual Direction*. Collegeville, Minn.: Liturgical, 1985.

Norris, Kathleen. *The Cloister Walk*. New York: Riverhead Books, 1996.

Nouwen, Henri J. M. *The Way of the Heart: Desert Spirituality and Contemporary Ministry*. San Francisco: Harper, 1981.

Payne, Leanne. *Listening Prayer: Learning to Hear God's Voice and Keep a Prayer Journal*. Grand Rapids: Baker, 1994.

Peterson, Eugene H. *Subversive Spirituality*. Grand Rapids: Eerdmans, 1997.

———. *A Long Obedience in the Same Direction: Discipleship in an Instant Society*. Downers Grove, Ill.: InterVarsity, 1980.

Powell, Samuel M. and Michael E. Lodahl, eds. *Embodied Holiness: Toward a Corporate Theology of Spiritual Growth*. Downers Grove, Ill.: InterVarsity, 1999.

Sanford, Agnes. *The Healing Gifts of the Spirit*. San Francisco: Harper, 1984.

Sheridan, William A. *The Fortune Sellers*. New York: John Wiley and Sons, 1998.

Silf, Margaret. *Sacred Spaces: Stations on a Celtic Way*. Brewster, Mass.: Paraclete, 2001.

Vandergrift, Nicki Verploegen. *Organic Spirituality: A Sixfold Path for Contemplative Reading*. Maryknoll, N.Y.: Orbis, 2000.

Vanier, Jean. *Becoming Human*. Toronto: Anansi, 1998.

Veith, Gene Edward, Jr. *The Spirituality of the Cross: The Way of the First Evangelicals*. St. Louis: Concordia, 1999.

Von Balthasar, Hans Urs. *Prayer*. San Francisco: Ignatius, 1986.

Ward, Benedicta, ed. *The Lives of the Desert Fathers*. Kalamazoo, Mich.: Cistercian, 1981.

———. *Sayings of the Desert Fathers: The Alphabetical Collection*. Kalamazoo, Mich.: Cistercian, 1975.

Wesley, John. *The Nature of Holiness: Wesley's Message on Christian Experience.* Compiled and edited by Clare George Weakly Jr. Minneapolis: Bethany, 1988.

Willard, Dallas. *Hearing God: Developing a Conversational Relationship with God.* Downers Grove, Ill.: InterVarsity, 1999.

————. *The Spirit of the Disciples: Understanding How God Changes Lives.* San Francisco: Harper, 1988.

————. *The Divine Conspiracy: Rediscovering Our Hidden Life in God.* San Francisco: Harper, 1998.

————. *The Spirit of the Disciplines.* New York: Harper and Row, 1988.

Zizioulas, John D. *Being as Communion: Studies in Personhood and the Church.* Crestwood, N.Y.: St. Vladimir's Seminary Press, 1985.

Chapter 13—Worship Leaders: From Program to Narrative

Berglund, Brad. *Reinventing Sunday: Breakthrough Ideas for Transforming Worship.* Valley Forge, Pa.: Judson, 2001.

Hurtado, Larry W. *At the Origins of Christian Worship: The Context and Character of Earliest Christian Devotion.* Grand Rapids: Eerdmans, 1999.

Otto, Rudolf. *The Idea of the Holy: An Inquiry into the Nonrational Factor in the Idea of the Divine and Its Relation to the Rational.* Second edition, New York: Oxford University Press, 1950.

Liesch, Barry. *The New Worship: Straight Talk on Music and the Church.* Grand Rapids: Baker, 2001.

Jasper, R. C. D., and G. J. Cuming, eds. *Prayers of the Eucharist. Early and Reformed.* 2d ed. New York: Oxford University Press, 1980.

Webber, Robert E. *Worship Old and New.* 2d ed. Grand Rapids: Zondervan, 1994.

Chapter 14—Artists: From Constraint to Expression

Apostolos-Cappadona, Diane. *Art, Creativity and the Sacred: An Anthology in Religion and Art.* Revised edition, New York: Continuum, 1998.

Begbie, Jeremy, ed. *Beholding the Glory: Incarnation through the Arts.* Grand Rapids: Baker Academic, 2000.

————. *Voicing Creation's Praise: Towards a Theology of the Arts.* Edinburgh: Blackwell, 1991.

————. *Theology, Music and Time.* Cambridge, England: Cambridge University Press, 2000.

Bond, Fiona. *The Arts in Your Church.* Carlisle, England: Piquant, 2001.

Brand, Hilary, and Adrienne Chaplin. *Art and Soul: Signposts for Christians in the Arts.* 2d ed. Downers Grove, Ill.: InterVarsity, 2002.

Dyrness, William A. *Visual Faith: Art, Theology, and Worship in Dialogue.* Grand Rapids: Baker Academic, 2001.

MacGregor, Neil, with Erika Langmuir. *Seeing Salvation: Images of Christ in Art.* New Haven: Yale, 2000.

Nichols, Aiden. *The Art of God Incarnate: Theology and Image in Christian Tradition.* New York: Paulist, 1980.

Navone, John. *Toward a Theology of Beauty,* Collegeville, Minn.: Liturgical, 1996.

Rookmaaker, H. R. *Modern Art and the Death of a Culture.* Downers Grove, Ill.: InterVarsity, 1971.

————. *The Creative Gifts: Essays on Art and the Christian Life.* Westchester, Ill.: Cornerstone, 1981.

Scarry, Elaine. *On Beauty and Being Just.* Princeton, N.J.: Princeton University Press, 1999.

Schaeffer, Francis. *Art and the Bible,* Downers Grove, Ill.: InterVarsity, 1973.

Wolterstorff, Nicholas. *Art in Action: Toward a Christian Aesthetic.* Grand Rapids: Eerdmans, 1980.

Chapter 15—Evangelists: From Rallies to Relationships

Abraham, William J. *The Logic of Evangelism.* Grand Rapids: Eerdmans, 1989.

Brueggemann, Walter. *Biblical Perspectives on Evangelism: Living in a Three-Storied Universe.* Nashville: Abingdon, 1993.

Chang, Curtis. *Engaging Unbelief: A Captivating Strategy from Augustine to Aquinas.* Downers Grove, Ill.: InterVarsity, 2000.

Coalter, Milton J., and Virgil Cruz, eds. *How Shall We Witness? Faithful Evangelism in a Reformed Tradition.* Louisville: Westminister John Knox, 1995.

Collins, Kenneth J., and John H. Tyson. *Conversion in the Wesleyan Tradition.* Nashville: Abingdon, 2001.

Conn, Walter E., ed. *Conversion: Perspectives on Personal and Social Transformation.* New York: Alba, 1978.

Dupre, Louis. *Religious Mystery and Rational Reflection.* Grand Rapids: Eerdmans, 1998.

Gelpi, Donald L. *The Conversion Experience: A Reflective Process for RCIA Participants and Others.* New York: Paulist, 1998.

Green, Michael. *Evangelism in the Early Church.* Grand Rapids: Eerdmans, 1970.

Posterski, Donald C. *Reinventing Evangelism: New Strategies for Presenting Christ in Today's World.* Downers Grove, Ill.: InterVarsity, 1989.

Richardson, Rick. *Evangelism Outside the Box: New Ways to Help People Experience the Good News.* Downers Grove, Ill.: InterVarsity, 2000.

Scifnes, Mary J. *Searching for Seekers: Ministry with a New Generation of the Unchurched.* Nashville: Abingdon, 1998.

Swanson, Roger K. and Shirley F. Clement. *The Faith-Sharing Congregation: Developing a Strategy for the Congregation as Evangelist.* Nashville: Discipleship Resources, 1999.

Stone, Bryan P. *Compassionate Ministry: Theological Foundations.* New York: Orbis, 2001.

Webber, Robert E. *Journey to Jesus: The Worship, Evangelism and Nurture Mission of the Church.* Nashville: Abingdon, 2001.

Wells, David F. *God the Evangelist: How the Holy Spirit Works to Bring Men and Women to Faith.* Carlisle, England: W.E.F./Paternoster, n.d.

Wells, David F. *Turning to God: Biblical Conversion in the Modern World.* Carlisle England: W.E.F./Paternoster, n.d.

Chapter 16—Activists: From Theory to Action

Cahill, Thomas. *How the Irish Saved Civilization: The Untold Story of Ireland's Heroic Role from the Fall of Rome to the Rise of Medieval Europe.* New York: Doubleday, 1995.

Clapp, Rodney. *A Peculiar People: The Church as Culture in a Post-Christian Society.* Downers Grove, Ill.: InterVarsity, 1996.

Guroian, Vigen. *Ethics after Christendom: Toward an Ecclesial Christian Ethic.* Grand Rapids: Eerdmans, 1994.

Hauerwas, Stanley. *After Christendom: How the Church Is to Behave if Freedom, Justice, and a Christian Nation Are Bad Ideas.* Nashville: Abingdon, 1991.

Hauerwas, Stanley, and William H. Willimon. *Resident Aliens: A Provocative Christian Assessment of Culture and Ministry for People Who Know That Something Is Wrong.* Nashville: Abingdon, 1989.

Johnston, Robert K. *Reel Spirituality: Theology and Film in Dialogue.* Grand Rapids: Baker Academic, 2000.

Sine, Tom. *Mustard Seed vs. McWorld: Reinventing Life and Faith for the Future.* Grand Rapids: Baker, 1999.

Van Gelder, Craig. *Confident Witness—Changing World: Rediscovering the Gospel in North America.* Grand Rapids: Eerdmans, 1999.

Index

Robert E. Webber is Myers Professor of Ministry at Northern Seminary, president of the Institute for Worship Studies, and emeritus professor of theology at Wheaton College. He is the author of a number of books, including *Ancient-Future Faith* (Baker, 1999).

ALSO BY ROBERT E. WEBBER

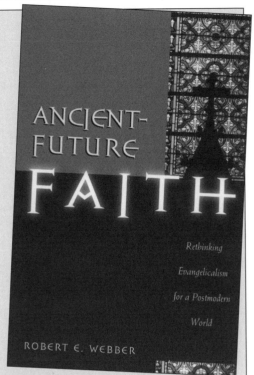

ANCIENT-FUTURE FAITH
*Rethinking Evangelicalism
for a Postmodern World*

IN THIS PROVOCATIVE WORK,
Robert E. Webber contends that
present-day evangelicalism is a product of modernity. The way forward
for evangelicalism begins with looking at the resources the early church
tradition provides for making faith
relevant in a postmodern world.

"This book makes an important
contribution . . . as a call for theological renewal within evangelical
churches . . . timely, practical, and
persuasive."
—*Publishers Weekly*

"[A] well written and readable
scholarly work with some interesting insights into this important
segment of religion in America."
—*Library Journal*

"*The Agenda for Theology*, which I attempted to set forth in
1979, is here being significantly extended by Robert Webber . . . in a way that is profoundly gratifying."
—**Thomas C. Oden,** professor of theology and ethics, Drew University

"Here is a faith for our time that finds in the ancient traditions the power to speak to
the postmodern world. This book amounts to an introduction to Christianity from
the theme of *Christus Victor*. It draws from Webber's own experience of growth as a
hearer of God's Word and is backed up with an impressive set of endnotes, charts,
and a bibliography."
—**Clark H. Pinnock,** professor of theology, McMaster Divinity College

"Robert Webber substantiates the vision of an anciently rooted and forward-looking
evangelicalism that marks all of his work. *Ancient-Future Faith* works as a narrative-
oriented Christian primer and as a road map to the promise of catholic evangelicalism. . . . Webber shows what it means to take seriously the character of Christian testimony as Christ-following church-formed story."
—**Gary Dorrien,** author, *The Remaking of Evangelical Theology*

"Now, more than ever, with the culture wars of a dying modernity cutting deeper and
more darkly into desperation and anger, all evangelicalism needs to hear Bob
Webber. Take up, read, pray, and consider: in this direction lies the most hopeful
future of our faith."
—**Rodney Clapp,** author, *A Peculiar People*